Hertfordshire
COUNTY COUNCIL
Community Information

7/12

08 OCT 2002
29 Oct

B/SHI.
STE

14 DEC 2002

4 - DEC 2000

1 2 JAN 2001

1 5 MAR 2003

2 6 MAY 2001

1 8 FEB 2008

D0493598

- 7 JUL 2001

2 9 SEP 2001

2 6 AUG 2002

14 Sept

Please renew/return this item by the last date shown.

So that your telephone call is charged at local rate,
please call the numbers as set out below:

	From Area codes 01923 or 020:	From the rest of Herts:
Renewals:	01923 471373	01438 737373
Enquiries:	01923 471333	01438 737333
Minicom:	01923 471599	01438 737599

L32

Eric Shipton

Also by Peter Steele

Two and Two Halves to Bhutan
Doctor on Everest
Medical Handbook for Mountaineers
Atlin's Gold

Eric Shipton

EVEREST AND BEYOND

———

Peter Steele

drawings by Bruce Paton

Constable · London

First published in Great Britain 1998
by Constable and Company Limited
3 The Lanchesters, 162 Fulham Palace Road
London W6 9ER
Copyright © Peter Steele 1998
Reprinted 1998
ISBN 0 09 478300 4
The right of Peter Steele to be identified as author of this work
has been asserted by him in accordance
with the Copyright, Designs and Patents Act 1988

Set in Monotype Garamond 12 pt by
Servis Filmsetting Ltd, Manchester
Printed in Great Britain by
St Edmundsbury Press Ltd
Bury St Edmunds, Suffolk

A CIP catalogue record for this book
is available from the British Library

In memoriam

BILL TURRALL
JOHN EMERY
GEORGE FRASER

'I will venture to say that he will be seen in this work . . . as he really was; for I profess to write not his panegyrick, which must be all praise, but his Life.'

James Boswell of Dr Johnson

Contents

Illustrations

Maps

(maps drawn by the author)

HIMALAYAN TRUST

CHAIRMAN:
SIR EDMUND HILLARY,
278A REMUERA ROAD,
AUCKLAND 5. NEW ZEALAND.
TELEPHONE: 520-3169
FAX: 64-9-520-7847

July 30th 1997

Dr. Peter Steele,
138 Dalton Trail,
Whitehorse,
Yukon Y1A 3G2,
CANADA

Dear Peter,

    In my younger days Eric Shipton was a hero to me.
He did all the things I wanted to do - exploring remote
areas, crossing unknown glaciers and passes, and forcing a
way through incredibly rough and unknown country.

    When I was invited to join his British Everest
Reconnaissance in 1951 it was like the answer to a prayer.
And Eric lived up to what I expected of him - tough and
determind, incurably inquisitive about unvisited remote
areas, and yet gentle and kind to young companions.

    He was a great explorer and a great man and I will
always remember him.

                                    Sir Edmund Hillary

Author's Note

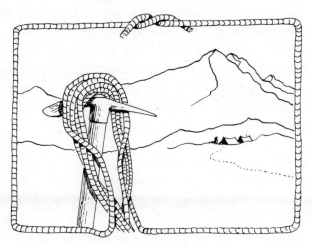

This is the story of a quiet, modest man acclaimed by many as one of the world's greatest mountain explorers. Eric Shipton's life, appropriately for a mountaineer, had steep peaks and valleys; it was constantly in the shadow of Mount Everest, a symbol of the fading British Empire. Ultimately his achievements were acknowledged by the mountaineering community, however he never received the public recognition he deserved, but did not seek. Lasting fame passed to others.

Eric Shipton laid the foundation for the climbing of Mount Everest over two decades from 1933 to 1953. He accumulated unique experience of the mountain before the Second World War with four expeditions from Tibet on the north side; afterwards he was instrumental in bringing New Zealanders into the team which discovered a viable route up the southern, Nepal flank of the mountain; he was appointed leader of the 1953 expedition to Everest, only to be supplanted a few weeks later; then he disappeared into obscurity, surfacing again in his late fifties to do some of his toughest journeys of all – in Patagonia.

I first met Eric Shipton when, as a boy, I joined a course at the Outward Bound Mountain School where he was Warden. He had become my hero since reading his books *Upon That Mountain, Nanda Devi* and *Blank on the Map*; several years passed before, in my maturity, he became my friend.

In the mid-sixties my family and I were invited to Bhutan to do research on thyroid goitre. On frequent visits to the Royal Geographical Society to search for maps I re-met Eric Shipton, who proved unstinting in his encouragement of our enterprise. We planned together that if I could get permission, Eric would join us for the second half of the traverse of the country. Sadly he never received my telegram affirming royal assent for his entry.

In the following decade we stayed closely in touch, especially when his latter-life companion, Phyllis Wint, would visit her lady friend across Bristol Downs. A soft knock on the door would herald Eric hoping to stay, and my wife, Sarah, (who loved him dearly as did every woman whose path he crossed) welcomed him warmly.

In 1971 I was invited to go as doctor to the International expedition to Mount Everest. As a family man I had severe doubts about accepting because of the dangers involved. So I went up to London to ask Eric's advice. As usual he was generous at someone else's good fortune, although the scale of the enterprise, so contrary to his basic philosophy of small being beautiful, horrified him. He told me to seek the opinion of others besides himself, and sent me to North Wales to see Charles Evans, who forwarded me on to Jan (then James) Morris. As a result I went to Everest, and no one was more pleased than Eric.

In 1975, at a barren crossroads in my surgical career, Sarah and I decided to move with our family to Canada. Eric, having made a journey to Alaska and relished its wilderness, was delighted and encouraged us, especially when we told him we were heading for the Yukon. But sadly our plans for him to visit us never came about because he died soon after.

Four years later I came over to England to see if, in the shadow of his excellent autobiography, *That Untravelled World*, there was enough material to write Eric's biography. After doing thirty interviews I returned to the Yukon (now my home of twenty-three years) to ponder the question. For personal and professional reasons I decided I could not undertake the project and handed it back to the putative publisher.

The years rolled by and, on long journeys overland by local transport which Sarah and I undertook every few years, we visited most of Eric's stamping grounds – Kenya, western China, Tibet and the north side of Everest, and Patagonia. I also came across treasure troves of his letters hoarded by various lady loves. In 1996 I returned to England to reassess the possibility of writing a biography. After another thirty interviews (half of the 1981 interviewees having died) I knew I had enough new material to tell a story that Eric never told about himself. (Sarah was always urging me to take on the biography, but she died in 1995 before this book got underway.)

During this absorbing project I have got to know Eric in a way that I never had the chance during his life. I have heard it said that biographers often end up disliking, or losing respect for, their subjects after the close scrutiny a biography entails. Nothing could be further from my present experience of Eric Shipton, familiar though I have become with his faults and weaknesses. He was a great man who has become an icon for climbers of the present generation, but who never achieved the place in history that I believe he deserves.

During the writing of this book Eric's sons, Nick and John Shipton, have given me unreserved encouragement. Several people gave me unrestricted access to many of Eric's letters: Madge Bridgman, of Vancouver, covering his Kenya, Kamet and early Everest years; Celia Armitage to a lifelong correspondence with her mother, Pamela Freston, starting in 1936; Nick and John Shipton to Eric's letters to their mother, Diana.

My profound thanks go to many people, some no longer living, for their help, whether by interviews, correspondence, advice, phone calls, loan of photographs, or checking the manuscript. My enjoyable and fruitful encounters with some of them – and indeed with Eric himself – are noted in Appendix 1. Their names are gratefully listed here:

Archivists of the Alpine Club, the Royal Geographical Society, the British Library, the Whyte Museum in Banff, Alberta, and the library of the University of Victoria, British Columbia, Rosemary Allott, Celia and Tony Armitage, David Attenborough, Bob Bates, Jennifer Bourdillon, Chris Brasher, Tom Brocklebank, Chris Bonington, Peter Bruchhausen, Roger and Ann Chorley, Nick Clinch, Robert Cross, Frank Dowlen, Norman Dyhrenfurth, John and Pauline Earle, Emlyn

Jones, Denise Evans, Irene Fleming, Pamela Freston, Eduardo García, Olivia Gollancz, Raymond Greene, Roy Greenwood, Alf Gregory, Ed Hillary, Peter Hopkirk, Tom Hornbein, Charlie Houston, Philip Hugh-Jones, John Hunt, Joan Mary and Maybe Jehu, Edwin Kempson, Larry Kirwan, John Lagoe, Peter Lloyd, Jack Longland, George Lowe, Beatrice and Joanna Lumley, Cedomir Marangunic, Nea Morin, Jan Morris, Margaret Mossop, Bill Norton, Noel Odell, Pat and Bruce Paton, Roger Perry, David Prysor-Jones, Peter Radcliffe, Bob and Vera Ransom, Mary Rawlinson, David Ridgeway, Jimmy Roberts, Barney Rosedale, Scott and Anne Russell, Audrey Salkeld, Brownie Schoene, Diana Shipton, Sarah Steele, Wilfred Thesiger, John and Phoebe Tyson, Walt Unsworth, Michael Ward, Charles Warren, Ken Wilson, Phyllis Wint, Charles Wylie.

My guides through the hills and valleys of biography were Maggie Body and Carol O'Brien, to whom I owe deep thanks for skilful navigation.

Whitehorse, Yukon, Canada, 1997

CHAPTER 1

Discovering Mountains

1907–27

ERIC SHIPTON was born in 1907 in what was then Ceylon – today Sri Lanka – where his father, a tea planter, died before Eric was three years old. His mother, a reserved and aloof lady, buried her grief by travelling constantly, accompanied by Eric and his sister, Marge, who was two years older than he was. Their travels took them round Ceylon and southern India, with frequent train journeys and sea voyages back and forth between Europe and the East.

Young Shipton delighted in the nomadic life and never missed having a settled home. Being a solitary child, he was uninterested in socialising with the games and parties common among colonials. He preferred to daydream about nature, with which he was closely in touch in the jungles and forested hills of Ceylon, particularly watching birds, a favourite pastime of his father, whom he could barely remember.

But his mother, thinking he needed civilising, brought him 'home' to England at the age of eight to a boring flat in London with lessons from a governess and walks in the park. His lack of progress with his studies, especially reading, persuaded his mother to send him to a preparatory school as a boarder. She did little to boost his childish confidence and her icy detachment, as he told a friend later, made him 'feel like a worm'.

Being extremely shy, he suffered from 'an aching loneliness', convinced he was generally scorned by adults and his fellows alike. His self-esteem was worsened at his prep school by frequently being put in the dunce's corner because of his slowness in learning to read. For this and other crimes, like 'impertinence' and 'cheating', the punishment was beating with a wide leather strap, a ritual then favoured by British boarding schools for making boys into men with stiff upper lips. He comments in his autobiography, *That Untravelled World*, 'On the whole we were not unkindly treated; but I am inclined to think that the frequency and severity with which we were flogged was a bit excessive.' His stoic attitude to this abuse may have contributed to the toughness he developed in his subsequent mountaineering days.

His slowness to read, and especially his inability to read aloud, led to derisive applause from his fellows, which was encouraged by the masters. When obliged to do so he would stammer, misread, or remain silent, which convinced him he was abnormally stupid. He describes how 'the words continued to get hopelessly tangled when I tried to read aloud.' In his day, and until very recently, such people were punished for their laziness and poor performance, which led in turn to wracking self-doubt and low self-esteem. This is the classic pattern of dyslexia, a neurological condition whereby the brain has difficulty in relating written symbols to sounds. Dyslexics hear words faultily and twist the symbols that represent those words. Legions of slow-learning children have been mistreated because of lack of understanding of a condition which is now thought to affect to some degree one child in every ten.

Like other dyslexics, Shipton learned tricks to cope with his learning disability, then known as 'word-blindness'. He discovered that piano lessons coincided with morning prayers (where he could be expected to read from scripture), so he became an avid pupil of music, for which he had negligible aptitude. Quickly realising that buffoonery was a passport to acceptance by his peers, he acquired a reputation for drinking the contents of ink-wells.

When he failed the Common Entrance Exam to Harrow, his mother decided to send him to Pyt House, a school for failing or delinquent boys who either had been thrown out of their public schools or, like Shipton, had never even got there. It also boarded a number of 'black princes' sent to learn English. The school was in a grand Palladian house with a pillared portico, set in parkland of oak and beech trees, looking across manicured lawns, a carp pond and a ha-ha ditch to a wide Wiltshire valley. School food, however, was scanty, and an old gardener at the school recalled how the boys used to steal bread from the back of the baker's van.

He continued to live reclusively, dreaming of exotic far-off places, stimulated by his own reading to himself which, though slow, had improved considerably. Edward Whymper's *Travels Amongst the Great Andes of the Equator* focused his attention on mountains, about which he began to devour any books he could find. In a hideout at the top of an enormous tree in the school grounds he used to share his adventurous dreams with Gustav Sommerfelt, a Norwegian friend who had been sent to the school to learn English. Together they would climb on the crumbling Purbeck marble walls of the ruined keep of nearby Old Wardour Castle, at first looking for birds' nests, later for the pure pleasure of climbing itself. Nowadays a Department of the Environment plaque reads, 'It is forbidden to climb on the walls.'

But, as with many English schoolboys who survived boarding school, Shipton's memories remained quite fond. He retained a lifelong affection for the headmaster's assistant, a starchily military gentleman nicknamed the Bum Skipper, whom he used to visit whenever he passed through the West Country. As he wrote, 'Being in the company of boys, as, or even more, stupid than I, did something to dispel my deep-rooted sense of inferiority.'

Shipton's first real encounter with mountains was when he was fifteen years old on a holiday spent in the Pyrenees with his mother and his older sister. Inspired by such sights as the Cirque de Gavarnie, he hankered after more than just reading about mountains. Soon his chance came when Sommerfelt invited him to Norway to spend a holiday wandering in the Jotunheimen mountains. An enormous rucksack, with a kettle clanking on the outside, cut into his shoulders but did not prevent him coming under the spell of crossing passes and looking towards distant horizons – a passion that was to last his lifetime. For the

time being Shipton had found an activity at which he excelled; it
involved no competition, satisfied him deeply, and bolstered his self-
confidence.

His first experience of the Alps was on a family winter sports holiday
in Adelboden. It was marred for the skiers by lack of snow, but was a
joy to Shipton who found an excuse to climb the Gross Lohner, a
10,000 foot mountain above the village, sharing the expense of hiring
two guides with some fellow hotel guests. He was deeply satisfied
cutting steps in the ice of the last slope to the summit, which revealed
a view of the great peaks of which he had read in Whymper's *Scrambles
Amongst The Alps*. He was also impressed by the guides' easy rhythmic
movements over difficult ground which he tried to emulate and which
in later life became his hallmark.

Unexpectedly, his austere and reticent mother never tried to stand in
his way of pursuing this supposedly dangerous sport, and did nothing
to discourage his infatuation with it. She continued to take her children
on holidays abroad which, for the era, were quite adventurous, and
pursued travel all her life.

Shipton was now seventeen and ready to branch out on his own.
Leaving his mother and sister ensconced beside Lake Como, he hired a
guide and a porter to climb neighbouring Monte Disgrazia. After a
night in a hut they set out for the top in foul weather and, on cresting a
ridge in blinding snow, the guides shouted ecstatically, wrung his hand
with congratulations for reaching the summit, and plunged down the
other side of the ridge, dragging him behind them. Despite his doubts
about the veracity of their triumph, it had been a great outing (on
repeating the climb forty years later with his younger son, John, he was
sure they had got no nearer than 2,000 feet from the top).

Now he was hooked on mountains, but with special interest in
volcanoes. So in the summer of 1925, aged eighteen, he went alone on
a Robert Louis Stevenson-like walking tour in the Auvergne and
Cevennes of the Massif Central. His plan for the second part of the
holiday (but not divulged to his mother) was to visit the Dauphiné Alps,
the site of his hero Whymper's adventures which were much more dramatic than his later competitive exploits on the Matterhorn.

At La Bérarde he met Elie Richard, 'a bandy-legged little man, barely
more than five feet tall', who was a second-class guide in need of filling

his quota of peaks so he could qualify for the first-class rank. The season had been poor and clients few, so Shipton's arrival, despite not looking like rich pickings, was a boon to Richard. Shipton was fit from his walking tour, and for each of the next ten days they climbed a peak or crossed a pass, sleeping and living frugally in alpine huts.

Back at home he faced the formidable obstacle of cramming for a Cambridge University college entrance exam. Despite nine years at school studying Latin, it was still his biggest stumbling block, so he set out to learn by heart (a common trick of dyslexics) his own paraphrase of the *Odes* of Horace. He passed the set-book paper with glory, but failed the 'unseen' exam miserably. Sitting again next year, he had to repeat the learning ordeal with Cicero's defence in the trial of Milo. This time he scraped by and was given an interview with the Master of his prospective college to whom he earnestly suggested that he should study geology. The Master poured scorn on the idea and told him its only worth would be for becoming a lecturer, and that, only if he got a first class honours degree. This damper finished any aspirations Shipton held for going to university, something that would dog him for the rest of his life and always give him a sense of inferiority in the presence of the university men who filled the ranks of the top British climbers at the time.

But at the age of nineteen those long-term prospects did not stand in the way of his far more immediate aspiration – to become an alpinist. Another rendezvous with Elie Richard in the Dauphiné produced twenty ascents in six weeks of almost continuous climbing, including the classic traverse of La Mèije. As with the Sherpas later in his life, Shipton treated Elie as a peer rather than a servant, and they both enjoyed the exploration as much as the climbing itself. By comparison with the élite alpine climbers of the day, Shipton's type of mountaineering was quite old-fashioned in style and undeveloped in technique, but he was enjoying himself far too much to mind, or to have ambition to join their ranks.

In the summer of 1927 Shipton returned to the Alps, this time with Gilbert Peaker, a friendly mathematician and a meticulous climber who he had met in Wasdale. Twenty years later Peaker and Shipton were climbing together again in Wales along with Peaker's teenage nephew, David Attenborough. The young tiger could not understand why

Shipton always called his uncle 'George', until it was explained to him that Shipton originally thought that was his name, but by the time he discovered his mistake ten years later it was too late to change.

They planned to climb without guides, which for the twenties was considered very risky. Starting in the Graian Alps they made their way via the Gran Paradiso to Chamonix, heartland of the great granite spires that attracted many expert rock climbers. Finally he did guided climbs on three of the great mountains surrounding Zermatt – Zinal Rothorn, Obergabelhorn, and Matterhorn.

Shipton's last alpine season – before life became serious – was the next year, 1928, when he and 'George' Peaker packed three cloudless weeks with uninterrupted climbing of classic routes around the Zermatt Valley. There he joined some of the Cambridge University Mountaineering Club climbers who had become his idols – Jack Longland, Lawrence Wager, Graham MacPhee and George Trevelyan. Longland, the ace rock gymnast of his day, remembered how Shipton 'moved very fast and safely on alpine ridges', but described him as 'only a reasonably good rock climber'.

Shipton's salad days were now over and he had to turn his mind to more mundane thoughts of earning a living. He wrote in *Upon That Mountain*, 'I left the Alps with a heavy sense that I was breaking with an episode in my life that would not be repeated. If I had been able to foresee something of what the next twelve years would bring I should not have been depressed.'

Without any academic qualifications to speak of, there seemed something to favour following in the footsteps of his father, a colonial entrepreneur. Gustav Sommerfelt was also thinking of emigrating, so Shipton enrolled in a course in estate management with a view to running a coffee plantation in Kenya, a land said to hold great promise for enterprising and adventurous young people.

CHAPTER 2

The Kenya Planter

Mount Kenya – Kilimanjaro – Ruwenzori, 1928–32

KENYA in the 'twenties and 'thirties, following the First World War, was a paradise for energetic people intent on living free from the constraints of formal society. Game abounded in expansive veld and savannah, land for farming was cheap, and the climate pleasant. Many white settlers were remittance men, the second sons of wealthy families, paid an annual sum to stay away so as not to upset the tradition of primogeniture. Kenya also drew, as did other colonies, its fair share of undesirables and fugitives from the law, and created its own alcoholics and wastrels. For a decade one settler community at Happy Valley in the Aberdare Hills brought opprobrium on the colony for its licentious ways and free interchange of spouses. These scandals culminated in the worldwide publicity surrounding the murder of Lord Errol in 1940 and the caste of aristocrats who assembled in the High Court in Nairobi. But libertines were a minority compared with hard-working immigrants from many nations bent on carving a new life out of untamed country.

Eric Shipton went to East Africa in 1928, planning to settle there for the rest of his life. He arrived with an ice axe, climbing boots and several hundred feet of rope, which he admitted seemed rather ridiculous in the heart of Africa. On the map he had noticed some high mountains, though he held out little hope of any serious mountaineering comparable to what he had tasted in the Alps during several past summers. Knowing nothing about agriculture, he apprenticed on a large coffee farm at Nyeri, north of Nairobi. Lying between the Aberdare Highlands and Mount Kenya, which sits astride the equator at 17,040 feet above sea level, it was an idyllic spot for a mountain-lover. Fifteen glaciers flow from Mount Kenya's twin summits, Batian and Nelion, named after two Masai chiefs.

Shipton describes the view from the balcony of his bungalow in *Upon That Mountain*.

The mountain was usually clear in the morning when the swiftly-forming clouds clustered round the peaks and extended far down the great volcanic cone. In the evening the clouds would dissolve and the peaks unveil. Sometimes the two tips of the twin peaks would appear above the cloud mass – incredibly high they seemed; sometimes the lower glacier skirts would come first into view, grey and cold under the dark pall; sometimes a window would open and show a section of flying buttress and deep ice-filled couloir, steep and forbidding; sometimes the western clouds would break before the southern, and the peaks would emerge already bathed in the sunset glow, shreds of rose-coloured mist clinging to their sides. Each evening, week after week, it was different, though I had learnt to know every detail of ridge and corrie. After a while the rains broke and the peaks remained hidden for weeks at a time. Those were dull days.

Shipton wrote a letter to introduce himself to the Colonial Service Assistant District Commissioner in Kakamega, Percy Wyn Harris, a Cambridge University mountaineer who had already garnered a reputation of several good alpine seasons. Wyn Harris suggested that at the end of December, before embarking for his home leave, they should make a joint attempt to climb Mount Kenya, on which he had failed the previous year. Finding a fellow climber in Africa was manna for

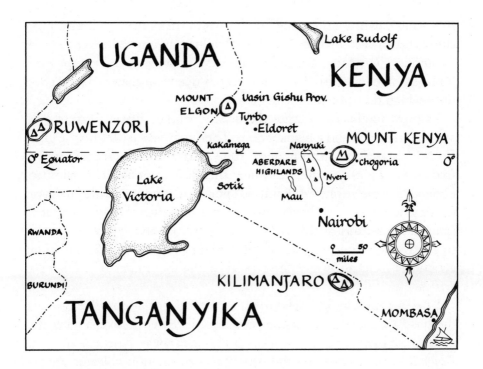

Shipton. Theirs would, they hoped, be a second ascent, the mountain having lain fallow since the first ascent of Batian in 1899 by Sir Halford Mackinder with two alpine guides, César Ollier and Joseph Brocherel. Nelion, the lesser summit, yet remained unclimbed.

Shipton's old school friend, Gustav Sommerfelt, had also emigrated to Kenya and was working on a farm near Eldoret. Although no mountaineer, he was a good athlete, so the climbers invited him to join them. But fate conspired to delay the enterprise. While practising climbing on a cliff, Shipton fell into the fork of a tree and broke his ankle; then Wyn Harris sent a telegram reporting a tribal disturbance in his district that would prevent him from getting away. Fortunately both these problems resolved themselves, and the three men met in Nairobi on New Year's Eve. There they shopped for supplies to last three weeks, rented a truck, and set out for the mountain. They drove, or rather lurched, from pothole to pothole, incurring one burst tyre and one puncture, to Chogoria, a village in the forest at the eastern foot of Mount Kenya. At midnight they billeted in a comfortable mud hut. The

following dawn, a welcoming host of Meru tribesmen, each carrying a
spear and a rolled blanket over one shoulder, assembled eager to work
for money. The long-limbed, barefoot Meru were naked except for a
loin cloth and brass arm bangles, their red-dyed hair thatched into a bun
onto which they hoisted their loads.

Shipton and his two friends recruited a band of fifteen porters, paid
at a shilling a day and a blanket each. Then they all set off into the giant
forest, entangled with monkey rope and tropical creeper, where
Colobus monkeys swung through the dark canopy. The climbers
entered a dense zone of bamboo, which gave way shortly to giant
heath where moss and lichen hung in swathes; then they emerged into
spacious parkland with thickets of bamboo and massive solitary
trees. Above 10,000 feet grew tall, lush grass, giant lobelia and giant
groundsel (senecio) which are typical of the mountains of Equatorial
Africa.

They camped in full view of the twin peaks of Mount Kenya near
the head of a gorge at 14,000 feet, and delighted in exchanging unaccustomed mountaineering gossip about faraway North Wales, the
English Lake District and the Alps. The central, non-volcanic granite
core of the mountain stood high above the ancient volcanic crater,
making an impressive array of sawtooth ridges and gulleys filled with
glaciers. They paid off most of their porters because the nights were
intensely cold and they had passed the upper limit of giant groundsel
which they could burn to warm themselves.

Mackinder's party had climbed Batian from the south-east; Shipton
and Wyn Harris went round to the north-east to have a closer look at
the network of ledges and gulleys that broke up that face. Next day, only
400 feet below the summit, they were rebuffed by a smooth granite
bulge and the sudden onset of equatorial night. They moved their camp
round to a frozen lake beside the Lewis Glacier, in which they found
embedded hundreds of wind-borne locusts from a plague the previous
year. They gained the southern ridge and were again impressed that the
mountain showed no easy breach in its defences. While contemplating
the difficulties ahead they saw a Brocken Spectre, a clear rainbow
framing their own silhouettes.

Next day Sommerfelt was sick with an altitude headache and stayed
in camp, so the others set off early across the glacier towards the moun-

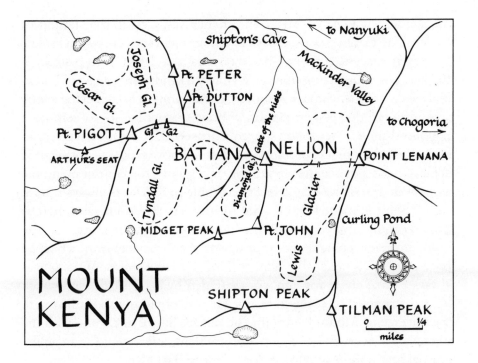

tain; Wyn Harris led off up the lower part of the face of Nelion with the skill of an alpine guide. Then Shipton took over the lead, entering a gulley that became the key to the lower part of the face. At the top they found a threadbare piece of rope left behind by Mackinder's party. They were now both climbing strongly and feeling fully alive after a lethargic start to the day. Through the clear African air they could see the summit of Kilimanjaro, a great dome of shining ice nearly 2,000 feet higher and 250 miles away to the south.

Not liking the look of the Diamond Glacier, across which Mackinder had traversed by cutting steps in the hard ice, they decided to try going directly up the face of Nelion. They climbed a chimney, followed by a shallow crack, then they turned the base of a large bulging overhang in a series of technically difficult rock pitches which Shipton compared with the traverse of La Mèije. They reached a smooth perpendicular cliff which they thought would be the crux of the climb, only to find to their surprise that easy broken rocks led to the virgin summit of Nelion. Then they descended into the gap between the twin peaks, named by

Mackinder the Gate of Mists, and thence easily up to the summit of Batian. The climbers walked back to Chogoria in snow, tired but replete with their success, and hitch-hiked (after a two-day wait) to Nairobi in the truck of a Dutch missionary. Wyn Harris and Shipton had unknowingly set a new benchmark in mountain exploration by achieving a long and difficult alpine-style climb, without crampons, in so remote a region. Although they found subsequent ascents of the mountain easier and easier, their first exploration of that unknown route was a gigantic achievement. For the first-timer, the uncertainty, the commitment, the anxiety of retreat all exaggerate the problem; followers always have it easier. Shipton made this his style for the rest of his life, and thereby carved his undisputed place in the history of mountaineering.

He started keeping diaries (but few of them survive) from which he began writing publishable accounts of his adventures. Writing was always a great chore for him, compounded by his dyslexia with which he had struggled to come to terms. He was obviously so thrilled with the traverse of Mount Kenya that he fills his tale of the climb with the minutiae of every difficult step and problem, interesting for an alpine journal but more than enough for a general narrative.

In Nairobi Shipton diffidently sold the story of their climb to the *East African Standard*. Banner headlines, which appalled Wyn Harris, announced, 'The Twin Peaks Conquered', and photographs covered an entire back page. Shipton was paid £2 10s which went towards his total expenses of £15 for the trip.

In April 1929 Shipton moved to Turbo in the Uasin Gishu region bordering Uganda. He and Gustav Sommerfelt got work on a large farm and shared lodgings in a sparsely furnished, one-room bungalow. By living frugally they could afford between them to run an old station wagon, which allowed them at weekends to explore the surrounding country, particularly to the north of the farm in the forests of Mount Elgon where wildlife abounded.

Farming was a very insecure business for most East African settlers, who were honest hard-workers trying to build this potentially fruitful land into a prosperous and developed country. However, a mood of optimism induced otherwise level-headed people to sink all they possessed into dodgy schemes. Banks advanced huge sums to farmers who lacked the technical expertise in what, when and how to cultivate their crops. Many farmers grew high-priced flax but the market suddenly slumped, leaving them with unpaid mortgages and expensive machinery standing idle. For the first five years coffee grew well in Uasin Gishu soil and on the slopes of Mount Elgon, but on reaching maturity, despite lavish nurturing, no beans appeared on the woebegone bushes. Others tried farming dairy cattle, sheep, maize, pyrethrum and sisal with similarly discouraging results. A rare plague of locusts devastated the crops in 1928, and the rains failed, causing widespread drought. Next year came the Wall Street crash heralding the Great Depression.

'But for all that it was a good life,' wrote Shipton, 'full of interest and variety, and there was a great sense of freedom. Each day's work showed a concrete result in so much land cleared or ploughed, a drain dug, trees planted, a wall built.' People were always dreaming up money-making schemes and experimenting – breeding ponies for the Indian polo market, big game hunting, forestry, prospecting for gold on the shores of Lake Rudolf, exploring the Turkana Desert.

Despite being out in the bush (even by Kenya standards), Shipton started to live quite a social life especially under the influence of Sommerfelt, who was outgoing, confident of his handsome looks, and liked the limelight on the dance floor where he excelled. Shipton was more retiring and content to stand in his friend's shadow, but soon he had a widely scattered circle of acquaintances. One particular girl caught his eye, and his fancy – Margaret 'Madge' Anderson, acclaimed the most graceful ballroom dancer at the Turbo Club. When she and suave Gustav (whom she called the Lounge Lizard) took to the floor to waltz people stopped dancing to watch them.

'I could follow anybody because I had good rhythm,' Madge said, 'they could stand on their head, and I would do the same. I think it comes down from my Welsh relations. Henry VIII was one of them.'

She recounted how at one dance a handsome young man sidled up to her and said he had been trying unsuccessfully to get an introduction. He asked her to dance, but she had no pencil to book her dance card, so he marked it with his thumbnail. The couple evidently hit it off because he also danced well. This was the new, emerging extrovert Eric Shipton.

'We danced and, as usual, sat out in the car and chatted, which was the custom then,' she said. 'He was about twenty-two and had lovely, deep set, blue eyes and a nice expression. He was a very sensitive, well behaved boy.'

Thus began a friendship and a romance that lasted for the next four formative years of Shipton's life, during which Madge Anderson was his main confidante and correspondent. Her friends had warned her against marrying tall, dark, handsome, witty Murray 'Andy' Anderson because he drank too much. 'But like all young girls,' she said, 'I wouldn't listen to their warnings.'

Soon after their wedding Andy became manager of the Eldoret Hotel, and he started having alcoholic blackouts. After one Christmas party he took six people in his car to a dance at a neighbouring hotel; on his return two extra men asked for a lift, which overloaded the car. Driving too fast down a corrugated road to a bridge, he struck the balustrade, the car plunged over the bank and ended upside down in the river. One of the passengers thrown clear saw bubbles in the water, rushed down and hauled Madge out by her hair. She was unscathed, but Andy died shortly afterwards, leaving her a widow at the age of twenty-two.

Eric Shipton and Madge Anderson soon became a pair and saw each other most weekends either at tennis parties or picnics. However, theirs was a very chaste friendship, perhaps because Madge's mother would always sit up until 5 a.m. after a dance waiting for her to come in.

'She was very strict with me, even as a child. If I did anything wrong she always found out. It was very good for me because it kept me pure, you see,' she said with a chuckle.

One day Shipton decided to host a party at Turbo, where his mother had bought him a farm from the proceeds of selling her house in London. He asked Madge to bring the girls and he would find the boys. As ever, her mother was there to see fair play and to help with the food. They intended to picnic and have a pyjama party on top of a rock behind the house. When Madge told the invited girls they would have to climb a hill and sleep in the open, half of them backed out. But for the remaining bold girls Shipton built a large fire on the rock slab, and they all spent an enthralling night out under a full moon.

Shipton became very fond of Madge's mother, who reciprocated. But she was always there chaperoning the young lovers, something they just accepted even when they went on long trips to the Aberdare

Highlands or to Uganda. Conversely Madge found Shipton's mother very cold, aloof and distant; they were civil to each other, but never became close. Between her travels, Shipton's mother used to stay with her son, who was always intensely loyal to her, even though she never liked his partners-to-be (nor those of her daughter).

'The only time she really took any notice of me,' said Madge, 'we were walking across the garden and Eric took my hand. She got wise, as if to say, "There's something going on here." But there wasn't.'

Madge and Shipton talked a lot about his climbing adventures on Mount Kenya, for which he had become quite famous. He used to write long screeds to her at home in Eldoret, both from his farm and whenever he went away on trips into the mountains.

As a result of the article in the *East African Standard*, Shipton received a letter from a stranger asking about the possibilities of climbing in Kenya. His name was H. W. Tilman, a farmer in Sotik, sixty miles south of Turbo. Older than Shipton by ten years, Tilman had emigrated to Kenya in 1919 soon after returning from four years' distinguished service in France in the Royal Artillery (incidentally serving under a battery commander, Major Norton of later Everest fame).

In a lottery for ex-servicemen, Tilman drew a farm in East Africa. Finding himself on the south-western slopes of the Mau forest near Lake Victoria, not far from the Uganda border, he climbed a tree to view the square mile of land which was to be his home for the next ten years. In *Snow on the Equator* he wrote, 'This unusual method of inspection was adopted because heavy bush, through which there were no paths for there were no inhabitants, prevented access to it . . . True, it was in the back blocks fifty miles from the railway, a journey of three or four days for ox-wagons, which were then the only means of transport; no Europeans had grown anything there before, and the clearing of the land would be an expensive business; but all that weighed light in the balance against the ardour of the pioneer.'

Tilman and Shipton had little in common apart from their desire to climb mountains, which Kenya society considered quite peculiar. Tilman's interest in mountains had been fired up by a holiday in the English Lake District, but he had not yet done much climbing. They agreed to meet in Nairobi and drive down to Tanganyika to climb the extinct volcano of Kilimanjaro, the highest mountain in Africa (19,340 feet), a great inverted pudding basin, technically easy apart from the altitude.

Tilman's account of their adventure on Kilimanjaro is twelve times as long as Shipton's. Throughout, he refers to his partner as S. – laconic to the point that even the full stop seems an extravagance. Shipton says of him, 'I soon realised that my new companion (it was many years before I called him "Bill"), though having virtually no mountaineering experience, was ideally suited to the game.' Tilman complemented perfectly the now gregarious and garrulous Shipton, who was a hedonist by comparison with Tilman who became renowned as a recluse, a misogynist, an astringent, tough companion, yet humorous and sensitive.

On their drive to Kilimanjaro they met lions and elephants, such as one reads of in Livingstone's and Stanley's travel tales, or in *Boys' Own Paper*. But Tilman was an experienced 'white hunter' and was quite unperturbed by this addition to their adventure. Once on the mountain they walked to Peter's Hut, now Horombo Hut, and pushed on to reach a cave which they knew lay in a windy valley. Tilman had a headache

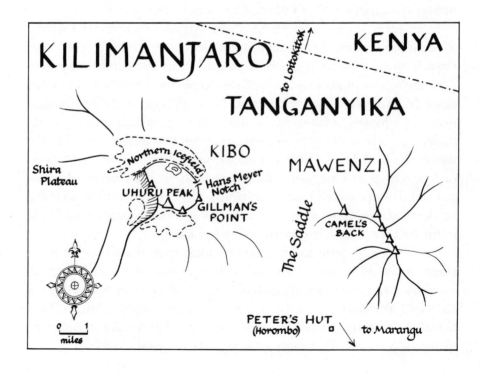

from the altitude, which was to be a recurring problem for him since he became sick on nearly every other climbing expedition they did together. Shipton by contrast acclimatised easily to the cold thin air on high. 'S. was fit enough,' Tilman wrote.

They sent most of the porters down to the comparative comfort of the hut, together with a little white donkey 'who had the legs and lungs of us all'. Solomon and one other porter stayed and suffered the cold together, speechless because of their chattering teeth. Next morning they began the long, tedious slog through waist-deep snow to the rim overlooking the giant, flat-bottomed crater of Kilimanjaro, towards Kibo, the highest of the twin summits. Tilman stopped frequently to vomit so, according to him, they decided to retreat from Kibo for the simple reason that they could go no further, though Shipton's account claims that they had reached the top.

While floundering around near the summit in thick cloud they had discarded their sunglasses, unaware that ultraviolet rays penetrate haze insidiously. On return to the cave their eyes began to smart and feel as though sand had been rubbed in them, a characteristic sensation of snowblindness. When they returned to Solomon, who had stayed behind at the hut, he was 'the colour of a mottled overripe plum'. This sounds as if he was dangerously short of oxygen, for Kilimanjaro claims several climbers' lives each year because they ascend too rapidly. At Peter's Hut they rested for their eyes to improve before trying Mawenzi, the satellite peak of Kilimanjaro. Snow was falling through thick mist, the rock was rotten, and the whole mountain was rimed with ice. Nevertheless they struggled up to the jagged teeth on the summit ridge and so to the top. They had no cause to dally there and descended at speed, as did, separately, Tilman's hat and snow glasses.

Once down, Shipton was in a hurry to get home, so they set off to drive back to Nairobi. But at a washed-out bridge when they tried to drive across the swollen river it swirled over the car's floorboards. Eventually, some Africans standing nearby pushed them across. Soon afterwards they drove through a deep mud puddle and the car stopped with the back axle firmly stuck on a ridge between the ruts, while the wheels spun in the smelly mud. This emphasised something they already knew well – the futility of ever being in a hurry on African roads.

They returned to their respective farms for six months before getting together for another climb. Shipton wrote to Tilman telling him that the coffee had grown so well in his absence he was now ready to carry out his long-nurtured plan of traversing the twin peaks of Mount Kenya. 'I already had some land in Sotik,' wrote Tilman, 'where with a newly acquired partner there would be no danger of becoming enslaved by the farm. If either of us wanted a holiday, it could be taken; all that was needed between the two of us was the sort of understanding that John Jorrocks had with his huntsman, James Pigg, to wit, "that master and man should not both get drunk on the same day."' So from this convenient ability to abandon their farms and have compatible trips together whenever it took their fancy burgeoned one of mountaineering's historic partnerships.

They drove to Nanyuki, Shipton burning with impatience to reach Mount Kenya, and again the car got stuck with its axles deep in some muddy ruts. So they abandoned it and walked to the Silverbeck Hotel at the bar of which representatives of the northern and southern hemisphere once played a famous chess match, with the board straddling the equator. Here Shipton and Tilman rented pack ponies from the proprietor's brother, Raymond Hook, legendary big game hunter and outfitter. After meeting a rhinoceros, and then a big bull elephant, they wended their way up the Mackinder Valley. At 14,000 feet near the foot of Batian, they found a cave where the porters annexed the only dry part. Shipton and Tilman were left out in the wet, but they found adequate groundsel nearby to make a big fire. Next day, by way of reconnaissance, they made the first ascents of Point Dutton and Point Peter. They then saw they would have to cut steps up the steep part of the Joseph Glacier to reach the col on the ridge.

'We would have been saved a great deal of trouble if we had had crampons, but as I had hardly ever used them, I did not regret their lack,' Shipton wrote in *That Untravelled World*. 'I know of no mountain in the Alps, with the possible exception of Mont Blanc, that presents such a superb complexity of ridges and faces as the twin peaks of Mount Kenya.' They named two spires on the ridge the Grand and Petit Gendarmes, which were evidently going to pose difficult problems. Beyond that they could not get a good view of the ridge, but it appeared formidably complex, as Shipton wrote, 'certainly not the place to take a novice [Tilman] for his first serious mountaineering exploit, and it was stupid of me even to think of doing so.'

They retreated to their cave, prepared to launch themselves at the mountain the next day. 'It would be August 1st, but, though the fact that this was S.'s birthday (his 23rd) was not given undue weight,' Tilman wrote, 'it would be a very nice birthday present if we pulled it off.' They left their cosy, warm cave at 3 a.m. under a bright moon. Shipton, however, regarded his companion much less charitably at that moment. 'How I hated Tilman in the early morning,' he says in *Upon That Mountain*.

Not only on that expedition, but through all the years we have been together. He never slept like an ordinary person. Whatever time we agreed to awake, long before (how long I never knew) he would slide from his sleeping bag and start stirring his silly porridge over the Primus stove. I used gradually to become aware of this irritating noise and would bury my head in silent rage against the preposterous injustice of being woken half an hour too soon. When his filthy brew was ready he would say 'Show a leg,' or some such imbecile remark. In moments of triumph on top of a peak I have gone so far as to admit that our presence there was due in large measure to this quality of Tilman's, but in the dark hours before dawn such an admission of virtue in my companion has never touched the fringe of my consciousness.

On a glorious crisp dawn they quickly gained the ridge, using steps they had cut the previous day. They climbed over and round the gendarmes and then came to another obstacle, a red pinnacle, flanked on both sides by vertical drops. By standing on Tilman's shoulders, and with a final kick off his companion's head, Shipton just reached two finger holds and pulled up to a more secure stance. As they were wearing boots with tricouni nails in the soles, it is surprising how little Tilman complained. This pitch was obviously technically difficult by any modern climbing standards. Now they could not retreat by the way they had come because their rope was not long enough for the abseils that would be necessary, so they were committed to following the sound granite ridge which continued, narrow and difficult, to the summit.

Suddenly at 4.30 p.m., twelve hours of continuous climbing after setting foot on the mountain, they stood beside the cairn Shipton and Wyn Harris had built on top of Batian the year before.

With only two hours of daylight left – and tropical night falls like a curtain – they gulped a tin of meat essence, and started down. But first, Tilman twisted off the point of his ice axe, next, he dropped it several hundred feet to the glacier below. Soon after, Shipton vomited violently (probably from the meat essence), and he was forced to halt frequently, becoming progressively weaker and suffering the hallucination of seeing an extra member in the party. But in their accounts each of them unreservedly praises the other. Shipton: 'Bill had been magnificent; he had shown no sign of anxiety throughout the climb, and his stoicism no less than his innate skill in climbing and handling the rope made a vital contribution to our success.' Tilman: 'The most vivid impression that remains in my mind of this grim ordeal is how S. in the feeble state he was, not only climbed, but led the way unerringly and safeguarded his companion.'

Crossing the Lewis Glacier, they descended to a small hut at the Curling Pond, or Skating Lake. At first light they headed for their cave (since officially named Shipton's Cave), where they collapsed into their sleeping bags, placing a ten-pound Cheddar cheese and a bottle of pickled onions between them, and gorging themselves until they fell asleep.

They still had another six days' holiday so, after recuperating, they set off to explore a prominent slender rock spire set apart from the south side of the mountain which they climbed with some difficulty. But on their way down snow began to fall heavily, causing Tilman to slip on a sloping ice ledge and knock himself out. Shipton held him on the end of a tight rope but was unable to see him or talk to him. He climbed down a gulley, still with Tilman tight on the rope, and found him looking a bit strange, half conscious and with no idea where he was, or what had happened. They continued their descent. After each abseil they had to cut off three feet of rope (using a sharp stone for lack of a pocket knife) to make a sling through which to thread the rope. After pulling the doubled rope through, they left the sling in place with each abseil, so by the time they were finished their 120 foot rope was reduced to about forty feet in length.

Shipton regarded the traverse of the twin peaks of Mount Kenya as one of the most enjoyable, and one of the hardest climbs he had ever done – 'a perfect and wholly satisfying episode, shared with an ideal companion'. As for the rock spire on which Tilman knocked himself out, it now appears on all the maps as Midget Peak, Shipton fondly having used the nickname of his petite, beloved Madge Anderson. For someone so recently a dreamy loner, it was quite a flamboyant gesture.

At this time some prospectors discovered gold in a stream bed near Kakamega, a small town roughly halfway between Shipton's farm at Turbo and Tilman's in Sotik. A mutual friend, one of the syndicate that made the original discovery, beguiled Shipton and Tilman with tales of a cornucopia of riches lying just below the ground they were walking on. But Shipton had just received a flattering climbing invitation from Frank Smythe in England to join his expedition to Kamet. 'I was far too dazzled by the glitter of the Himalaya to be much tempted by the lure of gold,' he wrote. 'It was a shortsighted choice, no doubt, but not one that I have greatly regretted.'

Tilman fell for the bait of gold fever, mainly because he was at a loose end having abandoned coffee planting. So he, somewhat reluctantly, joined his friend 'D.' in the goldfields. 'That I was not infected [with gold fever] the first year,' he says, 'seems to argue the tranquil mind of the philosopher or the apathetic insensibility of a blockhead.' He spent the next six months living first in a tent then in a mud and wattle hut, digging trenches across ground they had staked, dealing with jiggers between their toes and rats under their mosquito nets. After six months they began to doubt themselves because it seemed a little odd that none of the expert prospectors thought it worth staking their land. So they sold out to gullible neighbours who they impressed with tales of a rich quartz vein under their ground.

The year after Shipton returned from Frank Smythe's Kamet expedition, he and Tilman paired together for what proved to be one last African venture to the Ruwenzori, the Mountains of the Moon, that lie in a remote corner of north-east Uganda almost straddling the border with present day Zaire, formerly the Belgian Congo. They set off in Tilman's car to the roadhead access point at Fort Portal. There they bought bananas and beans for themselves; and blankets, cooking pots and cigarettes for the fourteen Bakonjo porters. One porter went ahead

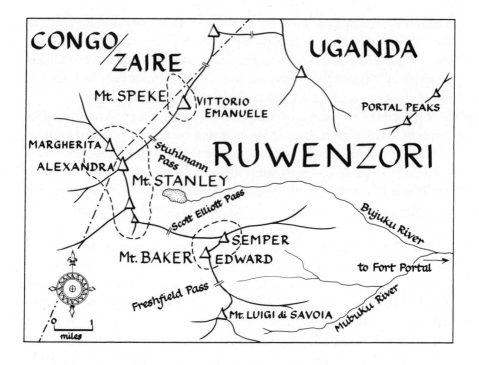

with a heavy panga bush-knife to clear the overgrown track, while the rest followed carrying fifty-pound loads on their heads. Shipton and Tilman really enjoyed this weird, wet mountainscape for the sheer pleasure of exploring its unusual beauty – country that had a vague resemblance to the Patagonia of their separate travels three decades later.

Shipton kept a running diary for 'Midget Dearest'.

You would love this forest, without the least sign of man anywhere, and the beautifully complicated and unexplored valleys and the continuous sound of waterfalls. There are lots of clear streams running over rocks, with great deep pools. Whatever the high peaks may be like, this is a real mountain range with savage rock peaks and crags. You would love it!

For this degree of wilderness he may have misjudged the enthusiasm of Madge Anderson, who was in her element on the dance floor of

Eldoret, at garden tennis parties and on little hikes up Mount Elgon behind Shipton's farm. He continues quite poetically.

I wish you were here to see it with me, when everything is shining and soft. But not when it is raining, as then things are too hard and wild, and there is too much work to do; but perhaps again when we are in the tent or under a rock shelter, and the rain had eased off, looking across the valley at a great rocky peak with the clouds blowing wildly off it with every little gully trying its hardest to hold a wisp of cloud which is trying to escape, listening to the drip of the trees. You like all that don't you, Midget? But I want more than anything else to show you a storm amongst the peaks. I wonder if I ever will!

Shipton's writing became fluent and more evocative than in his earlier accounts of climbing on Mount Kenya and Madge encouraged him strongly to keep on writing.

He and Tilman walked for long spells without touching ground, on top of thickly-matted vegetation. The Bakonjo porters climbed up and down formidable slopes, or sprang from one tree to another, their loads still balanced on their heads. Whenever they wanted fire they would blow on a cigar-shaped package of leaves they carried containing smouldering moss or lichen tinder. Rain fell continuously, so the climbers were glad to find caves and rock shelters for their camps.

The upper slopes of Ruwenzori (wrote Tilman in *Snow on the Equator*), from 10,000 feet to the snow-line, comprise a world of their own – a weird country of moss, bog, rotting vegetation, and mud, on which flourish grotesque plants that seem to have survived from a past era . . . gaunt giant groundsel crowned at the top with spiky heads like half-eaten artichokes; tough, leafless shrubs with white everlasting helichrysum; grey, withered, and misshapen tree heaths, tumescent with swollen growths of moss and lichen oozing moisture; monstrous freaks of nature bred from the union of mist and morass; a slimy barrier serving to enhance and make more desirable the fresh purity of the snows which lie beyond . . . by their position, mystery, traditions, and matchless scenery, ranking, surely, amongst the wonders of the world.

On they went through the senecio forest. 'Moss, moss, moss, nothing but moss,' bemoans Shipton. Their tent, sleeping bags, and kit were water-logged, but even these discomforts (which are hard to imagine Midget enjoying) did not dampen their admiration of the beauty of this unique country. One afternoon the clouds parted for a moment, revealing the great ice peaks of Mounts Stanley and Speke which they had come to find. 'When I see high peaks and their glaciers,' Shipton wrote in his diary to Midget, 'I always get the same odd thrill which has lost nothing since the first I ever saw, and has altered nothing with familiarity.'

He marvels at these snow peaks in the midst of thousands of miles of tropical swamp and regrets that the Duke of the Abruzzi, who first explored them, gave them all Italian names (but forgetting that he himself had named a peak after Midget). In the same breath he worries that if the Germans were to climb Everest first it might become named 'Bismark-spitz'.

At sunset a few days later the mists cleared and they looked down on the plains of the Congo which appeared a vivid blue against the blazing sunset, with the silver streak of the Semliki River cutting across the middle. They climbed the subsidiary summits of Mount Stanley, Alexandra and Margherita, a jumble of fantastic ice towers, ice caves and pinnacles; Vittorio Emanuele of Mount Speke; and Semper and Edward peaks of Mount Baker. Often they barely knew where they were, despite following a compass course, sometimes through snow and high wind, at others in clammy mist and brooding silence.

Tentbound on the mountain by vile weather, and bookless, they read and re-read the inside of the Ryvita packaging in German, Spanish and Italian, interspersed with singing to each other their small stock of songs. Floundering around the glaciers of the Ruwenzori on their descent, and squelching through the swamps at its feet, Tilman lost his watch and camera, and Shipton sprained his shoulder in a fall.

'Climbing in the Ruwenzori was a memorable experience and well worth the discomfort and the exasperating toil,' summarises Shipton. 'One has to go a long way to see nature at her most sublime.' This was their last African adventure together. Now their eyes were turned towards more far-flung mountains.

CHAPTER 3

First Footing in the Himalaya

Kamet, 1931

AFTER MOUNT KENYA, Eric Shipton's reputation as a mountaineer reached Britain through his and Bill Tilman's articles in the *Alpine Journal* and the *Geographical Journal*. As a result Frank Smythe, then doyen of British alpinists, invited Shipton to join an expedition to Kamet (25,447 feet) in the Garhwal Himalaya. Tilman meanwhile bought a bicycle for £6 and, living mainly off roasted bananas, pedalled across the waist of Africa – a 'most cheap and efficacious method' of getting home to Britain and a chance to explore new country.

Shipton was excited about his 'impossible dream' of this coming Himalayan adventure. Nowadays the Himalaya has become almost commonplace, with thousands of people trekking through the foothills each year; then it was as far off as Mars, and the few who had explored there, mainly military or administrative officers, and members of Everest expeditions, were as revered as astronauts three decades later.

In love with Madge Anderson, Shipton wrote her tender, never

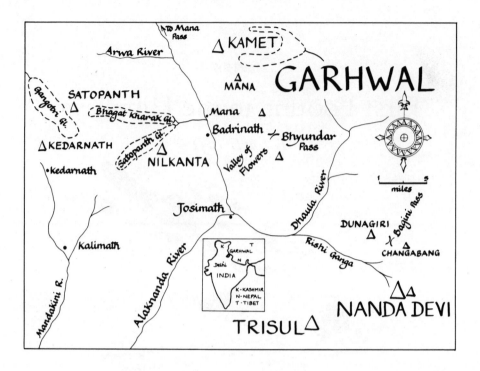

passionate, letters in somewhat Bertie Woosterish prose. He always sent his love to Midget's mother, of whom he had grown extremely fond. His own mother, who was living with him on the farm some of the time between her travels, remained quite demanding. 'While Mum is here,' he wrote, 'I simply can't leave her and she must have someone to take her about, besides.'

Before embarking for Kamet, he asked Midget for 'an enlargement (p.c. size) of the photo of yourself leaning up against the post outside your last residence, with your hat turned up, a small belt and a large grin'. Then he continued, 'Midget it's rotten things being as they are just before I'm going off. We'll do all sorts of things when I come back, won't we? As you say, perhaps this is good for us – but it hurts me awfully – and all I can do is try not to think about it. You are going to write to me lots, aren't you? This air mail is a splendid idea!'

Whenever possible he dashed into Eldoret from Turbo in his old car to meet Midget, holding his breath, 'in case the old bus would break down beyond repair, or a puncture would shorten my time with you by one moment. I think she must have had her heart in it too! Anyway she seldom – if ever – robbed me of the thrill of seeing you.'

Like anyone going off on an extended trip, the excitement of the adventure to come was tempered by what he was leaving behind – family, friends, lovers, home comforts and the security of things familiar. But it was heady stuff for Shipton being the youngest by seven years of an experienced group of British mountaineers led by the famed Frank Smythe, heading for what could be – were they successful – the highest peak in the world yet climbed.

Smythe had made a name for himself by climbing the exceptionally difficult (for those days) Lochmatter route on the Aiguille du Plan in the Alps, and had been on the 1930 international expedition to Kangchenjunga. A weakly child, owing to a heart murmur which restricted his physical activities, by dint of application rather than genius he became a proficient climber, mountain writer and photographer. Raymond Greene in *Moments of Being* caricatured him thus: 'Physically on mountains, intellectually in his books, Frank always tried to reach heights which were just a little beyond his powers, great though these were.'

Midget came to see Shipton off at Eldoret railway station. The train from Nairobi to Mombasa offered a glorious view of Kilimanjaro with the moon shining on its glaciers which he knew so well. He boarded the SS *Khandala* of the British India Steam Navigation Co. bound for India with only one fellow passenger on board. He found Bombay quite foul compared with Nairobi, itself no paradise, 'the streets crammed with limbless deformities and diseased people and crowds of smelly natives'.

Ensconced in the Taj Mahal Hotel looking out to sea beyond the Gateway of India, Shipton was well insulated from beggars. He played bridge and 'slosh' with friends till late at night, went to the 'talkies' (the first he had ever seen), and danced a lot. But he found his dancing partners not to be compared with Midget, for whom he was quite lovelorn, expectantly awaiting every mail. In Bombay, Frank Smythe and he got busy with expedition arrangements; then they caught the train across the Rajasthan Desert to Delhi and beyond. Being the hottest time of the year, Shipton still had not found the enchantment of the country, and wrote again to Midget, 'India is a vile place – hundreds upon hundreds of miles of hot, dusty ugliness.'

Once on the bus, passing through the foothills of the Himalaya with a ton of expedition kit, Shipton's spirits soared as the road wound steeply through forests of flowering trees. In Ranikhet they met their servants, Sherpas recruited in Darjeeling by Colonel Harry Tobin, co-founder of the Himalayan Club. Lewa, the expedition sirdar, or foreman, had been on Everest three times in the 1920s, as well as on Kangchenjunga the previous year.

The other members of the Kamet team assembled in Ranikhet were Wing Commander E. B. Beauman, an experienced alpine climber and skier; Captain Bill Birnie, of Sam Browne's Cavalry and the Governor of Bengal's Bodyguard, who had travelled widely in the Himalaya, spoke fluent Hindustani, and was a polo and squash rackets champion; Dr Raymond Greene, a six and a half foot giant with a matching intel-lect, a practising physician and researcher into acclimatisation to high altitude; and Dick Holdsworth, an avid athlete and skier, also the expe-dition's botanist (an important role in getting financial support).

Frank Smythe woke them all to see the sunrise as they dozed in their sleeping bags on the verandah of the tourist bungalow. Dawn touched Trisul and Nanda Devi, a green mist hung at the end of the garden and light filtered through the forests in the valley below. Raymond Greene described the scene, 'Then came ridge after ridge of rolling pine-covered hills, and, at last, apparently hung high in the blue sky above them, the edge of a silver saw. One tooth was bigger than the others – that was Kamet.'

Lying near the Tibetan border in the north of the Garhwal, Kamet had already been tried by ten previous expeditions, and the names of the participants read like a history of Himalayan mountaineering – Schlagintweit, Longstaff, Bruce, Mumm, Brocherel, Kellas, Morshead, Slingsby, Meade. Approaching it entailed wandering through gentle, flower-filled Himalayan valleys, ambling along well-made paths in the lovely foothills of Garhwal through woods of oak and pine, and climb-ing over high grassy downs, barren ridges, and along deep ravines.

Lewa led a team of seven other Sherpas, the group of Nepali people of Tibetan ethnic origin who live in the upland southern shadow of Mount Everest around Namche Bazar, and in the bordering hill stations of Darjeeling and Kalimpong. By reason of being genetically acclima-tised to high altitudes over many generations, they have become the

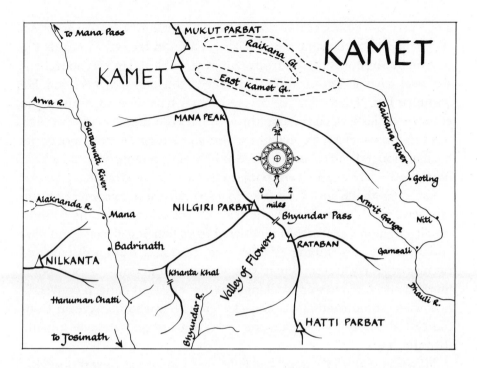

self-selected élite of high altitude porters. Shipton noted, 'The Sherpas saw to all our needs, acting as valets to look after our personal belongings, rousing us in the mornings with mugs of tea, pitching and striking our camps and even removing our boots'. Over the intervening fifty years little seems to have changed (apart perhaps from the boots) in the imperious march of expeditions through the Himalaya. Even trekkers in the high mountains expect such service.

On Smythe's Kamet expedition each climber had his own green canvas tent, they were generously provisioned with tinned delicacies, and in the mess tent in the evenings they listened to a gramophone with forty records provided by His Master's Voice. Shipton was in charge of stores and 'played at catering'. His most pressing job was encouraging the egg-wallah to scavenge in the villages for chickens and eggs to supplement their tins with fresh food. His cooking remained basic throughout his exploring life, as it did years later in his London flat where he still lived mainly on vegetable curry.

Shipton immediately hit it off with his companions, whom he found

a most cohesive bunch. Raymond Greene, a great talker, urbane, interesting, and witty, became a particular friend. On the walk towards the
mountain Shipton suffered from 'tummy troubles'. He was apprehen-
sive over what lay ahead, and could not get Midget out of his mind. He
wrote to her, 'I have just discovered that I have not been liking the
country we have been passing through. Heaven knows why, as it was
beautiful beyond my expectations! But something entirely spoiled its
beauty, though I can't think what.' Was he simply pining, or could it have
been the anti-dysenteric serum injected into him by Greene?

Crossing the Kauri Pass (12,800 feet), all the newcomers to the
Himalaya were impressed by the scale of the country and its complicated geography; avalanches thundered from hanging glaciers, and they
could see the sun shining through thin ice ridges from a distance of
twenty or thirty miles. But it was not all sauntering. At one point
Shipton and Greene were walking together engaged in deep conversation when some football-sized rocks fell with a whining scream from
the cliff above onto the path they were traversing, narrowly missing
them both.

However, Shipton's mood had lightened and he was now thoroughly
enjoying the beauty of the march, which for a week took them through
some spectacular gorges. They pitched camp in full view of Kamet
on a moraine near the foot of the Raikana Glacier at 15,500 feet.
Holdsworth and Shipton climbed a small peak above the junction with
the East Kamet Glacier and saw a gorge that would lead them towards
the foot of the peak.

They found a place safe from avalanches where they could pitch their
first mountain camp. The Sherpas were performing well, especially
Lewa, who would often shoulder a double porter's load, despite the fact
that as sirdar he was not obliged to carry a load at all. The climbers were
all beginning to notice some of the unpleasant effects of being in high
mountains – permanently cold feet, headaches, poor sleep and bad
dreams, and Cheyne-Stokes respiration which wakes people up in the
night because they have stopped breathing, only to start again with
ever-increasing sighs.

On the mountain they found a route up a couloir and pitched Camp
III in a blizzard. Acrid smoke permeated their tea, porridge and soup
as they huddled round a cooking fire of juniper carried up from the

valley. The only technical climbing lay between Camp III and Camp IV; Smythe called it a 1,000-foot precipice, but Shipton dismissed it as 'not unduly exacting'.

In fact, Smythe's account in *Kamet Conquered* has page upon page of step-by-step description, so one imagines the climb to have been dauntingly difficult. He wrote, 'The couloir allowed little latitude for life but an overwhelming margin in favour of death,' then continuing in characteristic purple prose, 'Night was draining the red wine of day from the peaks as we trod the glacier plateau; in the half-light the great wall on which we had laboured all day looked terribly forbidding. Above and behind it rose the huge peak of Kamet, blazoned on a shield of awakening stars.'

Meade and Kellas had got up the same 'precipice' two decades earlier without undue difficulty. Was Smythe painting this picture of incredible hazards for his intrepid climbers, laced with deeds of derring-do, in order to impress the armchair public who avidly read his books? Shipton remarked about the same episode, 'We've had a grand day's mountaineering.'

Smythe frequently notes how well and strongly Shipton was climbing, and how he was the fittest member of the team and had become one of the lead climbers, both for his technical skill and his easy acclimatisation. At every halt for a breather, contrary to modern views on lung health, the climbers dug out their tobacco for a smoke.

At great discomfort Holdsworth, the athlete and proficient skier, carried his skis for the chance to schuss down from Meade's Col. They pitched Camp IV where Smythe and Shipton stayed in a developing blizzard. Whenever possible in camp they donned pyjamas, crawled into their sleeping bags, smoked and yarned. 'By the time sleep claimed us,' wrote Smythe, 'we had come to the conclusion that the affairs of the British Empire should have been entrusted to a cabinet consisting exclusively of ourselves.'

Smythe thrived the higher he climbed. Raymond Greene said that at sea level he was very touchy and took offence easily. 'As soon as he became hypoxic the essential Frank came out and he couldn't have been nicer. At great altitudes a new force seemed to enter him. It was impossible above 20,000 feet to disturb his composure or his essential quietism and he became easy to deal with, and quite unquarrelsome.'

This is an uncommon beneficial effect of hypoxia, lack of oxygen causing the brain to function below par.

Shipton wrote, 'Smythe as a mountaineer was sound rather than brilliant, and he owed his outstanding success to his remarkable endurance. In adverse conditions he seemed to have a fakir-like ability to shut himself in a mental cocoon, where he was impervious to fatigue or boredom, discomfort or psychological stress, and thus emerged with his resources quite unstrained.'

They pitched Camp V on Meade's Col at 23,000 feet, ready to attempt the summit next day. Shipton was feeling unwell, and wrote to Midget, 'The evening before our climb I was in my tent changing the film in your camera when suddenly I felt the power going out of my left hand. I didn't think much of it at first, but it quickly spread up my arm into my jaw and down my left leg. I seized the rum and drank it, and after a while life returned.' This was probably a transient ischaemic attack, which is like a minor, quickly passing 'stroke', possibly due to thickening of the blood that develops at altitude. Shortage of oxygen stimulates the bone marrow to produce more red blood cells, which can then carry more oxygen, of which the body – especially the brain – is peculiarly short. But the increased stickiness, or viscosity, of the blood makes it more liable to form small clots which can clog small blood vessels in the brain. Such episodes are not uncommon in high altitude mountaineering.

Shipton felt better next morning, and a party of five left their camp on Meade's Col: Smythe, Holdsworth and Nima Dorje on one rope; Shipton and Lewa on the other. The funereal rate of their climb was due to them floundering in new snow, rather than the steep ground, and breaking through the crust prevented them from getting into a steady climbing rhythm. Crossing some windswept slabs, they reached the sharp final summit ridge after eight hours of continuous climbing. So that Lewa might be the first to tread the summit, they pushed him in front of them – a generous gesture of appreciation to the Sherpas for their contribution to the success of the climb. Smythe stuck a small Union Jack in the snow at 4.30 p.m.

'Here we are back at Base Camp with Kamet climbed,' Shipton wrote to Midget on 28 June 1931. 'On the highest summit ever reached my mind was too dull to feel any elation. The grandeur of the scene did not make a slight impression on me.' Time was short for getting back to Camp V before dark, so they could not dally long. 'I only remember a long muddle of driving myself to do things,' continued Shipton. 'We were all quite finished when we got back to camp.' Lewa's feet were coloured white and dark purple with frostbite; Greene predicted he would loose all his toes. Holdsworth and Shipton had minor frostbite of their toe tips. Beauman took charge of getting the porters and Sherpas to carry their sirdar, who resented being the cause of so much trouble, down the valley. He eventually lost the last joint of all his toes.

At base camp an evil-looking (and smelling) itinerant fakir entertained them for the sum of one rupee by contorting himself and standing on his head on top of a large boulder. Greene wrote in *Moments of Being* about their descent into the valleys, 'Grasses were beginning to sprout between the stones and a saxifrage was almost in flower. The wind up in the valley smelt of distant vegetation and had lost the cold virginity of the winds of high places. Water flowed again and the hills lost their silence, a strained silence broken only by the occasional crash and moan of an avalanche.'

Now that the hard work of climbing Kamet was complete, the exploration phase began. 'By far the most enjoyable part of the expedition, was the month that followed,' wrote Shipton. They set off to explore the Badrinath Range to the west of the Saraswati River that drains from Mana Pass to Badrinath and Josimath, spending several glorious weeks in an unexplored area near the Tibetan border, crossing passes and climbing peaks.

First they had to leave the Kamet watershed and cross over the Bhyundar Khanta Pass, a route that would short cut their way to Badrinath. On the pass they met sleet, biting wind and mist so thick they could barely see ahead. To add to Smythe's misery, he suffered severe toothache. Dr Greene had sent all his anaesthetic supplies round to Badrinath on an easier route down the Dhauli Valley. So he gave Smythe a shot of morphine and, while the drug took effect, left him to carve a dental gag out of juniper wood. Meanwhile Smythe topped himself up with half a bottle of rum in anticipation of the impending operation.

'I extracted the tooth,' wrote Greene, 'and Frank, after one screamed expletive, passed into oblivion.' They carried Smythe to his tent, where about 2 a.m., overcome with sickness, he stuck his head through the flap and was nearly strangled by one of the ties. He passed out, stopped breathing, and Greene had to give him artificial respiration for two hours before he resumed breathing spontaneously – not the sort of major medical emergency one would wish to handle in such a place.

Descending on the further side of the Bhyundar Pass, their world changed dramatically. The valley was carpeted with flowers growing in such profusion that it appeared as though someone had laid out masses of brightly coloured handkerchiefs. Holdsworth was in botanist's heaven – ankle-deep primulas, wine-red potentillas, purple irises, forget-me-nots, huge yellow lilies, orchids of all colours, green fritillaries, pansies, geraniums and, most special of all, the Himalayan blue poppy, *Meconopsis baileyi*. Smythe and his companions could not put a foot down without trampling a dozen blooms in this Eden, which they named, the Valley of Flowers. They lay around the campfire beside a mountain torrent utterly content in this paradisal place.

In Badrinath they met His Holiness the Rawal Sahib, the local equivalent of the Pope, who invited them to give an account of their 'brilliant victory in having succeeded in climbing the renowned Kamet peak for the first time in history'. This was the era when mountains were viewed in terms of siege and conquest and victory, both by indigenous inhabitants and by mountain climbers.

Going north to Mana, they then turned west up the Arwa Valley where, climbing to a pass of over 20,000 feet, they discovered that they were standing on the watershed of the Saraswati-Alaknanda and Gangotri Rivers, looking into a jungle of peaks never before explored. Being supremely fit and acclimatised, they climbed eleven peaks over 19,000 feet and crossed five passes in small groups – a mountain frenzy that delighted Shipton. On one peak, Smythe was swept up in a snowslide and fractured a rib, which curtailed his feverish activity. He and Shipton, his partner, named the mountain Avalanche Peak. Smythe generously wrote, 'No one who climbs with Shipton can remain pessimistic, for he imparts an imperturbability and confidence into a day's work on a mountain that are in themselves a guarantee of success.'

On their return, while crossing a river, the egg-wallah nearly drowned when he let go of a hand rope. He was swept down several rapids and came to a stop in an eddy from where he was hauled by Greene, who observed regretfully, 'But the eggs were lost.'

While Shipton and Holdsworth continued climbing, Greene and
Smythe went up a side valley of the Alaknanda River, under a beautiful
triangular peak, Nilkanta, to try to find the source of the River Ganges.
This most auspicious water in the world burst unromantically from
beneath a dirty glacial moraine snout. On impulse they and the porters
washed themselves in the silty, muddy stream. Later when the Rawal
Sahib heard of their holy ablution he explained that it had washed away
not only all their past sins, but also their future ones. 'A dispensation,'
says Greene, 'of which I regret to say I have taken too little advantage.'

Badrinath spelled the end of Shipton's first taste of the delights of
Himalayan wandering that was thenceforward to colour all his climbing
expeditions. Generally he would rather wander along valleys and cross
passes than be stuck on some mountain of rock, snow and ice.

But the idyll had to come to an end. Soon Shipton returned to Africa
and to work on his farm at Turbo. From there he wrote regularly to
Midget in Eldoret only twenty miles away, his mail being dependent on
the whims of the goods train. 'I have been having an exciting day – my
first brood of chicks have been hatching out – huge fun! So far ten have
come out, out of thirteen, and two more are just about to. They are
ripping little fellows – so small, warm and squeaky! I am as proud of
them as the old hen.' The domestic life evidently appealed to him, and
he continued, 'Of course I suppose it is asking too much to expect it to
rain when one wants to plant coffee! But one has got a lot to be thank-
ful for in a life full of dewy mornings and soft, colourful evenings. The
black cat now comes for long walks with me.' Quite a change from wandering the valleys and passes of the Himalaya, let alone climbing the
highest mountain in the world so far climbed. But this was only just a
beginning.

CHAPTER 4

A Grim and Joyless Business

Everest, 1933

IN THE AUTUMN of 1932 Eric Shipton was in Kenya, 'peacefully occupied with problems of manure, soil erosion and farm politics,' he wrote in *Upon That Mountain*. 'I received a note from a neighbour who had a wireless set, saying that he had just heard that Lhasa had consented to allow another expedition to go to Mount Everest, and that this was being organised under the leadership of Mr Hugh Ruttledge, and would set out the following year. This news was deeply disturbing, and a storm that carried away a long job of terracing that I had completed passed almost unnoticed.' He was in love with Midget and was deeply embroiled with her in a social life of house parties, picnics, tennis foursomes and dancing – always dancing. He could hardly have guessed that this piece of news about Everest would turn his life on end for the next two decades.

After a gap of nine years the Dalai Lama of Tibet had granted 'reluctant permission' to the British Government, 'in order that friendly relations may not be ruptured'. The reason for the gap was as follows: Captain John Noel, the photographer on the 1924 expedition, had made a movie film of their journey through Tibet, which contained some footage on the mountain, but not enough (in the light of their failure to reach the summit) to draw the crowds back home. So the film became a travelogue of Tibet. As an introduction to the showing of the film, and to enhance its appeal, Noel invited some lamas from Gyantse Monastery, who performed religious rituals on the stage and danced, accompanied by thigh-bone trumpets, cymbals and drums.

This exhibition, when reported back to Tibet, caused great offence on two other counts. First, some shots in the film showed a Tibetan 'eating fleas'. In fact, fleas colonise only the body, never the head; what he was doing was picking the head for lice and biting them, which is normal and common practice in Tibet. Second, Colonel Norton, the leader of the expedition, had allowed some members to visit the Rongshar Valley (just across the Nepal border) in order to recuperate. Although they had permission from the dzongpen, or governor, of Xegar to do so, it was not written into their passport.

Correspondence about these complaints from the Tibetan Government was channelled to the Everest Committee via the India Office through Major F. M. Bailey, the Political Officer in Sikkim, also responsible for relations with Tibet. Bailey, one of the foremost Himalayan explorers of his day (and collector of *Meconopsis baileyi*, the Himalayan blue poppy), once confided to Noel's wife that he did not like Everest expeditions because of the trouble and work they gave him. Another reason could have been thwarted ambition, for he once wrote a note, recorded by A. Swinson in *Beyond the Frontiers*, concerning Everest: 'It must be climbed one day and I hope I will be one of the men to do it.' Whatever his motives, Bailey effectively blocked the way to any subsequent expeditions for nearly a decade.

Colonel Leslie Weir took over Bailey's job in 1928, at a time when the affair of the dancing lamas still rankled in Tibet. However, in 1932, to everyone's surprise and pleasure, permission for the next year suddenly arrived. So Everest was on again, and the Mount Everest Committee, composed of Fellows of the Royal Geographical Society and members of the Alpine Club, and presided over by Admiral Sir William Goodenough, met without delay.

When the news about Everest came through, an excitable Irishman staying on Eric Shipton's farm at Turbo became wildly optimistic about his host's chances of being invited. Soon afterwards, returning to his house, Shipton met his Irish friend brandishing a pink telegram that read, 'MOUNT EVEREST COMMITTEE INVITE YOU JOIN EXPEDITION SUBJECT MEDICAL APPROVAL PLEASE REPLY GOODENOUGH.'

'To save time, and mistaking Sir William's name for a kind of code word,' Shipton recalled, 'my enthusiastic friend had sent the telegraph boy back with the cryptic reply, "GOODENOUGH – SHIPTON". I managed however to intercept the message.'

Because of the sinister proviso 'subject to medical approval', he went to the local doctor in Eldoret in some anxiety, knowing that he had an irregular heartbeat. Under the stethoscope his heart 'performed a wildly erratic syncopation', and he promptly fainted. Later he sought solace from Midget who, noticing how shaken he was, put him to bed at her mother's home.

Despairing of Shipton's prospects, and discouraged by her mother, Midget had met another beau to whom she became engaged briefly. However, as on similar subsequent occasions in his life, Shipton was not deterred by such a trifle and continued to meet Midget and her new man together. Indeed, they often went out as a threesome, which was less than satisfactory to anyone because, hardly surprisingly, the two men did not like each other. Despite his unpropitious behaviour at the doctor's surgery, Shipton appears to have got through his medical and was summoned to England. When he set off, Midget drove him to Eldoret station where they said goodbye, never to see each other again. But they remained friends and continued an affectionate correspondence intermittently for many years, which was characteristic of Shipton, who rarely ditched his lady loves, nor they him, and the correspondences which have survived provide an engaging insight into an outwardly undemonstrative character.

This was the end of the African chapter in Shipton's life (apart from a brief visit there to sell up the farm). His mother had bought a house, which became his base, in Lexham Gardens, London. Although he had little sign of visible income, presumably his mother must have financed him for the next few years until he acquired a proper salary after joining the Consular Service in Kashgar. Certainly his writing royalties were not enough for him to live on during this time of almost constant expeditioning, parsimonious though his lifestyle was.

On reaching England, Shipton discovered that the entire Everest team had to undergo another medical examination. Fortunately his inquisitors were distracted from his errant heartbeat by discovering that his spleen was enlarged owing to recurrent bouts of malaria; but they passed him fit.

The party was a mixed bag of fourteen climbers, all good upper-middle class stock, with an average age of thirty-four; at twenty-six Shipton was the youngest. On one hand were the military servants of the Raj, preferred by the expeditions of the 'twenties; on the other the brash young climbers – Smythe, Longland, Wyn Harris, Crawford, Wager and Shipton; also there was the usual support team of doctors (Greene and Maclean), wireless operators, transport officers – and then there was Brocklebank.

Tom Brocklebank's selection exemplifies the bizarre ways of the Establishment of the day. Walking to his office at the *Financial News*, Brocklebank had dropped in on the Athenaeum where he noticed Tom Longstaff, luminary of the Himalaya, sitting alone in a corner. Brandishing an envelope covered with Tibetan seals, the diminutive Longstaff thrust his red beard forward and said in a conspiratorial voice, 'Don't tell *anyone*, old chap, but Sir Charles Bell says there's going to be an Everest expedition next year.' Whereupon Brocklebank asked him (cheekily he admitted) if there would be any chance of his being considered. Tomstaff (as he was affectionately called, or simply TGL) immediately put a word in the right places because he approved of Brocklebank on the strength of his three climbing seasons on standard guideless routes in the Alps, his being a master at Eton, his having an Oxford rowing blue (as had Sandy Irvine, another non-climber, in 1924), and his ability to ride a horse 'more or less'. So Brocklebank got the nod from the Everest Committee – for who dared gainsay TGL?

'I was a complete amateur,' Brocklebank said modestly, 'and chosen quite wrongly in every possible way.'

For the early expeditions the Everest Committee had sought good travellers, explorers and linguists rather than skilful climbers. By 1933 Shipton had become associated with a cadre of ace rock climbers, from the Cambridge University Mountaineering Club, led by their president,

Jack Longland. They were mostly disciples of the legendary Geoffrey Winthrop Young, who pioneered lightly laden, long, fast traverses, in the Alps, the yardstick of contemporary climbing. Longland felt that Shipton rued not having the academic training the others took for granted, and Shipton himself admitted, when pondering his future, that for the first time he regretted not having gone to Cambridge to study geology. But he had already made his mark as a climber. 'Of magnificent physique and a beautiful rhythmical mover on difficult ground,' noted Ruttledge in *Everest 1933*, 'he was certain to go high.' This makes him sound like some sort of Hercules, which was far from the case; in fact he was rather slight of build but strong withal.

The team travelled out first class to India by P & O steamship. Shipton wrote, 'As we sat deep in deck chairs, listening to the gentle swish of the sea, a cool drink within reach and with the comfortable prospect of a large lunch and a sleep to follow . . . gasping toil, blizzards and the like were hard to visualise in true perspective. No one, I think doubted for a moment that we would succeed.'

On arrival in Calcutta, Ferdie Crawford, the joker in the pack, decided to test Shipton's reputedly calm disposition. Crawford had noticed that the keepers at the zoo, where he went for his early morning walk, let the tigers frolic on the lawns. So he took Shipton there and sat him on a bench. The tigers duly appeared and gambolled round the feet of Shipton who, unblinking, just went on puffing at his pipe.

The expedition soon moved up to the hill station of Darjeeling, riding in the famous Toy Train which used to convey the memsahibs and their families away from the heat of Calcutta up into the cool mountain air. Shipton and Longland were sent to nearby Kalimpong to acquire the 350 baggage animals needed to transport the expedition's stores and equipment through Tibet by the lengthy route round the back of the north side of Everest. This was the only feasible approach for all pre-war expeditions because Nepal, which gave access to the south side, was closed for political reasons. Among the loads were cases of champagne to celebrate their victory, Stilton cheeses from Fortnum & Mason's, tins of lobster and crab, herrings and cod roes, smoked salmon, asparagus, caviar, foie gras and Carlsbad plums. They also took boxing gloves for bouts between members of their retinue.

To ease strain on accommodation, the expedition moved off in

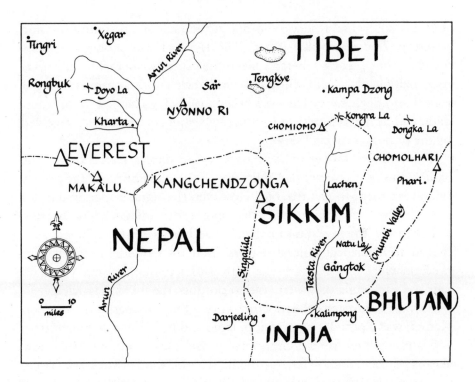

two groups, Shipton being in the first party along with most of the youngsters – Crawford, Longland, Wyn Harris, Wager, Greene and Brocklebank. They were an amenable group of disparate characters which made delightful the six weeks of 'luxurious lounging' on foot or pony, covering about fifteen miles a day across the highlands of Tibet, 'a world of wide horizons and ice-blue skies, always in sight of great peaks, following valleys through russet hills and along frozen rivers, the winter homes of huge numbers of wildfowl'. Occasionally they were lashed by blizzards and sand-laden, freezing wind, which alerted them to the conditions they might expect ahead.

Every sahib had his own pony, and Birnie, the cavalryman, was appointed Master of Horse. Each climber also had a large Whymper tent to himself with plenty of room for a Trojan camp bed and for suit-cases and kitbags. A marquee served as mess tent. Ninety servants accompanied them, mostly Sherpas recruited in Darjeeling by Karma Paul, the expedition interpreter.

But Shipton had reservations about the scale of the enterprise and noted in *That Untravelled World*, 'The sight of our monstrous army invading the peaceful Tibetan valleys, the canvas town that sprang up at each halting place and the bustle and racket that accompanied our arrival and departure gave me a feeling of being chained to a juggernaut, and I longed to return to these lovely places free and unshackled by the trappings of civilisation.'

The Tibetan Government passport specifically stated that, 'The Sahibs must not roam about, must not shoot, must not beat the people or subject them to any trouble.' However, the same evidently did not apply to the local governors or dzongpens, one of whom, on hearing that some of the expedition baggage had been seriously pilfered, sentenced four suspect animal drivers each to a hundred lashes with rawhide whips on bare buttocks, with pauses to pull the accused men's hair and ears while they were told to produce the missing articles.

Raymond Greene, the doctor whom Shipton had first met on Kamet, was a popular companion, large and handsome, sophisticated, and witty with his 'rolling Gibbonian prose'. He caused one of the few alarms of the march when, on the high, cold, windy plateau of Tibet, he gave one of the porters an anaesthetic to set a broken collarbone. The man went to sleep well enough, but would not wake up, so Greene had to use coramine and artificial respiration to bring him round. The team's own medical problems arose mainly from constant coughs and sore throats, worsened by inhaling the ever-swirling dust, a recurring and persistent bother on all subsequent approaches from the dry Tibetan side, which lies in the rain shadow of the Himalaya. 'This bugbear contributed largely to our general weakness,' wrote Shipton, 'which was a potent factor in our failure to reach the summit.'

On 7 May, the Head Lama of Rongbuk Monastery, home to 300 monks and headquarters for all the expeditions of the 'twenties, blessed the party in full view of the north side of Mount Everest. In 1852 Peak XV was computed by officers of the Trigonometrical Survey of India to be the highest mountain in the world. Thirteen years later it was officially named after Sir George Everest, the Surveyor General at the time of its discovery. Sadly the eponym stuck in general parlance, rather than its more euphonious Tibetan name, Chomolungma, or the less dulcet Nepali word, Sagarmatha. At the turn of the century many people had seen the mountain from a distance, but only in 1921 was it first approached by a British expedition intending to explore it at close quarters, and even perhaps to climb it. The British gained permission from the Dalai Lama to return in 1922 and 1924, and they made serious attempts to climb the mountain, getting within 1,000 feet of the top.

By then Everest had become, in the eyes of the British at least, their own preserve. The pre-Second World War expeditions were conducted in the umbra of an Empire which, though evidently waning, was still enjoyed under the peepul trees shading the lawns of the Tollygunge Club in Calcutta and from the mountain eyries of Simla and Darjeeling.

Attempts to climb Everest were followed intently by armchair travellers across the globe who read reports in *The Times*, nor did failure deter each expedition from producing its Everest book. The early expedition leaders were all soldiers: Lieutenant Colonel Howard-Bury (1921), Brigadier General Bruce (1922) and Lieutenant Colonel Norton (1924). The mountain took a place in British mythology and some of the climbers, like George Mallory who lost his life there, became idols.

A few miles up the Rongbuk Glacier an insignificant creek issues from a slot in the left-hand wall. This is the entrance to the East Rongbuk Glacier, found by Major E. O. Wheeler of the 1921 expedition to be the key to the approach to the North Col. Shipton and Smythe moved up through a forest of fantastic ice pinnacles (mostly 100 feet high, but some more than 300 feet) to the foot of the North Col. By cutting a road of steps and placing fixed ropes and rope ladders up an ice wall about twenty feet high, they quickly proved their reputations as experienced mountaineers. Finally they climbed a steep ice slope to a campsite just below the North Col.

Shipton in his autobiography describes the actual attempt on Everest from Base Camp upwards as 'mostly a grim and joyless business, chiefly because of persistent physical infirmity'. They spent much of their time on the mountain in their sleeping bags, 'waiting for supplies to be carried up the glacier, waiting for the weather to clear, waiting for our red blood corpuscles to multiply. I sometimes thought that bedsores were a more serious hazard than frostbite or strained hearts, and these conditions gave rise to some spectacular outbursts of ill-temper for which we used to blame the altitude.'

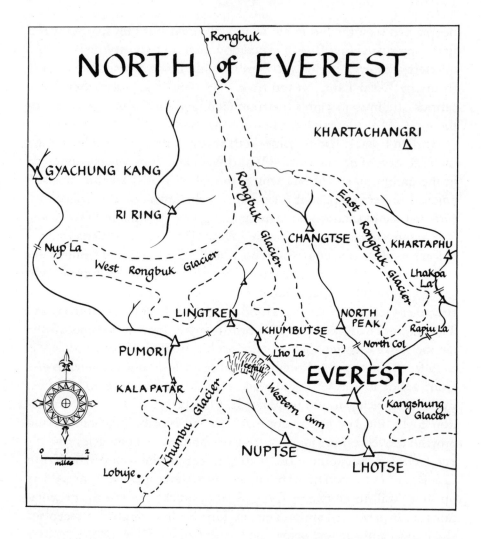

Gradually the climbers worked their way up the mountain, placing and stocking strategic camps on the long ridge leading upwards from the North Col. These military siege tactics were the common way of attempting to climb high mountains right through into the 'seventies when fully acclimatised, alpine-style, quick dash climbing became the vogue. Then came the most crucial day of the expedition, upon which much hinged. Wyn Harris, Birnie, Boustead and ten porters set off with orders to pitch Camp V at 25,000 feet or higher, as a launching place for an assault on the top. The weather was good and the going easy, but at

24,000 feet, Birnie, who was in command, decided that the porters were exhausted and could go no further.

Raymond Greene, who was at Camp IV, described the returning porters 'bouncing and leaping down the mountain'. Birnie limped into camp, claiming his feet were frostbitten (Greene says they weren't), and went off to sulk in his tent. Wyn Harris arrived furious, muttering to Longland about 'the fucking soldiery' whom he never forgave for their timidity. Ruttledge, in a rare show of leadership, came up to read the Riot Act, and put Wyn Harris in charge of the next attempt to place Camp V.

News crackled over the wireless set (the first time radio was carried on the mountain) that the monsoon had arrived in the Bay of Bengal some weeks earlier than usual. In fine weather Wyn Harris and Wager occupied Camp VI, placed by Longland and six Sherpas at 27,400 feet, the highest ever pitched. They made the first attempt at the summit following Norton's traverse line well below the ridge, and there they found an ice axe that must have belonged to either Mallory or Irvine, who disappeared near the top in 1924. This axe has fuelled debate ever since as to whether or not they reached the summit and slipped to their deaths on the descent.

But Wyn Harris and Wager were turned back by new snow lying on a rock stratum that dipped to the north like tiles on a steep roof, where handholds and belays were practically non-existent. Soon afterwards Shipton and Smythe climbed to Camp VI and a blizzard broke. The mountain, caked in fresh powder snow, was 'a terrible sight' according to Ruttledge. Tentbound for two days, sleepless because of cramped space, and their strength sapped by the altitude, they both realised that their slender chance of reaching the summit was quickly disappearing. But during all these tribulations they still got on well together.

The third morning was clear. They thawed their boots over a candle and forced their five-sock-covered feet into them; they each dressed in two pairs of long woollen pants, seven Shetland wool sweaters, with a loose, hooded windproof over the top. 'I felt about as suitably equipped for delicate rock climbing,' wrote Shipton, 'as a fully rigged deep-sea diver for dancing the tango.' They both set out without oxygen and climbed delicately across the shelving ledges where they had to rely largely on the friction of their bootnails.

After about two hours Shipton began to feel sick, possibly because the night before they had eaten meat essence, a standby in the days before dehydrated foods (shades of Mount Kenya). He decided to stop, descend to Camp VI and let Smythe go on alone. Smythe reached the same point as Wyn Harris and Wager in the Great Couloir at about 28,100 feet. Finding it deep in new snow and late in the day, he turned back. 'In all probability the summit can be reached by an acclimatised man without oxygen,' wrote Smythe in *Camp Six*, 'but the odds against him are great. The difficulty of the mountain, the evil effects of altitude, the possibility of being benighted, the risk of sudden storms and the dangers of exhaustion are so serious that oxygen should be taken if it can aid the climber. Those who tread [Everest's] last 1,000 feet tread the physical limits of the world.'

To let the exhausted Smythe get some rest in the tiny tent, Shipton descended to Camp V alone, but he became lost in a howling storm that nearly cost him his life. He sat down helplessly and waited, 'incapable of strong emotion of any sort, and blissfully resigned to whatever the fates chose to do with me'. Further down he became unable to articulate his words properly – possibly dyslexia surfacing in his oxygen-depleted brain, possibly a form of migraine aphasia associated with a blinding headache, possibly a transient stroke. Brocklebank recalled meeting him at the North Col. 'He just gazed at me with those blue eyes, beaming a wide smile, but he was unable to speak for twenty-four hours.' He had also lost his voice from 'altitude sore throat', so Shipton could not communicate any news when he reached his anxious leader at Camp III.

By now the monsoon had truly arrived and they retreated to Base Camp. The general feeling was that pitching Camp V too low had set them back several days and cost the expedition their chance at the summit. 'The army haven't shown up very well,' was Shipton's laconic summary in a letter to Midget. 'We reached Base Camp, a set of crocks, what with frostbite, strained hearts etc. I had lost nearly 2½ stone.' By way of diversion, Shipton climbed the Rapiu La with Crawford and Brocklebank; from there they looked down into one of the world's most gigantic cirques enclosed by the great Kangshung Face of Everest, Chomolonzo, Makalu and Lhotse.

After the expedition returned to England, a confrontation boiled up over Hugh Ruttledge's indecisive leadership between the RGS Establishment on the one hand and, on the other, the young bloods spearheaded by Crawford, Longland and Brocklebank. Shipton avoided becoming embroiled in the controversy because he had remained for two months on the Lashar Plain observing the monsoon weather patterns along with Wager, the geologist who was collecting rocks, and Sen Tensing. They concentrated their work two marches west of Tengkye, near Changmo and Kellas Peak. There they were entertained by the local dzongpen, 'whose hospitality was so lavish and his chang so powerful that our 3.00 a.m. breakfast was more than usually unpleasant.' Shipton goes on to note in the *Alpine Journal* that, 'To start an ascent by cantering on horseback across dimly lit plains to the foot of one's climb was a novel experience.' Eventually, he returned by double marches down the Lachen Valley into Sikkim, 'to the comforts and worries of civilisation', leaving Wager to obtain one more glimpse of his beloved Tibet from the Dongkya La.

Shipton's quarrel with the 1933 Everest expedition, expressed in *Upon That Mountain*, was that it was far too large and grossly overburdened. 'I was convinced that a small party, lightly equipped and shorn of supernumeraries and superfluous baggage, would not only be just as effective but would have several positive advantages.' But he continues, 'I would not have forgone a single friendship that I made in 1933.'

CHAPTER 5

Into the Sanctuary

Nanda Devi, 1934

AFTER KENYA, Kamet and Everest, Eric Shipton's standing as a mountaineer was beyond question; he had yet to make his name as an explorer. His foray with Wager after the Everest expedition into some unknown valleys of Tibet sparked his interest in exploration, and set him pondering how he might pursue this as a chosen way of life. Most of his companions on the recent trip had university degrees and were embarked on professions that would comfortably support their expensive mountain habits. Shipton had no professional salary and only modest private means; but his will was strong and he deplored the notion of sacrificing his active years to the dignity and comfort of old age.

He summarised his feelings about big expeditions, such as he had recently been part of, in *Nanda Devi*: 'on each occasion I had a mighty longing to detach myself from the big and cumbersome organisation which for some reason has been thought to be necessary for an attack on the more lofty summits of the earth, and to wander with a small,

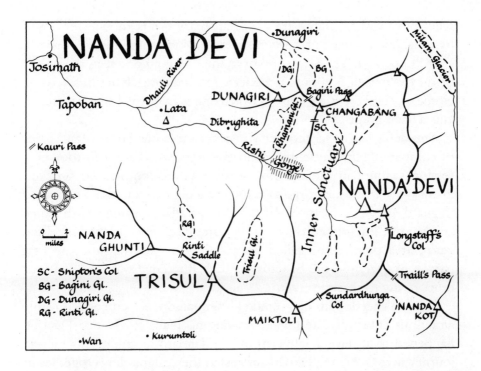

self-contained party through the labyrinth of unexplored valleys, forming our plans to suit the circumstances, climbing peaks when the opportunity occurred, following up on our own topographical clues and crossing passes into unknown territory.'

Tom Longstaff had whetted Shipton's appetite when he was invited to stay for a weekend in the country. TGL suggested he try to find a way into the Nanda Devi Sanctuary, which he himself had attempted twenty-seven years before from the north side of the Rishi Ganga Gorge; he advised Shipton to concentrate all his efforts on the southern side. Also staying that weekend was Everest jester, Ferdie Crawford, who told Longstaff's teenage daughters that Shipton was a brilliant pianist, but was so shy they would have to work hard to get him to play for them. Being musically almost illiterate (despite his piano lessons at school), Shipton had difficulty persuading the girls of his ineptitude, and urged them to turn their frustration onto Crawford, meanwhile his own thoughts winged back to the Himalaya.

Nanda Devi, in the district of Garhwal, rises to a summit at 25,660

feet from a vast amphitheatre – the Sanctuary as it is known – enclosed
by a gigantic rampart of curtain walls on which stand twelve peaks of
over 21,000 feet. The lowest point in the ring is 17,000 feet; the height
of the basin itself is about 13,000 feet. The only breach in this awesome
cirque is where the Rishi Ganga, which drains from the Inner Sanctuary,
cuts a deep gorge.

This defile had so far repelled all attempts to enter it by several parties
of competent Himalayan mountain explorers, who habitually took professional mountain guides from the Alps as their companions. Graham
in 1883 described the gorge as 'a mighty moat of nature's own digging
to guard her virgin fortress'. In 1905 Longstaff attempted it with Bruce
and Mumm, but immediately gave up; later he climbed to the rim of the
basin, at a point since called Longstaff's Col, and became the first
person to gaze into the Sanctuary. Hugh Ruttledge was rebuffed four
times trying to reach it.

Shipton needed a like-minded companion to embark on this
ambitious enterprise, and while making his plans for Nanda Devi he
happened to receive a letter from Bill Tilman describing his bicycle
journey across Africa. Tilman suggested they might climb together in
the Lake District for a couple of weeks; Shipton countered with the
proposal that Tilman should accompany him to the Himalaya for seven
months. To this Tilman agreed without persuasion.

This adventure was to set a course for the rest of both their lives. The
first lines of the preface to Shipton's *Nanda Devi* read, 'The greatest
asset a mountaineer or traveller can have when embarking upon a
difficult undertaking, more valuable far than any amount of money,
equipment or fine weather, is a companion in whom, both physically
and morally, he has implicit confidence.' He dedicated the book to
Tilman, whose name will always be linked to that of Shipton's when
people gather to plan small expeditions to remote and distant lands.

To accrue some much-needed cash, Shipton went off to Norway on
'the distasteful business of lecturing', at which he was somewhat self-
disparaging, and often inaudible because of his soft, clipped voice.
Tilman, meanwhile, took on the job of arranging return passages on a
cargo boat bound for Calcutta (£30 each), in stark contrast to the P & O
luxury of the previous year. They immediately wired to Darjeeling
asking Karma Paul, the previous year's expedition interpreter, to find

Sherpas Angtharkay, his cousin Kusang, and Pasang, who had all been on Everest in 1933. Shipton budgeted the cost at £300 in total for five persons in the field for five months (at the end £13 was unspent).

The only excitement on the month-long voyage was when Shipton jumped off an awning rigged up as a swimming pool and dislocated a toe, which was reduced by the purser. However, this limited their training of skipping and throwing medicine balls at each other. During the next few weeks, for comfort he had to wear a pair of tennis shoes with the toe cut out, even appearing in them at formal dinners.

Karma Paul put the three Sherpas on a train to Calcutta. They looked quite exotic with their Tibetan features, their long black hair in pigtails braided with pink ribbon, and wearing garish purple shirts. But if they turned heads, for their part they were unimpressed with their first visit to a big city, except for the zoo. Eventually the expedition of five reached Ranikhet, where they engaged a dozen lusty Dotial porters who shouldered their eighty-pound loads and set off on the march towards Josimath. The climbers had brought some provisions with them, but they intended to live mainly off local food. Angtharkay, an expert haranguing barterer, always found some eggs, chicken, flour and rice, although these commodities were scarce so close to the pilgrimage centres.

Their supplies were rudimentary. Various 'luxuries' included tea, sugar, lentils, and ten tins of pemmican to supplement their basic diet of flour, rice and ghee (liquid butter). Instead of Fortnum & Mason's Stilton, they took several ten-pound Cheddar cheeses sewn in cloth. They planned to grind roasted wheat or barley flour to make tsampa, which requires no cooking and slips down best when mixed in tea with plenty of sugar. Tilman favoured a vegetarian diet, having lost several teeth recently by falling from a horse while steeplechasing.

They estimated their food needs on the simple formula of two pounds per man per day. Therefore five men for six weeks (forty-two days) would need $42 \times 5 \times 2 = 420$ pounds. Their common equipment consisted of two small Meade tents, Primus stoves and kerosene, ropes, cameras and survey instruments, candle lanterns and matches. Each man, including the Sherpas, had a light windproof suit, sweaters, woollen pants, balaclava, puttees, socks, a double down sleeping bag, climbing boots and ice axe.

For nine leisurely days they walked through the foothills of Garhwal. Crossing the Kauri Pass they had striking views of the serrated Kedarnath and Badrinath peaks, which they hoped to explore later. This brought them to the Dhauli River from where they looked up part of the Rishi Ganga Valley to the summit pyramid of Nanda Devi. In somewhat purple prose into which he occasionally slips, Shipton described, 'The trees with their drowsy limbs still wet with dew, the song of the birds sharing with us the exaltation of the new-born day, the streams splashing down in silver waterfalls or lying dormant in deep pools'. Perhaps he fell under the influence of Frank Smythe's writing, which was notoriously verbose compared with Shipton's usually spare and lucid style.

At Josimath, ten of their Dotial porters, who were due to be paid off, were eager to remain with them, despite the gloomy picture Shipton painted of the perils and hardships awaiting them in the Rishi Gorge. But eight local men, who they had hoped would help them find the way, deserted as soon as they reached snow. This defection was serious and threatened to wreck the expedition at its outset. However, Shipton and Tilman re-divided the loads and carried huge weights themselves. At times they had to go ahead and stamp out a trail where the soft snow lay up to their waists, and even to their armpits. Repeatedly they came to impasses and had to retreat and try a different line. The cliffs they were traversing dropped 8,000 feet in an almost unbroken plunge, and the Dotials had difficulty on a narrow, icy ledge half a mile long, which was used by shepherds to reach their summer pasture. Tilman described Dibrughita, near the junction of the Rhamani Valley with the Rishi where the unpenetrated upper gorge began, as 'a horizontal oasis in a vertical desert'. Shipton appreciated this vividly when a falling rock struck him on the head causing his scalp to bleed profusely. Their legs, too, were scratched and bled from tangles of thorn and bramble.

At the junction they found a snug cave on a narrow strip of river shore, cached their loads, and paid off the loyal, indefatigable Dotials. Upstream the view of a box canyon with vertical walls was 'anything but encouraging'. However, they had food for thirty-five days and could take their time in tackling the problem. As it was, covering the remaining four miles of the previously untrodden gorge took nine full days.

Just above their camp a huge boulder straddled the river making easy crossing to the southern side up which, following Longstaff's advice, they intended to try forcing their way by traversing high on the cliffside. 'I found myself to be very nervous and shaky on the steep grass slopes and slabs on which we had to climb, not yet used to the immense scale of the gorge and its surroundings,' Shipton wrote. 'As we gradually became used to the gigantic depth of the ravine, the early feeling of nervousness changed to one of exhilaration.' Such an admission by a climber of his calibre means it must have been very steep.

They climbed one near-vertical scar of crumbling rock and hauled their loads up after them. One load overbalanced and crashed down into the gorge, taking two days' food with it. They frequently met precipices that looked impassable until a kindly fault in the rock allowed them passage, only to come to yet another barrier. Snow on some sloping ledges forced them to remove their boots in order to cross more sure-footedly with their heavy, awkward loads. But relaying had taught them the nature of the ground intimately, something that would make their return journey easier.

They tried to descend to the river at the very end of the gorge but found crossing it so dangerous they gave up and returned to the high traverse. This was just as well because on their return the swollen monsoon torrent would have been impossible to pass. Tilman lost his pipe (an essential soother) crossing one swollen stream. 'Fortunately for him,' said Shipton, 'I had been travelling in southern Tibet the previous year with Lawrence Wager, who insisted on my smoking a pipe in the evening to keep me from talking. Since then I had continued the habit.' By now being close travelling companions, they shared the remaining pipe.

Eventually they entered the Nanda Devi Sanctuary, the first human beings to set foot there, and their feelings of despondency changed to deep content. The magic of that moment is hard to appreciate in these days of satellite photos, global positioning mapping, and with almost every corner of the earth explored. The elegant spire of Nanda Devi rose 13,000 feet above the amphitheatre where the two main rivers draining the basin joined. Herds of tame mountain sheep, bharal, grazed the moorland pasture where alpine flowers, wild onions and rhubarb abounded. The Sherpas, ever pragmatic, announced that this would make good yak pasture.

Shipton and Tilman decided to spend the remaining three weeks in the northern half of the Sanctuary, exploring the network of glaciers that flowed down from the enclosing walls, and to return after the monsoon to search for a way out over the southern rim. To deepen a sense of harmony with their surroundings, when the weather was fair they slept under the stars beside a huge campfire made from juniper wood that was plentiful on the grassland. Shipton said of Tilman, a constant early riser with a passion for making bread, 'I have never met anyone with such complete disregard for the sublime comforts of the early morning bed.'

They surveyed the glaciers of the northern basin with the plane-table which they had laboriously carried in; then they climbed three saddles of over 20,000 feet, and a peak of 21,000 feet where 'it was exhilarating to see the Milam Glacier System beneath one heel and the Nanda Devi Basin beneath the other.'

Both Shipton and Tilman were generally extremely fit and thrived on their simple diet. However, one following the other, they suffered severe fever and chills which lasted for thirty-six hours and then stopped suddenly. Being ill so far removed from help, and with no idea what was wrong nor medicines to treat it, made for anxious moments. With the advent of the monsoon at the end of June they returned through the gorge, now so familiar that they did it in less than half the time of their way in. Flooded side-streams caused their main problems; wild flowers were their delight – forget-me-nots, potentillas, gentians and dozens of others. Kusang gathered some wild strawberries and gave them all to Shipton; when asked the reason for his generosity, he said he had damaged his knee and eating strawberries would make it worse. Tilman developed a painful carbuncle on the upper surface of his foot – and avoided strawberries.

For the next two months they explored the Badrinath-Kedarnath range to the west of the great Alaknanda River, one of the three main sources of the sacred Ganges, that cuts a swathe due south from the Tibetan border. First they forayed up the Bhagirathi Glacier and over a series of high passes into the Arwa Valley; then across the watershed to the upper Gangotri Glacier, and finally back to Badrinath.

Local legend told that the high priest of Badrinath used to hold services on the same day both there and at Kedarnath temple across the

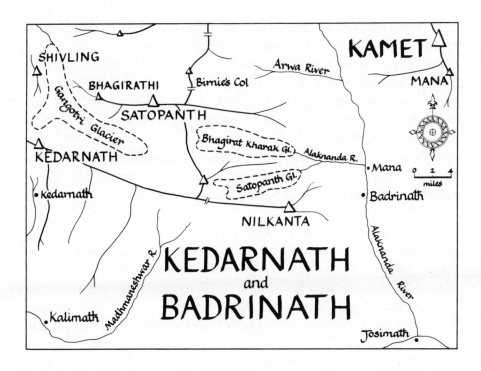

mountain range. So Shipton and Tilman's party set out to see how the holy man managed to make so speedy a passage of this twenty-mile distance, as the eagle flies. They travelled west up to the head of the Satopanth Glacier and climbed to the watershed saddle. Ahead an icy precipice plunged 6,000 feet into a lush-looking valley. It was so steep they had to rope down a narrow gulley, an irreversible move which heightened their respect for the Reverend who reputedly preceded them.

The gorge they entered was not the paradise they imagined; dense bamboo forest alternated with thorny bramble in the gulleys, so they progressed only about a mile a day. It rained so hard their gear became waterlogged and therefore doubly heavy, and they needed to bridge side streams in spate by felling trees. Their only remaining food, tsampa, became sodden and mouldy so they had to discard it. Thereafter their diet was of tree fungi and bamboo shoots, a delicacy also sought by bears whose tracks were everywhere. They saw one bear close-to, and the Sherpas were terrified, thinking it was a yeti. However, every night they built a bamboo shelter and started a fire by pounding sodden sticks of dead bamboo and lighting the pulp with matches.

On a positive note, Shipton observed, 'it was not on the whole an unpleasant experience; the days were full of vital interest, the nights warm and comfortable, and the forest was wild and beautiful.' The negative side of the picture was 'the prospect of retracing our steps and committing ourselves once more to the icy slopes we had just left'. The further they went the more desperate they became, and they even considered dumping their loads and pushing on without them. Then a falling boulder broke a small bone in Pasang's foot so he could not carry his pack.

Shipton wrote in his diary: 'Pasang is no better. The job is becoming very tedious; always wet, not enough food, and can't see where the hell we are going. If the bamboo were to fail us our plight would be serious indeed.' Eventually after five days in the forest they emerged and saw a distant farmstead. Tilman remarked laconically, as though he was looking down on Wasdale from Sty Head Pass, 'We shall be down in time for tea.'

They were worried how they could pay for food. 'A whip round amongst the five of us produced exactly seven rupees,' Shipton wrote. 'Kusang could juggle with three stones and Tilman and I had a varied repertoire of hymns.' However, they acquired four pounds of flour, a cucumber and some dried apricots, and had a feast. Soon afterwards they reached the Kedarnath pilgrim route at Kalimath. Their journey had persuaded them that if the Reverend had indeed done a puja at Badrinath and Kedarnath on the same day, he must have flown on the back of a tiger, like Padma Sambhava. Thereafter they travelled easily, and comparatively luxuriously, to Josimath.

It was now the end of August and Shipton and Tilman wanted to hurry back into the Nanda Devi Sanctuary to complete their survey of the southern half of the basin. Angtharkay went off to Mana village to recruit fifteen porters who proved to be just as reliable as the Dotials. Now that they knew the gorge so well they got through it in a quarter of their original time, while the simpler geography of the southern basin made for a speedy plane-table survey. Then they set out to climb Maiktoli, one of the peaks on the Sanctuary rim, though Tilman had to miss it because he became sick again with altitude. From the foot of

Nanda Devi they spied a possible route up the great south ridge of the main peak, but their boots were so worn and lacking nails they could not contemplate a serious attempt to climb it. However, they got high enough to have a good look and to confirm their opinion of a practicable route for a competent team.

Then they set about searching for an exit from the Sanctuary. The foot of the col down which Longstaff had looked in 1905 looked formidably steep. So they turned to the Sunderdhunga Col, whose eastern 6,000 foot glacial precipice had justly awed Ruttledge in 1932. Following one of the ridges they worried their way down by tedious trial and error 'in a day of toil over-packed with thrills'.

In several places they roped down from a bollard chipped out of the ice. Thus they became utterly committed to the descent and Shipton noted, 'It is not often that one had the opportunity of watching a display of ice avalanches from so close, and rarer still to see them breaking away from the very cliffs on which one is standing.' Once a cascade of huge ice blocks roared down the gulley they had just crossed. But they eventually reached the peaceful valley after 'perhaps the most exciting of our adventures'.

And so came to an end their season of freedom and perfect happiness, the best five months either of them had known; 'boots were ragged and funds running low.' They had lived, eaten and slept with the Sherpas as friends and equals, and Shipton never stints in praise of their toughness, humour, loyalty and comradeship. 'During the months we were together I never once detected the slightest sign of dissension among our three. With these allies we hope, one day, to reach the summit of Mount Everest; without them we would have little hope of doing so.' And of his companion he says, 'As we had done in Africa, we continued to address one another as "Tilman" and "Shipton"; and when, after another seven months continuously together, I suggested that it was time he called me "Eric" he became acutely embarrassed, hung his head and muttered, "It sounds so damned silly."'

The adventure was more successful than either of them had anticipated and certainly made their names in explorers' circles. Shipton lectured to the Royal Geographical Society on their return and received full praise from many distinguished Fellows, including Tom Longstaff and Brigadier Norton. Some of those present (they all seemed to be in a hurry to catch trains home) remarked how little they knew of Mr Tilman. When asked to say a few words, the latter admitted diffidently that he had never previously faced an audience.

On the homebound boat, Shipton began to write *Nanda Devi*, which has become a classic of mountain literature. As with all his books he resolved it would be his last. Unfortunately, there are no maps in the book, which makes some of the travelling hard to follow. But his writing is untutored and pithy, and his story riveting; his later writing became much more polished with the help of judicious editing, but the freshness of his first book remains.

CHAPTER 6

Old Leaders, Young Men

Everest 1935, 1936

ON EVEREST in 1933 the young climbers repeatedly asked Hugh Ruttledge to do something when he returned to England about changing the fossilised old men of the Everest Committee, especially Sir Percy Cox, President of the RGS, whom Longland described as 'a deeply deceitful diplomatic old soldier'. Eric Shipton, as we have seen, managed to avoid this divisive politicking by staying in Tibet. Back in Britain battle lines were drawn between the Old Guard, imperial explorer-proconsuls, and the rude, brash, ribald younger generation (Longland's words) of top climbers. The latter tended mostly to come from, or be affiliated to, the Cambridge University Mountaineering Club, Shipton and Smythe being notable exceptions. The university graduates arrogantly believed that, being intellectually trained, they were better at self-discipline than the army types who had discipline thrust upon them.

The leading revolutionary was Ferdie Crawford – the oldest of the youngsters. He had been on Everest in 1922, and was involved in the

North Col avalanche when seven Sherpas died. Longland strongly supported him, feeling that the climbers should have their own say in choosing a leader who at least should be a climber himself, instead of having him handed down by 'that self-perpetuating oligarchy', whose members had climbed nothing of note for years.

Brocklebank, having no intention of returning to Everest, and therefore nothing to lose by being a mutineer, spoke out against Ruttledge's leadership; Wager also expressed doubts about it. The main Ruttledge supporter was Smythe, who was desperately anxious not to be left out of the next expedition; 'Frank pretended to be on our side, but he wasn't,' said Longland, 'he behaved fairly dishonestly, but then Frank often did.'

The Everest Committee was taken by surprise again when permission for 1935–36 arrived unexpectedly from Tibet (unexpected because of the death of the thirteenth Dalai Lama and a devastating earthquake in Nepal). The notes of the Tibetan Ministers to Williamson, the Political Officer in Sikkim, read:

Kalon Lama said the Tibetan Government did not want any more expeditions at all because they caused offence to the gods and trouble to the country. No one could see these things which were invisible. The frequent travel of the expeditions has been a great source of trouble to the people residing on the road. In view of friendly relations, the sahibs should be accorded permission for another expedition in Wood-Pig year (1935). But the guardian deities of the mountain take great exception to such attempts and in their anger they render the weather very rough and the after-effects are very bad. Such attempts only work undesirably on the temper of the gods and guardian deities, which results in heavy snowfall and storms.

Ruttledge had already written resigning from the leadership of any future expeditions, knowing that Crawford had designs on it himself. Because there was so little time to organise a full scale expedition for 1935, Ruttledge suggested to the Committee that Shipton should lead a reconnaissance during the monsoon period. 'No better man could have been found than Shipton, whose temperament and abilities it exactly suited,' wrote Ruttledge in *Everest: The Unfinished Adventure*. 'His love of exploration is only equalled by his horror of large expeditions, and he is a past master in the art of living off the country and of exploring a mountain region at a minimum of expense but with utmost rapidity.'

The Committee agreed and drew up a set of objectives for the expedition: to study monsoon snow conditions; to seek an alternative route up the West Ridge or from the Western Cwm but without venturing therein since it was in Nepal; to examine ice conditions on the North Col; to try out new men, food and equipment; and finally to make a survey to the north of Everest.

'But I had a private motive,' Shipton wrote much later, 'my dislike of massive mountaineering expeditions had become something of an obsession, and I was anxious for the opportunity to demonstrate that, for one-tenth of the former cost and with a fraction of the bother and disruption of the local countryside, a party could be placed on the North Col, adequately equipped to make a strong summit attempt.'

Shipton asked to be allowed to choose a party of six climbers, budgeting at £200 each. Naturally, he asked Tilman, expecting him to be delighted at the chance of going to Everest; but Tilman, who had been looking forward to trying to climb Nanda Devi, was quite displeased by the change of plan. 'Though he did not say so,' wrote Shipton, 'I suspected the root of his objection was that, while he had been forced to accept the stark necessity of my company, the prospect of having five companions was scarcely tolerable.'

Shipton's other choices were Dr Charles Warren, a physician who had been with Marco Pallis in the Garhwal in 1933; Edwin Kempson, a master at Marlborough College and an alpine climber with fourteen seasons' experience; Edmund Wigram, a medical student of powerful physique; and Dan Bryant, a brilliant New Zealand ice climber. Shipton became specially fond of Bryant, who was both tough and competent, as well as having a mocking sense of humour and a huge fund of anecdotes and comic songs. This friendship was to have historical significance fourteen years later when Shipton, on the strength of this memory, made a momentous, if illogical, decision to include two New Zealanders in his team for the southern reconnaissance of Everest.

Another person whose name was to enter the history books – Tenzing Norgay Bhotia – appeared with the team as a nineteen-year-old porter, apprenticing to the now famous Sherpas, Angtharkay, Pasang and Kusang, who had all been with Shipton to Nanda Devi, and to Everest in 1933. This was Tenzing's first expedition, and his broad toothy smile and keenness for work left a lasting impression on Shipton. Another Sherpa who became his close friend, was Sonam (Sen) Tensing, the Foreign Sportsman, as he became known for his habit of swaggering round the Chowrasta of Darjeeling, or sweltering down-town Bombay, in cast off European clothing given him by departing expeditions.

An important member of the team, not himself a mountaineer, was Michael Spender, a specialist surveyor. Reputedly a man of overbearing conceit and arrogance, he became close friends with Shipton, who enjoyed his provocative way of expressing wildly unorthodox views. Shipton seemed to have the knack of being able to get on with 'awkward customers' like Tilman and Smythe, and now Spender.

Shipton and his mother, who had accompanied him out from England, met the party in Darjeeling. Tilman and Bryant had already been there for two days, having spent almost the entire time together in complete silence. Eventually Bryant's charm worked on Tilman, who responded 'with unwonted conviviality'. Their passport for Tibet had not yet arrived, so Williamson, the newly appointed Resident in Sikkim, gave them a temporary frontier pass. They chose to follow the Teesta River to the Kongra La, west of the usual Chumbi Valley route through Tibet.

Not long after starting, a deputation of Sherpas protested to Shipton against having to carry heavy loads until they reached higher altitudes. Shipton calmly told them if they didn't like it they could all go back to Darjeeling, and started collecting their ice axes, whereupon they quickly shouldered their loads.

Being in no great hurry, Shipton was keen to explore the Nyonno Ri Range lying halfway between the Kongra La and Everest. In his favoured manner he split the party into small groups and sent them all off in different directions. Tilman led one group to attempt Nyonno Ri itself, while Shipton led another that would try to circumnavigate that massif by crossing unknown passes, an occupation he loved. Spender went off mapping with a group of Sherpa helpers. Two weeks later they all met again at Sar where they were lavishly and boisterously enter-tained by the headman, a connoisseur of chang, Tibetan beer.

During this approach through Tibet the expedition lived mainly off the country. Using pressure cookers they tenderised mutton from sheep toughened by being driven over many high passes. In the villages butter, milk and eggs abounded; one group of four climbers broke the record for gluttony by eating 140 eggs in a single day; some were fresh, others stale, but indistinguishable when scrambled.

In perfect weather they made their way over familiar ground to Rongbuk from where they could see the top of Everest as a black triangle of rock with barely any snow on it. Had they missed their chance of a shot at the summit by dallying in the Nyonno Ri? They romped up the East Rongbuk Glacier to the old Camp III, near where they found the body of Maurice Wilson who, the previous year, alone, had tried to climb the mountain by divine faith, but failed even to reach the North Col.

Three days later, and less than a week after leaving Rongbuk, they had pitched a well-stocked camp on the North Col at the foot of the North-East Ridge. Shipton and Kempson, the most experienced men on snow, 'could not detect anywhere the slightest tendency to avalanche'. They planned to take a light camp up to 26,000 feet from where they could study snow conditions on the crucial upper pyramid of the mountain. Then the weather turned bad and the already late monsoon seemed to have arrived. The Sherpas, partly on account of the weather, partly from the bad omen of finding Wilson's corpse, refused to go further. Shipton again threatened to sack them and to carry their loads himself. Knowing he meant business, and was by far the fittest climber, 'they were all immensely contrite.'

Because the expedition's brief was to study the snow throughout the monsoon, they decided to go down and spend the time exploring other peaks in the vicinity while waiting for the weather to improve. Shipton was descending with Kempson and five Sherpas when they came to a place where an enormous avalanche had recently broken away. The whole face of the slope had peeled off to a depth of six feet, largely along the line of their ascending tracks, and stretching for several hundred yards in either direction.

Shipton reasoned that if the slope had avalanched, being a mixture of new and old snow, it was unlikely immediately to do so again and it was therefore safe to descend across its path. Kempson records in his diary,

'We had a colossal argument about the safety of the up and down route, Eric stoutly maintaining that the former was the more dangerous!' Ruttledge summarised the event in the *Geographical Journal*, 'Shipton displayed fine judgment in descending along the track of the avalanche without delay, assuming that another immediate fall was improbable.'

This sobering event, and his later experience, persuaded Shipton that monsoon snow in the Everest region neither disappears nor consolidates above 23,000 feet, and that the only time of year they could reasonably hope to reach the summit of Mount Everest was during the exceedingly short interval between the end of the cold north-westerly winter gales and the arrival of the monsoon with its warm air flowing up from the Bay of Bengal. The collision of these two air streams creates the disturbances which develop into storms that wander up and down, to and fro, till they strike the Himalaya.

Again the team split up into small groups and wandered off in different directions. Tilman and Wigram went to explore the possibility of descending from the Lho La to the foot of the Western Cwm, but they found themselves on the edge of a mighty precipice. Shipton and Bryant went up the West Rongbuk Glacier and climbed several small peaks near Lingtren. Descending one icy ridge, Bryant stepped on a cornice and fell with it, so the rope yanked on Shipton nearly cutting him in two. Bryant managed to hold on to his ice axe and with great skill cut his way back to the ridge.

From the col between Lingtren and Pumori they also looked into the Western Cwm, and photographed it, proving that there was no way to reach it down the southern precipices. But Shipton noted in the *Alpine Journal*, 'As far as we could see the route up it did not look impossible, and I should very much like to have the opportunity of one day exploring it.' Sixteen years and one war later, he did.

They moved into a galaxy of unexplored peaks north-east of Everest, between the Doyo La and Kharta. Shipton, in his element, wrote in the *Geographical Journal*, 'We had a delicious time crossing new passes, climbing peaks and unravelling the most interesting topography.'

The expedition that he had led so well (or rather that he had allowed to lead itself in his characteristic and preferred style) had been most congenial, with 'not a single quarrel'. Only one thing dampened

Shipton's happiness, the inability to acclimatise to altitude of Tilman and Bryant, both superb mountaineers and perhaps his closest friends. Bryant's altitude ceiling seemed to be about 20,000 feet; Tilman's was only a little higher. This meant that neither of them could be considered for the 1936 team, which in Tilman's case was a blessing in disguise because he went off to Nanda Devi again instead.

The expedition had reached twenty-six summits. After Shipton's lecture to the Royal Geographical Society, Tom Longstaff complimented him by saying, 'About as many peaks of over 20,000 feet were climbed in the Himalaya as have been climbed since the days of Adam, so far as I remember the list.' At the end of the lecture, with a metaphorical roll of drums, the President announced the names for the 1936 team. Then everyone rushed off to catch their trains home.

The composition of the team for the following year had not been achieved without grief, particularly in respect of the leadership. At No. 23 Savile Row, then the headquarters of the Alpine Club, noises of dissent on this score continued to rumble across Hyde Park towards No. 1 Kensington Gore, home of the Royal Geographical Society. The Everest Committee had hustled round desperately to find a leader, approaching Norton, Bruce, Wilson, Strutt, Longstaff, Greene and others, but all refused. Ruttledge had officially resigned; Crawford was an ambitious contender, and ironically they were together on the same Committee representing the Alpine Club. At an important meeting on 28 March 1935 both men were asked to withdraw while the rest of the Committee pondered the issue, which had come down to Ruttledge versus Crawford. Two AC members of the Committee, Strutt and Wager, voted for Crawford; the two RGS members, Cox and Mason for Ruttledge. Sir Percy Cox broke the tie by casting his Chairman's vote for Ruttledge.

So, with age winning out over youth, they were back to the old problem – a non-climbing leader whom everybody liked but nobody wanted. Cox peremptorily sacked the turbulent Crawford; however, Strutt, an old, fulminating diehard, surprisingly went out on a limb and resigned in sympathy for the younger man.

So Hugh Ruttledge, for lack of anyone better, became leader again and set about choosing his team, strongly influenced by Frank Smythe, who had become his self-appointed right-hand man. Ferdie Crawford, the mutineer, was obviously out; so was Jack Longland, who refused to give unconditional support to Ruttledge; Noel Odell, who had distinguished himself on Everest in 1924, was considered too old (he went to Nanda Devi with Tilman instead); Campbell Secord was passed over because he 'seemed a rather queer fellow'; Peter Lloyd and John Hunt, two hopefuls, failed to blow a column of mercury high enough to satisfy the RAF medical examiners; and Lawrence Wager was otherwise occupied. Eventually the climbing team comprised mainly old hands, Frank Smythe, Eric Shipton, Wyn Harris, Edwin Kempson, Charles Warren and Edmund Wigram, along with newcomers Jim Gavin and Peter Oliver. The non-climbers were Noel Humphreys (doctor), John Morris (transport), and Smijth-Windham (radio).

'When it became clear that the 1936 attempt was to be launched on the same massive scale as before,' Shipton wrote in *That Untravelled World*, 'I considered resigning my place on it, having tasted the joys of simplicity and freedom in two long seasons of unrestricted travel.' But, as Jack Longland said, 'For Shipton Everest came rolling round like some boring old clock, and it was difficult for him to refuse.' He did not know how to get off this particular roller coaster and, without a proper career to fall back on and only slender financial support from his mother, he had to keep climbing. In this respect he was virtually a professional mountaineer like Frank Smythe, who lived off his writing and mountain photography.

After the initial high expectations, Everest 1936 was variously described as 'a washout', 'a lousy failure', 'a bitter disappointment'. But for Shipton it had a consolation – he fell in love again. While in Kalimpong preparing for the expedition's departure, he went to dinner with Bunty and Norman Odling at their home, 'Glenrilli', set on a hill above the town with wide views of the distant snows. Kalimpong was the terminus of the Tibetan wool trade across the Natu La between Tibet and Sikkim, and Odling ran the godowns where the wool was stored. At dinner Shipton was seated next to a friend of the Odlings, Pamela Freston, with whom he struck an immediate chord, spending the evening discussing places they would like to visit. His travels and lifestyle epitomised all she loved, but she was then embroiled in divorcing her husband, an Indian Civil Service officer.

The expedition moved up to Gangtok, the stepping stone for travel through Sikkim, where they camped on the lawn of the Residency. Basil Gould, the British Resident, invited Pamela to stay, and every night Shipton climbed a drainpipe to visit her. 'Eric was very frightened of an affair,' Pamela Freston said forty-five years later, still with a sparkle in her eye. 'I said to him, "Don't be so stupid, Eric, it's as easy as falling off a log, and very much nicer." We had gorgeous fun.'

Pamela was nine years older than Shipton, but nevertheless their romance flourished for three years; their friendship and correspondence was to last a lifetime of ups and downs. Pamela, though no writer herself, was a good editor and had a profound influence on Shipton's writing. She took the perennially reluctant author in hand, edited most of his subsequent books and supervised his reading list. An affectionate yet restrained exchange of letters followed during the 1936 expedition, at the end of which, about 500–600 items of the expedition's mail disappeared. On the back of the 494 assorted letters subsequently found hidden in an outhouse behind the post office, was a copied typewritten note, 'Suffered detention in Gangtok post office owing to Postmaster's failure to affix postage stamps and to forward them in time. The Postmaster has been sent to jail for his offence.' Shipton and Pamela were fortunate because the majority of their letters survived to cement their bond of love.

So the usual military-style convoy lumbered through Tibet; and Shipton wrote to Pamela, 'I should like to do a long journey through Tibet with just a rucksack and a pony.' Undoubtedly he meant to add the words – and you.

On the march Shipton became particularly friendly with Dr Noel Humphreys, at fifty-three an elder statesman with a remarkable career as explorer of the Ruwenzori, pilot, botanist, surveyor and, later in life, medical doctor (in order to expand his exploring life). 'I don't think I have ever met anyone who has lived so thoroughly. He is a grand object lesson to anyone who, like me, is apt to take a rather weak line about things,' he wrote to Pamela.

Ruttledge had picked out Smythe and Shipton as the most likely first assault pair on the mountain. Together they went off climbing the hills beside the trail, 'so as to evolve a perfect harmony of movement'. In describing Shipton's mountain skills, people repeatedly extol his rhythmical, perfectly balanced, sure-footed pace uphill and over rough ground.

When the expedition reached Rongbuk at the end of April, Everest appeared in perfect condition, spirits were high, and of his companions Shipton wrote, 'They are a grand lot – one simply couldn't have better.' At Camp I, Smijth-Windham set up his wireless equipment comprising fifty-eight porter loads, some weighing over the standard eighty pounds. Already news of an early monsoon arriving at Ceylon started crackling across the air waves from the Indian Meteorological Office in Alipore, followed by reports of earlier than usual disturbances in the Bay of Bengal. Worse was to follow.

No sooner had they set foot on the mountain than snow began to fall heavily; it never really let up, and two feet fell on 18 May, showing that the monsoon had arrived several weeks early. Various climbers made forays up to the North Col accompanying loaded porters, but always the snow conditions were terrible. So Ruttledge recalled every-one from the mountain, and wrote remorsefully in *Everest: The Unfinished Adventure*, 'I could not help reflecting that, with a little luck, Everest might have already been climbed; and that we should now have been packing up here, in complete happiness, instead of morosely peering through the tent door at a landscape which became whiter as the hours dragged by.'

Eventually, Shipton and Wyn Harris, goaded by inactivity and sheer exasperation, persuaded Ruttledge to let them go up and have another look at conditions above the North Col. They knew they were taking an unjustifiable risk, and they nearly paid for it with their lives. Shipton in the lead set off an avalanche which carried him down towards the edge of a precipice; Wyn Harris jumped clear of the moving wind-slab, dug his ice axe into the lip of a crevasse and belayed the rope around it, just managing to slow Shipton to a halt. This undignified episode finally closed down the expedition, which made a subdued return across Tibet. Messages of sympathy arrived from their patron, King George V; more appropriate, had he known, would have been his condolence to the mother of Kusang Sete, a Tibetan porter, who fell off a rope bridge and was drowned.

In a letter to Pamela, after thanking her for 'a lovely box of pepper-mints from Firpo's' (a famous restaurant in Park Street, Calcutta) Shipton confessed, 'Now it looks as if we have failed once more, and this time without even coming to grips with the mountain. We certainly haven't done anything on this show (frankly I have never been on such a boring expedition in my life). From my point of view the one good thing that came out of it was a talk with John Morris which focused my attention on the Karakoram.'

In Darjeeling, after the expedition was over, Shipton met Gordon Osmaston of the Survey of India, who was on his way into the Nanda Devi basin to fill in gaps in his survey work. He asked Shipton to guide him up the Rishi Gorge. At Lata, near the mouth of the gorge, they met a bearded, tattered Peter Lloyd bearing the news that Tilman and Odell had reached the top of Nanda Devi. In his book, *The Ascent of Nanda Devi*, after describing the view, Tilman wrote, 'I believe we so far forgot ourselves as to shake hands on it.'

For Shipton this must have been a sweet-sour moment of pride mixed with agony and envy. In a letter to Pamela (which expresses his feelings much more frankly than do his autobiographical versions) he wrote:

> What a glorious effort of Bill & Odell to have climbed Nanda Devi. I am overjoyed that it was Bill who did the 'touchdown' – he so thoroughly deserves every inch of his success – and I gather from brief conversations that he was outstandingly good the whole time on the mountain, as well as having done the lion's share of the donkey work. I think the whole show was quite undoubtedly the finest achievement that has ever been done in the Himalayas. By Jove, it will shake the old fools at home [the Everest Committee] and will do far more good towards getting the right spirit in the Himalayas than anything else could have done. I confess I wished I had been with them instead of wasting my time on that ridiculous Everest business.

Shipton did not then have the chance of congratulating Tilman who, with his expedition's moving spirit, young American climber Charles Houston, was at that moment leaving the Nanda Devi Sanctuary by climbing over the col named after Tom Longstaff. In 1905 Longstaff had camped there, 'the first human beings to look down' into the Sanctuary. Tilman described the ascent as 'a little dicey in places'.

Shipton and Osmaston's party, including Sherpas Angtharkay, Sen

Tensing and Ang Dawa, went on up the Rishi Ganga. 'The route up the gorge is now dead easy,' he wrote to Pamela, 'the whole way is marked with cairns and all footholds on the steep bits are trodden flat by the passage of many feet. I feel rather superfluous in the capacity of "guide".' The sheep, which they drove in on the hoof, became firmly attached to Angtharkay, who carried the struggling animal when the ledges became too narrow. Nevertheless, finally they had to sacrifice their pet which thereafter constituted several excellent dinners.

Once in the Sanctuary, Osmaston concentrated his survey on the Great North Glacier, while Shipton went off to explore the peaks at the head of the Changabang Glacier from where he hoped to look down on the Rhamani Glacier and the Bagini Pass (now called Shipton's Col). A problem arose in naming the peaks because the villagers of each valley, having no economic interest in the mountains themselves, called them random names. Shipton concluded, in the *Geographical Journal*, forthright if undemocratic: 'the best solution is for the pioneer travellers to adopt the pleasantest sounding of the various names, for geographers to accept their suggestions, and for subsequent travellers to refrain from discussion.'

Leaving Osmaston to finish surveying the southern half of the Sanctuary, Shipton returned down the Rishi Gorge to Dibrughita. From there he, Angtharkay and Sen Tensing tried to climb the South-West Ridge of Dunagiri but they were turned back near the top. Then they crossed to the north over the Bagini Pass, the difficulty of which heightened his respect for Longstaff's passage thirty years earlier. A blaze of autumn tints filled the Bagini Valley. Shipton returned towards Josimath, from where he made a final journey, carrying the Watts-Leica photo-theodolite, to make his own survey of the Rinti Glacier, crossing the Rinti Saddle between Trisul and Nanda Ghunti. So he came to the end of another season of filling in blanks on his map of Garhwal, and of ensuring that the entire region of Nanda Devi was thoroughly explored and mapped.

He returned to Kalimpong to stay with the Odlings at 'Glenrilli', where Pamela Freston had spent the summer while he was away in the mountains. Together they planned a two-week trek to survey the Kurumtoli Glacier, south of Trisul, near where he had passed only a few weeks before. Again he took his faithful friends Angtharkay and

Sen Tensing, along with five Dotial porters.

It was a pleasant, lighthearted holiday for Shipton, and an exciting adventure for Pamela, who had never done such a demanding trek, and was often near her limits. But the romance of it compensated for all the discomforts – no tinned food allowed, sleeping out under the stars or in a cave, reading poetry aloud by the light of a campfire. Forever it remained the high point of her life.

At the end of the trip Shipton took the results of his work to the Survey of India offices in Dehra Dun, accompanied by Sen Tensing, while Pamela went with Angtharkay to see the Taj Mahal at Agra. Then they all met up in Bombay, where the Sherpas slept on the floor outside memsahib's hotel bedroom, and spent the morning going up and down in the lift. They all went sailing in a yacht on the Indian Ocean, went to 'the flicks' (a movie); and finally the captain showed them, from the bridge to the engine room, the boat on which Pamela and Shipton were returning to England.

'As the ship gathered way and the quay grew smaller and smaller,' Pamela records in her diary, 'we still could see two faithful dots waving, and the last sound we heard from India was Angtharkay's piercing whistle echoing over the water as we had heard it so often on the trek echoing across the hills.'

CHAPTER 7

Peaks, Valleys and Glaciers

Shaksgam, 1937

As MENTIONED in the last chapter, Eric Shipton considered the one good thing that came out of his frustrating 1936 Everest expedition was John Morris's suggestion of a journey from Hunza to Leh by way of the Shaksgam River valley on the northern side of the Karakoram Range. Before leaving India that year, Shipton went to Simla to interest the Government and the Survey of India in a projected expedition to the Karakoram and to solicit their help in getting permission.

The first lines of *Blank on the Map*, the book he wrote about this expedition, perhaps his most fulfilling and successful of all, read, 'A fascinating way of spending a few hours of leisure is to sit down with a paper and pencil and work out in minute detail the preparations for an expedition into unexplored country. The fact that there is very little chance of carrying out the project matters little.' In fact, his small party did accomplish the plan, and Tom Longstaff, in the preface to that same book, wrote, 'The combined party has surveyed 1,800 square miles of one of the most difficult mountain fastnesses in the world. Sums ten times as large have often been spent on expeditions which brought back one-tenth of the results.'

For this journey he chose first his well-tried companion Bill Tilman. Before his recent success in climbing Nanda Devi, Tilman was regarded as Shipton's apprentice, but now he had established his own reputation as a mountaineer. To add credibility and expertise to the party, Shipton invited two scientists; Michael Spender, the abrasive, tempestuous genius he had grown to like and respect as surveyor on Everest in 1935, and John Auden, a geologist with the Geological Survey of India, who had already worked in the southern Karakoram. Both, incidentally, were brothers of famous poets.

Shipton travelled out to India on the P & O *Strathmore* along with his rolling stone mother, who was on her way to China and Japan. On ship-board he, Tilman and Spender kept fit by throwing a medicine ball, skipping and swimming. The Captain invited them onto the ship's bridge to practise their surveying techniques using theodolites.

Shipton was working on the manuscript of his earlier foray into auto-biography, *Upon That Mountain*, 'knocking out my 1,500 words a day'. He wrote frequently to Pamela Freston, reminiscing over places and inci-dents they had shared, affectionate, cooing, and strangely coy, even allowing for the style of love letters of the day.

He planned this to be a lightweight expedition like their Nanda Devi trip, but longer and farther. The total budget was £855, of which three return passages to India consumed £200; the final cost was £15 less than he estimated. Angtharkay hand-picked six stalwart Darjeeling Sherpas and escorted them by train across the plains of India to Srinagar in Kashmir. Few of them had ever seen a railway bigger than the Darjeeling Toy Train, and they regarded it as quite an adventure.

By now Shipton and Tilman prided themselves on being able to 'organise a Himalayan expedition in half an hour on the back of an envelope'. But for this undertaking the scale and logistics were so massive that detailed planning was needed. To cross the main Karakoram Range would pose a mountaineering challenge of its own. But the real problem was to transport several tons of stores and equip-ment over a difficult glaciated pass early in the year when snow would still be lying deep. Current maps of the Karakoram accurately showed the southern side of the range, but to the north was a blank space across which was written the single challenging word, 'Unexplored'.

Once across the mountains the party would have to be entirely self-sufficient for four months. So they had to ration their food meticulously, using their successful Nanda Devi formula of two pounds per man per day. Their basic diet comprised flour, rice and tsampa, butter, sugar and dried milk, pemmican and cheese; no delicacies were allowed. They pruned their equipment and personal gear to the barest essentials. A vociferous debate ensued over whether to take a rifle in order to supplement their diet with fresh meat; the rifle won out and they were later to be glad it did.

For his survey Spender had to use a Wild theodolite, a plane-table and subtense bar instead of his fancy (and weighty) photogrammetric apparatus. They spent hours in the bazaar, as Shipton wrote in *Blank on the Map*, 'comparing the relative weights of various makes of spoons, plates and mugs, and debating whether each member of the party should be allowed a knife, or whether one knife was enough for two of

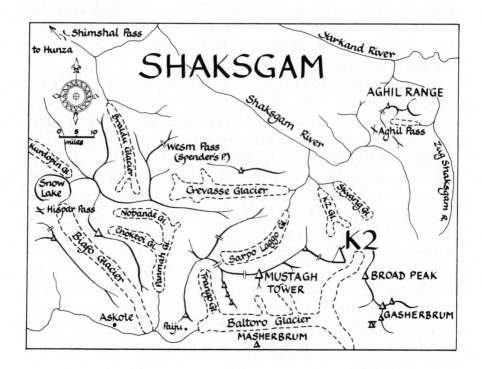

us. Tilman was strongly opposed to our taking plates, insisting that one could eat everything out of a mug. I maintained that if we happened to be eating curry and rice and drinking tea at the same time, it would be nicer to have them served in separate receptacles.' Spender sacrificed his extra tobacco.

From the comforts of the Srinagar home of Sir Peter and Lady Clutterbuck (who sent along a hamper of goodies) they set off from the Vale of Kashmir towards the mountains of the Karakoram. This country was new to Shipton, unlike the arid Tibetan uplands that lead to the north side of Everest, or the gentle alpine foothills of Garhwal. It is a barren region of desert and mountains interwoven with deep-cut valleys, braided rivers and some of the largest mountain glaciers in the world. Out of this starkness small oases suddenly appear whenever water springs out of the ground, with willows, apricot trees in blossom, corn and buckwheat. It is a land of austere contrasts, which he describes as 'like finding a corner of Kentish spring set in the midst of the arid crags of Aden'.

On 14 May 1936 he wrote to Pamela from Skardu, 'We have done 14 marches to here and have got another 5 to Askole. With luck we should be across the Karakoram and into our country in 3 weeks time. Expect to be back in October.' And so, as was his way, he put romance behind him in favour of the job on hand for as long as that should take.

At Dasso the party had to cross the river on rafts made of twenty bladders of sheepskins lashed together, and then to negotiate a gorge where the path clung to steep loose scree. In trimming their gear they had only one glacier lantern between thirty-eight of them. As Tilman predicted, the thirty-eighth man (himself) did not derive much benefit from its faint light.

Several side rivers were spanned by suspension bridges made of three huge ropes of willow wands – one for the feet, two for the hands – plaited and twisted together, suspended from heavy rock piers on either bank. These bridges sag towards the middle of the river, and as you approach the mid-point the hand ropes squeeze together, yourself sandwiched between, and the whole apparatus can suddenly turn turtle and pitch you into the torrent.

Askole is the last village on the way to the Baltoro, the mighty glacier flowing from K2 and other giants, the Trango Towers, Masherbrum,

Mustagh Tower, Gasherbrum and Broad Peak. There they bought two tons of flour, which they sewed into green canvas bags and made up into sixty-pound loads. With this weight they needed over a hundred porters; many porters were just carrying food for those who were carrying food. Their money had to be in silver coin because paper notes, being unfamiliar currency, would be useless beyond the range.

Angtharkay rounded up an unlikely looking collection of Balti porters. Many had goitres, some were cretinous and deaf mute, and they were reluctant to sally off into unknown territory with a bunch of scruffy sahibs and their frugal outfit. Angtharkay was dubious about them all and he made clear to Shipton his view that 'only three grades of humans should be included in a party. Firstly, there is the sahib, who is there to be satisfied. Secondly, there is the Sherpa, without whom no expedition could achieve its pointless objective; and lastly, there is the local porter, a greatly inferior being whom, unfortunately, it is necessary to employ when the party has more luggage than can be carried by the sahibs and Sherpas.' Fortunately the seventeen men brought from Skardu had no qualms about accompanying the expedition and were loyal throughout.

At Paiju Shipton decided to branch north up the Trango Glacier to try to find a way across a col, later named the Sarpo Laggo Pass, described by Professor Desio, who was on the Count of Spoleto's 1928 expedition. Both Sen Tensing and Tilman were sick with high fever; 'I still have a cold,' Tilman wrote to his sister Adeline, 'but that is not surprising as I crossed the Zoji La in shorts and sandals, and bathe every day' – and sometimes he dipped several times in a day. Because the caravan was consuming 220 pounds of food daily they could not afford to wait, so Shipton and Spender forged ahead up the Trango Glacier with the porters, leaving the invalids to follow with Auden.

After several minor fracas, the Baltis finally mutinied at the Sarpo Laggo Pass and most of them demanded to be paid off and sent back to Askole. They were poorly equipped for wading through deep snow, and seemed incapable of looking after themselves. Shipton's exasperation at the poor performance of these native locals was tempered by his thrill at standing on the Central Asian Divide. Descending the steep northern side of the pass his admiration rose for Francis Younghusband, who, in 1887, with no mountaineering experience, climbed over the neighbouring Mustagh Pass (19,000 feet), the traditional route from the north.

Starting in Peking, Younghusband crossed the Gobi Desert to reach Kashgar and Yarkand. His crew comprised Wali, a Balti guide; Drogpa, a Ladakhi leader of a caravan of ponies; and Turgan, a man he bought in the slave-market in Yarkand (along with a Certificate of Ownership), and finally some porters. They were all equipped with sheepskin coats, fur caps and smooth leather boots (Younghusband wore Yarkandi robes and an Englishman's solar topi). Patrick French in *Younghusband* describes how they bound handkerchiefs round the insteps of their boots for grip, roped themselves loosely together using pony reins, turbans and scarves, and, on a slope as steep as the roof of a house, Wali cut steps with a pickaxe they had bought in Yarkand. Having travelled already for many days through uninhabited country, Younghusband needed rare courage to have attempted such a difficult route nearly at the end of his journey and of his resources.

From Changtok, across the Sarpo Laggo Pass, Shipton saw K2, the world's second highest mountain. Spender based the whole of his survey on this fixed reference point visible from everywhere in the district. K2 has retained its original survey designation because there is no community within sight to give it a local name. Happily, an attempt to call it Mount Godwin-Austen after the then Surveyor General of India, did not catch on. Nowadays in the local Balti language the word *keitu* means a mountain – any mountain – not just the highest one in the region.

The expedition was in a hurry to relay their loads down the Sarpo Laggo Glacier to make a base camp at the junction of four large glaciers that feed into the Shaksgam River. The scale and barrenness of the country impressed Shipton deeply since these glaciers were bigger than any he had seen in other parts of the Himalaya. As he recounts in *Upon That Mountain*:

The valley of the Shaksgam River was a weird place, shut in on both sides by great limestone cliffs, slashed across with twisted streaks of yellow, red and black strata which gave them a bizarre appearance. The bottom of the valley was composed of gravel and sand flats, often a mile wide. Over these the river flowed, sometimes concen-

trated into one great body of water as it swirled round a bend in the
valley, sometimes split up into a dozen streams which sprawled their
independent courses across the flats. Spread out at intervals along the
valley we found jungles of grass, willow and tamarisk, natural
counterparts of the cultivated oases of the Indus Valley. The main
river was turbid, but, on each side of it, clear streams flowed through
a chain of deep green and blue pools. Steep, glacier-filled cores split
the vertical sides of the main valley, forming narrow openings into a
dark forest of Dolomite spires.

The Shaksgam River dictated their plans. Being early June it was low
and braided so they could ford it safely; but by summer, glacial melt
water would create raging floods. So they had only three weeks to complete their survey of the Aghil Range and be back on the south bank of
the Shaksgam, or risk having to stay into winter until the river subsided.
They crossed the Shaksgam River and followed it eastwards until a large
valley descended from the Aghil Range. The valley walls were made of
unclimbable, perpendicular conglomerate cliffs, and river terraces
which suddenly ran out into nothing. Beside a luxurious blazing fire,
Shipton reflected on his situation; 'East and west of us stretched an
unexplored section, eighty miles long, of the greatest watershed in the
world. We had food enough to keep us alive for three months in this
place of my dreams, and the health and experience to meet the opportunity. I wanted nothing more.'

They spent three weeks in the Aghil Range. Spender fixed the position of the Aghil Pass (which Younghusband had crossed), and mapped
the entire region. Shipton and Tilman crossed the mountains to the Zug
(or False) Shaksgam Valley and explored it thoroughly, discovering that
the water flowed north into the Yarkand River. Shipton shot two wild
sheep, which helped break the monotony of their diet and confirmed
the wisdom of carrying a gun. They also saw many snow-cock, and
occasionally wild asses, foxes and mountain wolves.

They crossed back over the Shaksgam River before its summer flood.
Even so, they had to take great care with river crossings because the
height of the water would vary according to the time of day, rising with
melt from the midday heat and falling in the freezing night. Lightly built
Angtharkay was nearly swept away in one crossing, emphasising the fact

ES with his mother and sister

ES (right) the neophyte climber with a friend, Charles Marriott

The farm at Turbo, Kenya

(Right) Mount Kenya with Midget Peak

Madge 'Midget' Anderson

ES on the summit of Kamet

Frank Smythe (left) with ES in camp-
boots, 1933

Everest 1933 team, with ES top row, sixth from left

ES setting off for Nanda Devi with Tilman

ES with Tilman on board ship

ES and Pamela Freston with Angtharkay and Sen Tensing on board ship

ES and Tilman with three Sherpas

Everest 1935 group. Back row (left to right): Dan Bryant, Edmund Wigram, Charles Warren, Michael Spender; front row: Bill Tilman, ES, Edwin Kempson

ES (seated extreme right) signing up Sherpas, including Tenzing (standing third from left)

Everest 1936 group. Back row (left to right): W.R. Smijth-Windham,
P.R. Oliver, G.N. Humphreys, C.B.M. Warren;
middle row: ES, F.S. Smythe, H. Ruttledge, C.J. Morris, P. Wyn Harris;
front row: J.M.L. Gavin, E.H.L. Wigram, E.G.H. Kempson

ES surveying the Kurumtoli Glacier   ES turning his back on the Karakoram

that mountain rivers are more of a hazard than the peaks themselves. After this incident they changed their technique, so one person would belay well upstream on a bend and let the man crossing use the rope as a pendulum. Even so, the raging torrent of muddy water hid boulders rolling along the river bed, which could injure the wader's legs.

Back in base camp at the junction of the Sarpo Laggo and Crevasse Glaciers, the whole party shared the excitement of a reunion and comparing notes and news, the Sherpas and the Baltis gossiping as much as the westerners. Shaded by willows, they lazed on glades of soft grass beside shallow pools edged with tall shrubs bearing pink blossom. Birds sang, a brook splashed from a spring, and hares darted across the meadows, in vivid contrast to the bleak mountain desert around them.

Shipton and Tilman next struck south up the K2 Glacier to explore the huge amphitheatre at the foot of the north side of K2 from which a single buttress soars 12,000 feet to the summit. Unfortunately, heavy mists hung in the upper glacier basin and a shifting drapery of cloud drifted across the massive face of K2 which never came fully into view. On their return to camp, they found Auden had left them a note in verse (a family trait) telling them that he was off alone again, but not much else of what he was doing. Spender was still out surveying. Shipton had realised that keeping the two scientists apart lent for harmony, and thereby the party was still remarkably amicable.

Now they had to undertake the final chapter of their exploration, travelling west over high passes parallel to the main Karakoram Range, and then re-crossing it. So Shipton decided they should split into three self-contained parties, each with its separate objective. They started together up the Crevasse Glacier through a forest of ice pinnacles, laboriously relaying 700 pounds of equipment and 1,500 pounds of food, enough to last another fifty-four days. Shipton and Spender planned to head north to explore the Braldu Glacier and find a way over the Shimshal Pass to bring them eventually to Hunza. Tilman, along with Sen Tensing and Aila would travel west, carrying food for twenty-three days, to try to solve the question posed by the early explorers, Conway and the Bullock Workmans, as to whether Snow Lake was the ice cap motherlode and hub of all the glaciers in the region. He discovered with some sadness that Snow Lake was a normal glacier basin that exited southwards to the Hispar Glacier. Then he crossed the contorted rock wall to the south of the Hispar Pass to reach Askole. Auden's time was nearly up, so he struck south down the Panmah Glacier to Askole, and so back to Skardu.

Of these journeys Tilman wrote to his sister, Adeline, 'We have had a very successful trip, and have settled a problem as to where a river went [Zug Shaksgam], fixed the position of an important pass [Aghil], explored this unknown glacier [Crevasse] – and of course, Spender has been mapping all the time. For various reasons, such as shortage of men, shortage of oil, and Eric's keenness on mapping, we have had very little climbing – only two peaks of about 20,050 feet. They were both difficult and gave us good days, but hardly worth coming all this way for.'

Tilman never hid his distaste for science. Of one occasion when they dropped the theodolyte while lowering it on a rope, Shipton wrote, 'He showed great self-restraint in not encouraging it to fall the rest of the way.' However, Tilman did come across some tracks, eight inches in diameter, which he categorically describes as of an Abominable Snowman. The Sherpas confirmed that they were definitely not of a bear, but were of the smaller man-eating variety of yeti, rather than the larger yak-eating beast.

By contrast, Shipton wrote about his own journey north with Spender, 'I found the survey so absorbing, it was enthralling to disentangle the geography of the region, to arrange the peaks and valleys and glaciers in their true perspective, and gradually to learn to know them with an intimacy and understanding that, for me, is the basic reason for mountaineering.' Shipton and Spender, together with Angtharkay and four Sherpas, took food for thirty days and crossed Wesm (later called Spender's) Pass; sometimes they carried loads of 130 pounds, almost Angtharkay's own body weight. Spender could be tactless and quick-tempered, which caused misunderstandings with friends and made him enemies, roughening his path unnecessarily. Under the surface, Shipton found a gentle, sympathetic, self-critical companion whose free expression of a lively imagination and intolerance of convention he admired. 'There was no man in whose company I found more pleasure,' he later wrote in the *Geographical Journal*, 'or with whom I would rather have shared the deep and varied experience of an exploratory journey.'

Having explored the length of the Braldu Glacier, they started up the
Shimshal Pass, an important link in the main Asiatic watershed; to the
west rivers flow into India, to the east into Turkestan and the deserts of
Central Asia. On the way up they met some yak herders and a cavalcade
of men armed with ancient muskets. Because the sahibs looked so disreputable they were escorted 'in a state of friendly arrest' across the
pass to the lambadar (or headman) of Shimshal, where they successfully reassured the headman of their good intentions and were allowed
to go on their way. Two 'minor considerations' that influenced their
decision to turn for home were the dilapidated state of their boots, and
the need for fresh supplies of food. In fact, they would both gladly have
spent the whole winter there. During the next four weeks they made
their way through a gorge of conglomerate cliffs beyond Shimshal to
Hunza, where the Mir lavishly entertained them, providing a feast of
grapes, pears, peaches and melons. Shipton also had a deadline to meet.
Having agreed to join the 1938 Everest expedition, he had to get back
before the passes to Kashmir closed for the winter in order to help
Tilman, the appointed leader, to organise it.

Shipton always gives credit to his Sherpa companions for their
contribution to the success of their shared adventures. 'They more than
justified their expense and without their support we would have accom-
plished little. During the expedition I frequently regretted that I had not
brought double the number of Sherpas.' He liked their boyish sense of
humour and love of the ridiculous, their loyalty and absolute friendship.
'I have often wondered,' he mused, 'exactly what the Sherpas think
during these long journeys in uninhabited mountain ranges so far from
their own homes. On earlier expeditions they often seemed worried,
but now they accepted the situation with philosophical resignation, and
displayed a touching confidence in our ability to find the way to
inhabited country before the food ran out.'

On preserving harmony among his own colleagues on an expedition,
Shipton details three essentials. First, every man should feel that he has
an important part to play. Second, each must be capable of deriving a
deep satisfaction from some aspect of his environment and sustaining
his enthusiasm. Third, all members of the party should agree on the
general policy and conduct of the expedition. He plays down the importance of the leader, whose primary task should be to select the party;

thereafter he should remain as inconspicuous as he can. Generally the leader will be the person with most experience of the ground to be covered.

By these criteria Shipton's leadership of the Shaksgam expedition was masterful; he thoroughly enjoyed himself, and summarises the journey in *Upon That Mountain* thus, 'Certainly no experience of mine has been fuller, no undertaking more richly rewarded than those few months among the unknown mountains beyond the crest of the Karakoram.'

This sketch of their journey understates the obstacles they had to overcome, the dangers that befell them (at different times both Shipton and Tilman plunged into deep crevasses), and the hardships they endured. In recognition of the outstanding merit of this journey the Royal Geographical Society awarded its Patron's Medal to Eric Shipton.

For ten days after their return to Srinagar, Shipton savoured the delights of autumn in Kashmir, along with beds, baths and clean clothes. There he met Colonel Leslie Weir, who had helped launch many of the early Everest expeditions, and his seventeen-year-old daughter, Beatrice, who described herself as 'a wild and woolly, bare-foot teenager'. She vividly remembered her first encounter with Shipton at a garden party: 'Suddenly there appeared this extraordinary brown-faced man, fairly small, with strong legs and a strong body, a shock of hair and a slightly weak chin. He had blazing blue eyes every-one used to talk about; he just sat and looked. It was indefinable. I melted like an ice cube and fell hook, line and sinker for him.'

Together they idled under the chenar trees of the Moghul Shalimar gardens, lounged in a houseboat on the Jhelum River and paddled on Dal Lake. But Beatrice's mother said to her, 'This man's a dreamer and just lives on a glacier. What good is he to my daughter?' To a woman, each of the mothers of Shipton's ladies seemed to have summed up his matrimonial prospects thus. As for Shipton, he was off to Everest again.

CHAPTER 8

A Vile Waste of Time

Everest, 1938

TILMAN begins his book *Everest 1938*:

> The story of the fifth abortive attempt to climb the mountain is only worth relating because a fairly drastic change was made in the methods used. That is to say we broke away from the traditional grand scale upon which all previous expeditions had been organized, and to that extent the story has novelty. I have no hardships to bemoan, no disasters to regret. Mr E. E. Shipton was possibly one of the first to doubt that in mountaineering the great and the good are necessarily the same. For financial reasons, if for no others, it seemed the time had come to give less expensive methods a trial.

Tilman budgeted £2,500 (following a theoretical exercise he and Shipton had undertaken in some idle moments the year before in the Karakoram) by spending a fifth of the money of previous expeditions

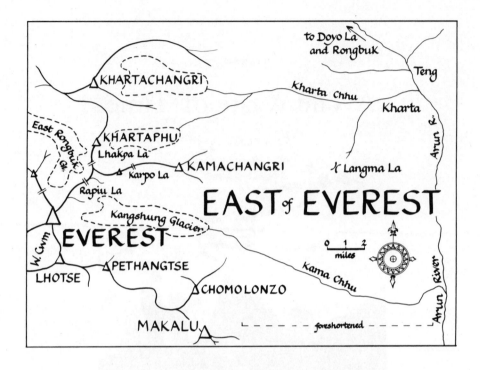

and taking a fifth of the gear – 'only essentials and not too many of those'. Money was tighter than ever because the Everest Committee's kitty was almost empty. The financial backing of newspapers, readily forthcoming until now, had dried up as interest in repeated Everest failures waned, or perhaps was diverted towards rumblings of war in Western Europe.

When it seemed possible the expedition might not get on the boat, Tom Longstaff offered to underwrite it himself. He empathised with the lightweight philosophy which was in tune with his own Himalayan travels, but he imposed three provisos: either Tilman or Shipton should lead it (he didn't mind which), there should be no advance publicity, and members would each contribute what they could afford.

Tilman was happy with this and expressed his hatred of newspaper razzle-dazzle, 'the lack of privacy is disagreeable and particularly so if, as usually happens, the newspaper gets hold of the wrong mountain wrongly spelt, adds or deducts several thousand feet to or from its height, and describes what the wrong man with his name wrongly spelt did not do on it'. However *The Times*, even knowing they would receive no regular dispatches from the mountain because the expedition carried no wireless, came through with a contract and £1,500.

Tilman chose a team of seven, numerous for a man who described an expedition as 'a party with too many people in it'. Odell, Shipton, Smythe, Warren and Oliver were all tried Everesters; Lloyd was a strong alpine climber. The average age of this 'socially harmonious' (Shipton's term) party was thirty-six, bumped up by Odell's forty-seven years. They were all primarily climbers with no supernumeraries – wireless engineers, transport officers or doctors. Wager and Longland, two powerful contenders for places in the team, were unavailable. Shipton gave Tilman his full support in planning a scaled down party on the latter's stated principle that 'the fewer the men to be maintained at each camp and the less food and equipment they need, the easier and safer it is for all concerned. No party should burden itself with a man or a load more than is necessary to do the job.' As to whether there were enough men for the hard work involved, Tilman's opinion was that underwork was more perilous than overwork; and Shipton had already published his views on the dangers of bedsores on Everest.

Only Tom Longstaff and Pamela Freston were at the station to see the expedition off. 'I wish Hugh [Ruttledge] had been there to see the lack of fuss. He always maintained that you could not avoid it,' Shipton wrote to Pamela from Paris en route to Marseilles to catch the boat to Bombay.

As usual Shipton used the voyage to try to catch up on his long-suffering publisher's latest deadlines (with the advent of jet travel his modern successors do not have this option). He retired into confinement, as Tilman said, 'for the speedier delivery of a book which he had carelessly omitted to finish before leaving home'. He wrote 15,000 words of *Blank on the Map* on the ship, and needed another 15,000 to finish the book. Despite the success of *Nanda Devi*, Shipton whines to Pamela, 'I am terribly sorry it is so bad – I feel that I have let us down. But the answer is that *I can't write.*'

She was now editing the book, and continued to have a strong influence on his writing and his reading (he took *Gone with the Wind* this time). The final typescript of *Blank on the Map* is very heavily edited – you might almost say re-written – by Pamela. She got him to use the active mood instead of endless passives that fudge his earlier writing. Moreover she took on his business dealings with Hodder & Stoughton to get the book published, and attended to all the details of assembling photos, acquiring illustrations, and commissioning maps.

The expedition arrived at Kalimpong to find Angtharkay and Kusang, dressed in long white aprons undergoing a cookery course from Bunty Odling. Angtharkay already made masterful stews, curries and rice, adequate for the austere palates of Shipton and Tilman. Noting that Kusang seemed less carefree than before, Tilman remarked, 'I think he had married.'

Shipton's letters to Pamela are still affectionate, even amorous, reminiscing euphemistically about the times and places of their initial romance in Kalimpong and Gangtok. 'I looked at the stairs that I crept up, and I'll go and see our room and write thinking of it all as if it were happening again.'

Shipton was obviously perfectly content to play second fiddle to Tilman as leader: 'Bill is shaping well as far as I can judge, and his exalted position does not seem to have affected him a bit. I suppose I am some moral support to him as he fusses rather about things. Also he *couldn't* have stayed in anyone's house for so long alone.' His letter to Pamela continues, 'The contrast and the general atmosphere of simplicity and genuineness that prevails is helping me to take a better view of the show – which otherwise is a bloody bore, and wasting much valuable time. This is a bad thing to say, I suppose, but it's the fourth time I have set out on this journey.' And this jaded note recurs in many of his subsequent letters.

Before setting off for Tibet the expedition members tidied up fine details. Regardless of expense, every European was given a plate in addition to a mug, and even dishcloths for wiping them. Odell was very critical of the Spartan 'provisioning', saying, 'the cult for lightness and mobility had been carried too far. A future expedition to Mount Everest will be best advised to adopt a compromise between the lavishness of some earlier expeditions and the frugality of this year's enterprise.' But as Tilman noted, 'Odell had not yet finished criticizing the food we ate on Nanda Devi in 1936 when, in spite of his semi-starved condition, he succeeded in getting to the top.'

They started off on the usual route to the north side of Everest through Sikkim and Tibet, soft with pastel colours and windless for once. Before Kampa Dzong, Odell strayed off from the party. The Sherpas went searching and found him wandering near the local nunnery (or gompa) so, much to their raunchy delight, they nicknamed him 'Gompa La Sahib'. Odell was often the butt of humour, which he took in his long stride, except on the occasion, during their return journey, when his rocks and fossils were stolen from outside his tent (the thief presumably thinking such a weighty crate must contain gold or silver).

Shipton was evidently fond of Odell who, he tells Pamela, 'almost never loses that courteous, gentlemanly manner, it used to be a joke in 1924 to try and get him ruffled out of it. He is terribly slow on the uptake, but he *never* obtrudes on one, or thrusts his views down one's throat. His most charming characteristic is his genuine and intense love for the country he is travelling in. He would be a *hopeless* leader, and I should not care to entrust him with scientific work on one of my shows. As a travelling companion he is grand. Also he never gets worried and is therefore a splendid person to have on a mountain.'

He also struck up a close friendship with Peter Lloyd, whom he knew previously only slightly. Lloyd had failed the medical exam for Everest in 1936 but was considered fit enough by Tilman to join his Nanda Devi team. 'Peter is a most unusually nice bloke. I like him far the best of this year's bunch,' Shipton told Pamela. 'Never for a moment did I get tired of him or lose interest in him.'

The expedition reached Rongbuk on 6 April, very early for Everest, which was still lashed by its usual spring gales. But Tilman wanted to be poised to make best use of the short pre-monsoon lull when the mountain might be calm enough for a week or so to allow them to rush the summit. They moved swiftly up the East Rongbuk Glacier, and stocked Camp III at the foot of the North Col.

'Frank & I are keen to delay things as much as possible,' Shipton wrote to Pamela. 'It will be fatal to get onto the mountain in April. If we try mucking about then, even if conditions look promising, we are liable to come in for such a hammering that we would be too weak to do anything when the warmer weather comes in May.' Shipton's and Smythe's opinion stood for a lot, being the two climbers most experienced on the highest reaches of the mountain.

The temperatures were extreme and many of the party were sick with the usual colds, sore throats and influenza. So they decided to leave all the equipment and food cached at Camp III, cross the Lhakpa La, and descend to the Kharta Valley 'to fatten up for the kill'. They had to rope down the steep eastern side of the pass, and then they romped down the Kharta Glacier. Kharta is 5,000 feet lower than Rongbuk, grassy instead of stony, and a far more suitable place to kill time and recuperate. 'We are camped in a charming bit of parkland,' Shipton wrote to Pamela, 'surrounded by tree-junipers and pink-barked birches, at the shore of a lake fringed with lovely green weed, gently sloping glades of soft turf, between banks of rhododendrons, a few of which are in full flower. Cowslips and primulas are out all over the place.'

Tilman had been ill during most of the walk in, and Warren was quite shaken after a fall crossing the pass. Unfortunately, Kharta was just too far away from the scene of operations on Everest to be used as a permanent base camp, preferable though it was in so many other ways. Nearby they bought eggs, chickens, vegetables and three sheep. Despite this, Smythe and Oliver complained continually about the food. Shipton was quite acerbic about them. 'Frank, of course, is about the worst traveller I have ever met.' And later, 'Peter (Oliver) has much more in him than the average bloke, but he is a great deal too neurotic for this game.'

Interspersed with rhapsodising about the scenery and the views of Everest and its neighbours, Shipton's letters to Pamela continue to bemoan his situation. 'This Everest business is all waiting about and one becomes very fed up with it,' and, 'What a vile waste of time this expedition is.' After ten days most of the climbers returned to Rongbuk via the Doyo La to find that 800 rupees had been stolen from their cash box left in a store room at the monastery.

Smythe and Shipton were told to rejoin the party at Camp III. 'Frank and I came back over the Lhakpa La and watched the others trying to get up a dangerous North Col,' he wrote to Pamela. 'Snow conditions were terrible everywhere. Weather seems to have been monsoonish since the *beginning of this month*. Peter Oliver came down in a small avalanche, lucky to get away with it. We got onto the Col to find terrific snow. Then the weather became HOPELESS. Frank and I decided to have nothing more to do with the East side of the col which is now a death trap. The weather this year has been MAD, it looks very much as if we are buggered again. I've *never* seen so much snow on the mountain as now.'

On 3 May snow started falling and continued for a week, covering the North Face with a deep blanket that 'looked like a sugar cake'; without doubt the monsoon had broken, and with it their chances of getting up the mountain. But Tilman would not give up so easily, and decided to move round to the head of the Rongbuk Glacier to try to reach the North Col from the west. Next day they climbed the west side of the col (a first ascent) with sixteen Sherpas, tediously cutting steps in glare ice left on the débris cone of 'the father and mother of all avalanches' (according to Tilman) that had come down a few days before.

'I was very frightened going up to the col,' Shipton admitted to Pamela. 'It was a bloody place. O.K. for a climbing party; but long, continuously exposed and very steep. A slip by one of the heavily laden porters would have been almost impossible to hold. However we got away with it. To my mind there is no question about the wisdom of Mallory's judgement in rejecting this route.'

They reached the North Col and climbed up to Camp V where they pitched the Pyramid tents. Shipton, Smythe and seven Sherpas went on to Camp VI (27,200 feet). 'I have never seen the blokes so completely corpsed as when we got there,' Shipton told Pamela. 'It was perfect weather and the views were glorious. But one is like a sick man climbing in a dream, too doped and sub-normal to appreciate anything on the upper part of Everest. It really is a mug's game for one is almost too weak to think, and one is always falling asleep and doesn't care a damn what happens. It would be a lovely way of passing out – just to let oneself go – rather like morphia.'

After a stormy night during which they slept well, Shipton and Smythe felt fit and optimistic for a chance at the summit which had eluded them for so long. Next morning they started early but soon became so cold they had to return to the tent to warm up. Then they tried again but found that 'conditions were HOPELESS. On the slabs we were up to our waists in powder snow, which threatened to come away with us. Even clear of snow those slabs are quite tricky, but with all that feathery powder into which we sank up to our hips –! My God she looked a real devil from where we got to. Norton's traverse (the only way I think) looked *formidable*, all hung with ice and snow. One just cannot climb Everest when it is like that – at least *I* can't! There was nothing for it but to turn our backs again. The old mountain has definitely rejected us.'

The snow showed no tendency to consolidate, confirming the experiences of every previous party that had gone above about 24,000 feet. It was bitterly disappointing, since Shipton and Smythe were both far fitter at these altitudes than they had been in 1933, and 'the glittering summit looked tauntingly near'. They descended in a blizzard, convinced they were climbing beyond all reasonable safety limits, an opinion confirmed by Smythe falling into a crevasse just before the North Col.

Smythe and Shipton met Tilman and Lloyd, experimenting with the open-circuit oxygen apparatus, on their way up for a second try. But they also were stymied by deep powder snow. At Camp IV they found Ongdi sick with pneumonia, and Pasang (one of the staunch Nanda Devi Sherpa trio) apparently 'off his head'. In reality he had suffered a stroke that paralysed the entire right side of his body, leaving him unable to speak and totally helpless. The other Sherpas, all close friends of Pasang's, including Angtharkay, calmly suggested leaving him where he was because evidently the gods of the mountain had summoned his soul. Tilman was furious and exhorted them to carry poor Pasang piggyback to the fixed ropes hanging from the col. They tied a bowline round his chest, lowered him down the steep sections, and hauled him like a sack of potatoes until they reached Camp III on the East Rongbuk Glacier.

Defeated and despondent, the expedition turned for home; yet again the Everest weather had won out. But to blame the weather when climbing Everest is like blaming the weather when sailing round Cape Horn. There's nothing you can do about it, and if you don't like it, stay away.

Tilman was very disappointed for his team; but Shipton writes charitably about his leadership to Pamela. 'Out of this party there is no one who would make as good a leader, except Peter Lloyd or myself. Bill has a number of silly faults, such as shyness in discussing plans & lack of mental flexibility, but he's got more guts than the rest of us put together.' Shipton had already decided he would not join Tilman on 'another

Everest show for next year', but he wanted to be around to help his friend prepare for it, despite possibly delaying his return to England.

Peter Oliver went ahead of the others because his regimental leave was up. In Kalimpong he stayed with the Odlings and discussed the expedition with them. Norman Odling rashly leaked Oliver's news to Reuters, who filed a dispatch that scooped *The Times*, thereby vitiating their exclusive contract with the expedition. Already upset about the 'lack of news', they were now apoplectic. Shipton had no sympathy with their wishing the expedition to fabricate endless dispatches when nothing was happening: '"The march across inhospitable lama-ridden Tibet", or "Hardships on the glacier", or "Brilliant work in establishing Camp I" (a walk as easy and a good deal pleasanter than between Lexham Gardens and Hyde Park Corner) etc. etc. etc.'

He continues to Pamela with a cynical attack on the public attitude towards the 'conquest' and 'attack' on Everest. 'I wish to God the Tibetans would prohibit any further attempts – they seem, like war, to bring out the worst in people – because they have become a pure stunt and nothing else, on no higher plain than dancing non-stop for a week.' Things haven't changed much in the intervening half century, and this rings true of the annual base camp circus of today.

Tilman wanted to cross the Zemu Gap into Sikkim and was keen for Shipton to accompany him; but the latter wanted to return to the Nyonno Ri Range where he was in 1935 with Edmund Wigram. So travelling light with two Sherpas he spent a week extending their survey of 'that glorious country'.

At the end of the 1938 expedition Shipton sums up his feelings about the past months on Everest, in *Upon That Mountain*: 'It is possible, even probable, that in time men will look back with wonder at our feeble efforts, unable to account for our repeated failure, while they themselves are grappling with far more formidable problems. If we are still alive we shall no doubt mumble fiercely into our grey beards in a desperate effort to justify our weakness. But if we are wise we shall reflect with deep gratitude that we seized our mountaineering heritage, and will take pleasure in watching younger men enjoy theirs.'

CHAPTER 9

Karakoram Survey

1939

ERIC SHIPTON left Everest with his head full of exciting plans for a much longer expedition into the massive, wild and barren mountains of the Karakoram Range which had so excited him the year before. This time Bill Tilman would not be with him. Whether they knew it or not, their amiable parting in the summer of 1938 – Shipton turning north to explore the Nyonno Ri, Tilman south to cross the Zemu Gap into Sikkim – signalled the end of an era of their major exploratory journeys together.

The two men were still close, if geographically distant, friends but their interests had reversed. Shipton had become fascinated by, and found an academic stimulus in, the technical aspects of surveying and mapping which compensated for his unscholarly background. No longer were peaks his main objective; more and more he saw, as the focus of his life, passes leading into exciting unexplored mountain regions. He expressed his philosophy in a lecture to the RGS. 'With such a vast area of unknown mountains to explore, the climbing of any of the countless peaks one sees offers little interest compared with the enthralling business of finding one's way about the country and crossing passes which lead from one region of mystery to another.'

Tilman, on the other hand, had become more interested in mountaineering itself, and thought they had climbed too few peaks on the Shaksgam expedition, which he felt was biased towards loathsome science. He had chewed on the Everest bone and was not going to let it drop. He thought the only way to climb the mountain was for a small lightweight expedition to be in position on successive years ready to take advantage of the short window of quiet pre-monsoon weather, when conditions might be perfect for a dash to the summit. Every ridge and gulley of the North Col and North-East Ridge route was known up to 28,000 feet; the bogey was the weather. He went to Yatung in Tibet to meet Basil Gould, the Political Officer, to discuss plans for an annual Everest expedition; but Gould was not encouraging about the chances of the Tibetan Government giving permission.

For Shipton, much remained to be explored before the map of the main features of the great Karakoram Range could be completed. 'From the experience gained in 1937,' he wrote in the *Geographical Journal*, 'it was clear to me that the task would best be tackled during the winter, when the rivers, instead of presenting the traveller with impassable barriers, might even be used as high roads by which to penetrate into the heart of the unexplored regions.'

Shipton invited Tilman on his projected Karakoram expedition but the latter declined politely. In the First World War, when still a teenager, Tilman had earned a Military Cross and bar in the Royal Artillery. Now threat of war again hovered over Europe; Germany had marched into Czechoslovakia, the Spanish Civil War was under way, Hitler had annexed Austria, and Mussolini had invaded Albania. Should war be declared, Tilman did not want to be cut off from news and thus prevented from joining the army. So he went off to Assam on what turned out to be an unsuccessful trip.

In order to plan his Karakoram expedition, Shipton returned home where Pamela Freston was waiting for him, but something was awry in their relationship. The last letter he wrote from Everest in the summer addresses her, 'My Darlingest', he plans trips they would do together when he returns, and ends sending 'All my love, Darling One'. By December he is writing 'frankly and bluntly' about their respective 'obligations' because a letter from her had made him 'bloody angry'. He declaims repeatedly his hatred of *writing* rather than *talking* together, and bemoans that he *can't* express himself on paper (his emphasis), despite achieving two publishing successes with *Nanda Devi* and *Blank on the Map*, published in 1936 and 1938 respectively.

After the passion of their letters written from afar had calmed, Shipton and Pamela evidently did not settle down to the realities of living close together and seeing a lot more of each other. They had experienced their troubles the previous winter, but these seem to have been resolved by Shipton's absence on Everest, making their hearts grow fond again. Pamela finds Shipton (so he deduces) 'cold, unimaginative, insensitive, rather selfish, overcautious, morally afraid, and proud of his reserve.'

To Shipton, Pamela is 'over-enthusiastic, emotional and oversensitive', and with 'ridiculous ideas about what (her) station in life demands'. He thinks she exaggerates: 'You say "devastating", or "the last straw", when I might say "a bit 'ard".' She fusses about small things like going to the theatre by tube train wearing an expensive evening dress; worrying about what his mother and sister think; about whether Tilman and Spender 'know about us'; and being left to walk home alone from Cromwell Road at 2 a.m. because he had 'promised to take some milk up to mother before she went to sleep'.

They row about dates and relations and friends, and Shipton tells Pamela she behaves like a spoilt child over money. He concludes that their temperaments are so widely different neither of them is likely to change. But he sees no reason why they could not get on with each other allowing sufficient give and take. 'I suppose if we *really* can't get over these differences there is nothing for it but never to see each other again, but honestly it seems to me to be making a blooming Everest out of an ant hill.' (Kenyan ants rather than English moles.)

Despite these rumblings of discontent he had enjoyed her company, sharing things together and being in love. But he continues quite definitively, 'As you know, I think it would be a mistake for us to get married. 1. Because I am not sure whether the difference in our

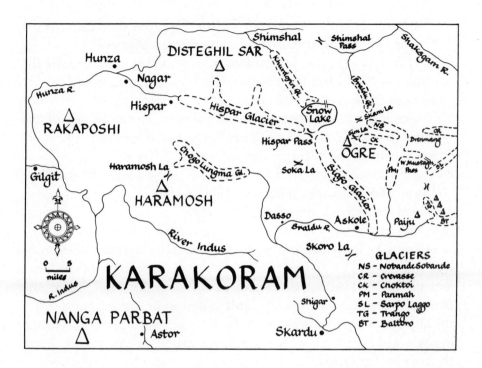

temperament is too great for us to cope with. 2. The difference in our ages [Pamela is nine years older]. 3. My present desire for complete freedom (which is a selfish reason) and 4. A silly notion that I ought to be able to support a wife if I marry one.'

In January 1939 Shipton and Pamela stayed at a pub in the Lake District, climbing together with Eadric Fountaine (who was joining the Karakoram expedition later in the year). 'Eric came to say good-night,' Pamela recalled. 'When I heard his footsteps going away down the corridor I said to myself, "That's for the last time", and I was quite right. Nothing was said; simply splendid to the end. We never had a bust up, no scenes, no trouble whatsoever. I didn't even go back to London with him. We were together for three years from '36 until the spring of '39; thereafter we remained tremendous chums.' But their correspondence was to last Shipton's lifetime, and became a special solace during the war when he was sequestered without news in Central Asia.

Shipton planned the Karakoram expedition to last sixteen months, divided into four seasonal parts:

1) Summer 1939 – to sort out the 'topographical confusion' of the Hispar-Biafo-Panmah Glaciers by accurate triangulation.

2) Winter 1939–40 – to explore the mountains to the east of the Shimshal Pass. Precipitation would be light, but they would require arctic gear for the extreme cold.

3) Spring 1940 – to journey from Shimshal to Leh by way of the Shaksgam River, using a small herd of yaks for transport and food, and to survey the northern part of the Aghil Range.

4) Summer 1940 – to travel from Leh to the source of the River Indus, exploring the unknown Aling Kangri Range on the way. 'Thence – well, who could tell?' he wrote.

Despite the imminent prospect of war and the attendant uncertainties, Shipton had surprisingly little difficulty in financing the expedition with grants from the Royal Geographical Society, the Royal Society, the British Museum, Kew Botanic Gardens and some private funds. After the Shaksgam expedition his reputation as a serious explorer was firmly in place. He even borrowed an extremely expensive photo-theodolyte from a firm in Germany.

He invited six people with different skills to join the expedition: Scott Russell – mountaineer and botanist; Eadric Fountaine – doctor and zoologist; Peter Mott – surveyor; and, to emphasise the scientific purpose of their travels, two Indian surveyors, Fazal Ellahi and Inyat Khan. Campbell Secord, a Canadian, joined the party for a brief spell, 'throwing everything into confusion'. Michael Spender, though sorely tempted, could not commit himself for a year and a half; and John Auden's bosses at the Geological Survey of India would not spare him. Shipton, as usual, left Angtharkay to choose nine Darjeeling Sherpas.

A scruffy bunch of climbers and Sherpas assembled in Kashmir and pitched camp on Lady Clutterbuck's lawn, soon taking over her whole establishment. One house guest was Diana Channer, whose father was in the Indian Forest Service, so she had spent much of her childhood in jungle camps, loved wild country, and was used to an outdoors life. Shipton fell ecstatically in love with her during the expedition's stay in Srinagar. It was mutual, as Diana's diary tells: '9th June 1939 – E. has very penetrating eyes. Looks attractive; 10th – I really flirted disgracefully with E. both teasing each other; 11th – had a dream about E. I like his quiet voice, quiet humour & eyes; 12th – lay out under the stars, sweet when he slept on my lap; 14th – out on Dal Lake, talked endlessly with lots of lovely giggles; 15th – helped E. pack. He is adorable & I love his vagueness and his worried look.'

Diana and Lady Clutterbuck accompanied the expedition for the first five marches. Another devoted Shipton admirer, Beatrice Weir, who had fallen for his blue eyes two years before, to her chagrin was considered too young (at nineteen) to go along, and was left kicking her heels in Srinagar. Diana's diary continues: '17th – E. refuses to walk with anyone else, which worries me, he is *so* loving; 18th – we both bathed naked and dried in the sun; 20th – I woke at 5 a.m. he looked so lost and adorable; 21st [their last day together] – E. looked so gloomy. Kissed E. passionate goodbye & burst into tears.' Then she and Lady Clutterbuck turned back. Thereupon Shipton wrote saying, 'I have been thinking about you every step of the way and wondering where you are and how you are getting on. Now you should be at Kurgabal where we sang songs on that heavenly evening.'

The expedition's gear posed problems of weight even more acute than in 1937 because they expected to be in the field four times longer and would be in almost uninhabited country with little chance of living off the land, and none of resupply. The only tinned food they took was pemmican. From England they also brought Cheddar cheeses, bacon sides (sealed in packages), slab chocolate and a little oatmeal. Their eight ounces of sugar per day proved insufficient; yet one wonders why they did not buy dried apricots that are abundant by the sackful in villages throughout the Karakoram – cheap, tasty, sugary sweet, and with kernels rich in protein and fat.

Scott Russell calculated their food needs, producing some sobering sums, recorded in his book, *Mountain Prospect.*

A coolie eats two pounds of food in a day, and the load he carries is 60 pounds. Thus one man's load is consumed by thirty coolies every day; or, viewing the problem from a different angle, if a porter is employed for three weeks in country where no food is available, only 18 pounds of his load benefits his employer; he consumes the other 42 pounds himself. Moreover, as he must be provisioned for his journey home, three weeks' employment means fourteen outward marches, it being assumed that unladen he will double his speed on the return journey.

Since expedition members and Sherpas were all living and working alongside each other equally, their equipment was to be identical. Windproof suits were made of royal blue, arctic-weight Grenfell cloth. An old lady in the Shetland Isles knitted them gloves and helmets, wool sweaters and pants – several each to be worn in layers, light in weight, and warm even when wet (the forerunners of modern polypropylene thermal underwear). 'Allowed but a single shirt, there would be no difficulty in deciding what to wear,' Scott Russell commented wryly.

From Srinagar they moved to Gilgit and then up the Hunza Valley to Nagir, where the Mir, a gracious old man, entertained them royally with exhibitions of polo and dancing. As a young man, in 1891, he had fought a British force of Gurkhas and Kashmiri troops under Colonel Durand who had been sent to subdue Safdar Ali, the ruler of Hunza. Shipton split the party into small groups, as he had done in Shaksgam two years previously, sending them off in different directions to survey the glaciers that flowed into the lower end of the Hispar. These glaciers made easy travel, being flanked by parallel ablation valleys which are formed by ancient lateral moraines left behind after a glacier has squeezed past a rocky projection. The ablation valleys provided idyllic campsites in meadows carpeted with wild flowers, and filled with willows and rose thickets which were then in bloom.

Shipton took thirty porters up the Hispar to make a food dump at Hispar Pass; he then continued down the Biafo another three days to Askole, a total distance of seventy miles without stepping off glacier ice, where skis might have made for quick travel had they thought to take them. In spite of fair weather and good travelling conditions, the Nagir porters made continual trouble. So he paid them off and sent them home; all except one, Mahmud, who remained faithfully with the expedition for the rest of the summer. Shipton and Fountaine left Askole with three weeks' food, bound for the Panmah Glacier, the lower part of which was desolate and barren, interspersed with oases. Angtharkay shot several ibex which provided meat for their entire time away. Fountaine followed the Chiring Glacier and climbed easily up to the New (or West) Mustagh Pass, which, Shipton pointed out in the

Geographical Journal, 'affords a very easy means of communication across the main Asiatic watershed, certainly the quickest and easiest known route between Askole and the Shaksgam River'.

From his camp on grass-covered slopes watered by clear streams, Shipton climbed a peak above Drenmang. He and Fountaine ascended the Choktoi Glacier to reach the east side of the Ogre; then they both crossed different passes westwards towards Snow Lake. Meanwhile Russell and Mott had crossed the Sokha La to the Cornice Glacier, descended the Basha Valley and, almost completing a circle, reached Askole. The party was beginning to settle down well together. Shipton increasingly enjoyed Scott Russell's enthusiasm, generosity and consideration, despite the flow of 'inarticulate vombosity' the latter employed while incessantly arguing trivialities with Mott, yet remaining firm friends. A disaster happened when Mott dropped the precious theodolyte because the top of a small peak, on which he had placed a survey station, collapsed.

Returning up the Biafo from Askole to Snow Lake, they met Fazal Ellahi, who had completed the survey and mapping of the entire Biafo Glacier and its tributaries from source to snout. He bore a Kashmir Government, yellow foolscap envelope, addressed to Shipton and marked 'Urgent'. A message inside (dated September 2nd) told them that Germany had invaded Poland, and had made a pact with Russia. They realised that war must follow and would stall their best-laid schemes. But the Sherpas were delighted because in the pre-war years a number of their friends had been killed needlessly on German expeditions to Kangchenjunga or Nanga Parbat. 'However,' says Russell, 'they did not fully understand the implications for themselves regarding the inevitable fate of the expedition.' Meaning that they would be out of a job.

Russell hurried down to their camp at Shenishish to collect the wireless set, which they had used to get accurate time signals for their astronomical work. Tuning to the BBC Overseas Service, the chimes of Big Ben heralded news of war. Russell trudged back up the Hispar in new-fallen snow and met Shipton at their Snow Lake camp where they lay talking of the future for half the night. Shipton admitted, 'I felt for a moment as though one of the crevasses had opened and that I was dropping into a bottomless pit.' They decided forthwith to return to

Gilgit to seek instructions from the Government of India, 'to be employed in any manner which authority might decide.'

But the survey parties were still widely scattered. To fill the time before they could foregather, Shipton and Russell climbed to the rim of Snow Lake looking for the pass which would lead to Shimshal by way of the Kurdopin Glacier. 'As if to point to the contrast,' wrote Shipton in *Upon That Mountain*, 'the mists cleared and for a moment the glacier was bathed in a sunset glow reflected from the high peaks. The granite spires of the Biafo stood black against a deep blue sky. At least this mountain world, to which I owed so much of life and happiness, would stand above the ruin of human hopes, the heritage of a saner generation of men.'

While Scott Russell set off for Gilgit, Shipton went north to help Fazal Ellahi finish his glacier mapping project. The surveyor 'worked like hell between dawn and dark each day' and, due to his 'amazing energy and guts', their results were more promising than Shipton had expected for the expedition's short time in the field. During the summer they had surveyed in detail 1,750 square miles of country and crossed several new passes. Shipton's disappointment was profound at having to shut down an expedition that bore so much promise. He tried to be pragmatic. 'For my part I found solace in the realisation of how incredibly lucky I had been in making nine expeditions to the greatest mountains on earth, which had yielded a wealth of experience and happiness that I could hardly have dreamed of ten years before.'

It was now November and the expedition members returned to Kashmir by various routes. Shipton was deeply saddened to discover that Diana Channer, whose loving correspondence he had relished, had returned to England to be part of the war effort. With war afoot people's futures were in limbo, and it must have seemed uncertain whether he and Diana would ever see each other again.

However, he met again Beatrice Weir, who had adored him since their meeting two years before. While trying to decide what to do next he lived for 'three golden weeks' on a houseboat moored alongside the Residency in Srinagar. No setting could have been more perfect for romance, and Shipton states laconically in *That Untravelled World*: 'Then for the second time in Kashmir that year, I fell in love.'

Half a lifetime later, Beatrice was able to put Shipton's relationships with his women in some sort of perspective. 'Great parts of himself he kept in separate compartments,' she said, 'you went into a compartment and for all you knew, you dwelt there like a queen. All these girls were swooning round him. He only had to crook his finger and they came running. He had charisma which bowled people over so they gave him what he wanted.

'He didn't really let you know him,' Beatrice continued, 'I doubt whether people could ever get to know him. If you were in love with him it didn't matter because you were so besotted and enjoying it, so happy living in the present doing wonderful trips up mountains with no need to talk or to analyse things. He had a faraway, bewildered, "little boy lost" look. But he had a mean streak, and he was an extraordinarily iceberg-like lover.'

About his own social life at the time, Shipton wrote, 'Though my chosen way of life made it impossible to contemplate marriage, it did not prevent my falling in love from time to time as I had done since the age of twelve. This, of course, presented problems and caused me, as a defensive measure, to adopt a light-hearted attitude towards sex, not quite in keeping with my temperament.'

Stuck in India without definite instructions from the Indian Government authorities on what he should do next, Shipton tore himself away from Beatrice, and left Kashmir for the Survey of India offices in Dehra Dun to continue working on the results of the previous summer's Karakoram expedition. He admitted, in a letter to Pamela Freston, to a feeling of profound hopelessness and futility about the war and the future.

So he joined the Indian Army, took a course of riding lessons at the Indian Military Academy, and was sent for three months to Officers Training School in South India, at Belgaum, mid-way between Poona and Mysore. His natural antipathy towards the military resulted in only a mediocre performance as an officer cadet. He got into trouble by championing the cause of an Anglo-Indian who had done extremely well on the course (far better than Shipton) and was dumped on the pretext of 'not being officer material'. Incensed by this blatant racial prejudice, Shipton encouraged his fellow trainee officers to protest, tantamount to mutiny under military law and a serious offence especially in wartime.

He was bored by the school, which constantly reminded him of his earlier scholastic failures. Nevertheless he scraped through the course and was grudgingly commissioned as a 2nd lieutenant. He was posted back to the Survey of India and sent on another three-month course in triangulation, a subject with which he was already familiar from his Karakoram expeditions. Then he had to await instructions on his future.

CHAPTER 10

The Consul-General

Kashgar, 1940–42

IN AUGUST 1940, halfway through his triangulation course, Eric Shipton was summoned by the Viceroy to Simla, headquarters of the Government of India, where he was offered the post of His Britannic Majesty's Consul-General in Kashgar, Sinkiang. It came like a thunderbolt. 'Had someone invited me to go to the moon, I could hardly have been more astonished,' he wrote, 'and for the next few days I was in a turmoil of incredulity, elation and doubt.' The prospect of being paid to trek for two months across the Karakoram Range that he had begun to know so intimately in recent years, and to spend unhurried time living on the edge of the Takla Makan Desert and the Tarim Basin beside the mountains of Central Asia, was a dream come true. His excitement was tempered by realising his lack of qualifications (seemingly of little consequence) for the job.

Also there was the prospect of a long spell of isolation from Beatrice to whom he had unofficially proposed marriage, which she had

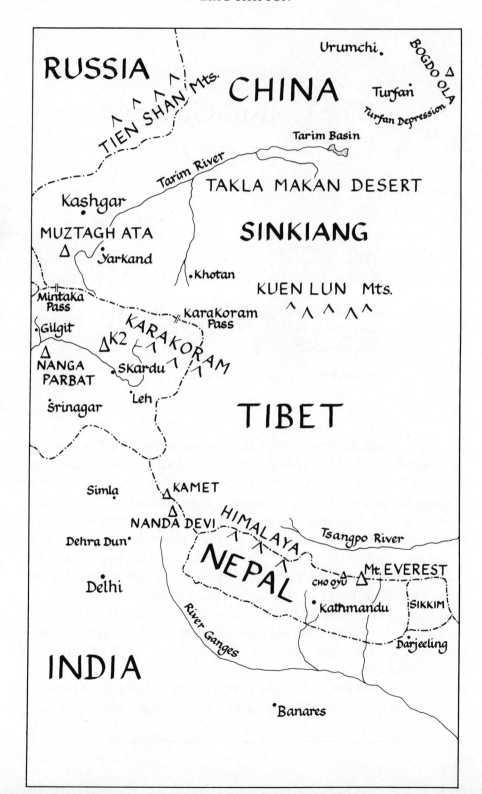

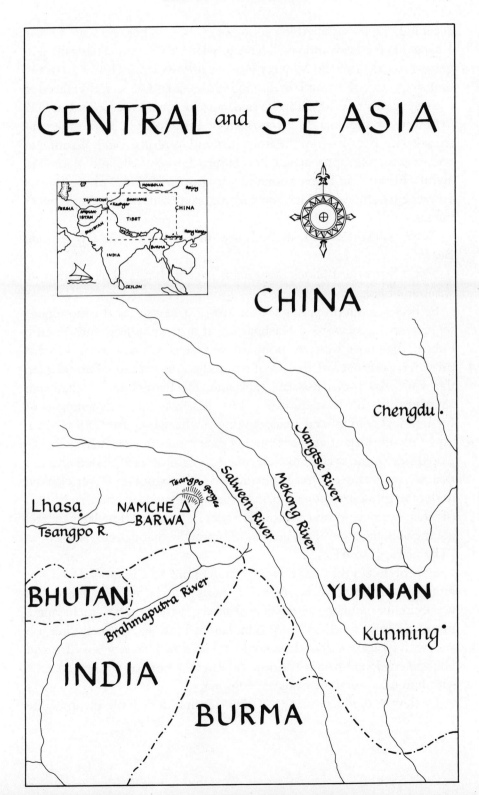

accepted. 'Don't say anything about it yet,' he told her, 'I'll write to you. Kashgar is far away, and you'll have to wait a long time.' They talked of getting married on the Mintaka Pass (that leads from Hunza across to Sinkiang), and of naming their children Kara and Koram. 'We lived in a lovely fantasy world,' Beatrice said, 'and he taught me Lewis Carroll's "Hunting of the Snark".' As a token of his affection, Shipton left his ice axe with Beatrice (not the first girlfriend to receive one). Wanting to reciprocate, she approached her father, Leslie Weir, and said, 'I'm awfully broke. Can I have something to give Eric?' Her father gave her a silver cigarette case which she had engraved with hers and her lover's initials.

'What will you say if somebody sees that and asks who BW is?' said Beatrice.

'Oh, I'll say the Bullock Workmans gave it to me,' replied Shipton, without a blink.

So he set about preparing for the long journey across the mountains to take up his new post. Kashgar lay at a geographical and political hub at the most westerly point of Sinkiang, China's most western province. South across the Karakoram, the greatest mountain range in the world, lay India; Russian Tajikistan, the Pamirs and Afghanistan were just to the west. Situated thus, Kashgar was a listening post for political activity and manoeuvring in the whole of Central Asia, especially important at that time because it was unclear where Russia would side in the war against Germany. It cannot have eluded Shipton that he was to be a rather sophisticated information-gatherer cloaked under the grandiose title of British Consul-General; as he wrote, 'part of that strange, semi-clandestine web of activity, intelligence and counter-intelligence, intrigue and diplomatic manoeuvre, known as "The Great Game"'.

Shipton heard that Angtharkay was in Simla, so telephoned to invite him to be his bearer in Kashgar. 'He fairly yelled down the phone and was quite inarticulate,' he wrote to Pamela, 'I thought he was having a fit he was so excited.' Sadly, Angtharkay had just accepted another job and, with typical loyalty, felt he could not let down his new boss. Instead Shipton engaged Lhakpa Tenzing and Rinzing, both of whom had been with him on several previous expeditions.

He flew in a military plane to Gilgit (his first time in the air, and quite unimpressed by the experience) over country he knew intimately on foot. The main trade route from India to Sinkiang went north from Gilgit across the Mintaka Pass to Tashkurghan, and thence to Kashgar. The whole journey normally took about a month. In Gilgit they were delayed because passports for the mule drivers had not arrived. In frustration Shipton planned, with the help of the two Sherpas, to drive the beasts themselves, 'though combining the two offices of H.B.M.'s Consul-General and mule driver might have looked a bit odd'. Eventually the caravan of new consulate staff set off. After two weeks they crossed the Mintaka Pass and, standing on the watershed of Central Asia, once a snowstorm had cleared, looked into that promised land. Shipton saw lots of ibex and a couple of snow leopards at close quarters. But his delight was short-lived.

A troop of Chinese mounted soldiers arrested the consular party and confined them to their camp for three days. Then they were locked up in a fort at Tashkurghan under armed guard for another three days while the soldiers repeatedly and meticulously searched their baggage. This was not the welcome Shipton had expected, but nevertheless it did not diminish his delight at viewing Muztagh Ata and other giants of the Chinese Pamirs. Eventually they were released and proceeded on their journey. After ten days, during which they met only hospitable Kirghiz shepherds, they left the mountains behind and moved out onto flat and fertile plains which led to the walled oasis city of Kashgar.

The Consulate was a large enclosed compound inside which lived a staff of over 200, including a doctor, Indian and Chinese secretaries and interpreters, an accountant and clerks, a scarlet-uniformed troop of Hunza gatekeepers, and a dozen mailrunners. The castellated house of the Consul-General had more than twenty rooms, some of which were huge empty reception rooms (one housed the ping-pong table), but Shipton lived in a few of the numerous smaller ones. The house was comfortably furnished and carpeted. Various predecessors had collected a library of Central Asian literature and other books reflecting a wide range of subject and taste, light and heavy. Among several bizarre inheritances were a black stallion named Tungan, a Russian carriage, a gramophone and a collection of records ranging from symphonies to dance tunes, enough toilet paper to last a couple of decades, and a cellar of French wine. Large photographs hung on the walls, and shooting trophies were stored below stairs. A terrace commanded a wide view over the river, fields and hills to distant snow-covered peaks. In the grounds were a mud tennis court, squash court, offices, garages, and a village of bungalows and huts for various retainers and their family hangers-on.

Despite all this unaccustomed consular luxury, Shipton's life was far from ideal. Forbidden by the Chinese authorities to travel outside the environs of Kashgar, about the most isolated major city of the world, he was virtually a prisoner in his own palace. He was 'crushingly lonely', worsened by his gnawing regret at having decided to join the army in India instead of going straight home when he had the chance, and somewhat guilty at being left out of the war when other people he knew were having to cope with the blitz.

On top of all this he received a telegram from Beatrice Weir break-ing off their engagement. He had written to her shortly after arriving in Kashgar officially proposing they get married in Gilgit the following spring, and had received her acceptance ten weeks later. But although they wrote to each other regularly thereafter, Beatrice's letters never reached him. Shipton's, apart from the first few describing his journey across the Karakoram, were intercepted by Beatrice's mother, who had discovered what was going on and, like a covey of mothers before her, did not approve of her daughter's relationship, nor of the ice axe beside her bed. Mrs Weir objected to his eccentric way of life and lack of a pukka job, and threatened to disown Beatrice, who could not face the prospect of family furore.

The terse and final telegram rejecting his love (which took three weeks to reach him) depressed Shipton into a 'slough of self-commiseration' from which he extracted himself with difficulty. 'In other circum-stances,' he wrote to Pamela, 'I might have been tempted to follow Lhakpa Tenzing's example by seeking consolation with a local mistress, for the Turki girls were very attractive. But the delicate political situation demanded immaculate behaviour and I was too scared of the possible consequences.'

He was able to pour out his heart to Pamela Freston. 'I think B. and I would have made a good job of it left to ourselves, but I know I could not have stood for one week the kind of world she comes from.' Pamela offered him solace and advice, which was gracious of her since their own affair was but two years severed. Her letters were a source of most of his news and contact with the war and the world outside. He constantly asked her advice on what books he should read, and complained (not for the first time) what hard work writing was. He eagerly awaited the weekly mail, his lifeline, which usually came via Gilgit, two and a half months being about the fastest he ever had a letter from England.

Bill Tilman wrote from France complaining he was very bored and pining to be sent somewhere more interesting; then he wrote from Iraq, before he was moved to Persia, still bored stiff with army life and general inactivity. Shipton heard, too, from Ferdie Crawford, teaching at Eton with Tom Brocklebank; from Tom Longstaff, fed up with the Home Guard; and from Lawrence Wager, a flying officer serving under Flight Lieutenant Michael Spender, both interpreting air photographs. Shortly afterwards Spender, in characteristic fashion, was chucked out of his job for telling his bosses how to do theirs.

Shipton had little contact with anyone outside the Consulate. The Russians and the Chinese did not respond to his friendly overtures, although the Chinese Administrative Commissioner eventually let down his guard whenever the Russians were absent. Every morning Shipton rode Tungan for a couple of hours. Some local Hunzas suggested reviving polo which had been in abeyance since a player was killed on the field just before Shipton arrived. Within minutes of starting their first game, in which he reluctantly took part, Musa Beg, a popular member of their team, was thrown, dragged by his stirrup, and died a few hours afterwards. So polo, confirming its deadly reputation, was no more.

For leisure, Shipton occasionally went duck shooting, once a week he played football with the staff, and he took language lessons from the Chinese secretary, Mr Chu, whom he repaid in kind with numerous games of chess. He wrote weekly dispatches to the Government of India and to the Foreign Office, and began working once more on his memoirs, *Upon That Mountain*, of which he was constantly self-critical, asking Pamela if the instalments he sent her were worth keeping. His dyslexia still made assembling words exceedingly laborious, despite his natural aptitude for them.

On most days in winter a drab dust haze hung over Kashgar, obscuring any view of the mountains. But on a clear day the views stretched

from his immediate flat surroundings towards the great peaks of the
Pamirs to the south and west. The winding rivers, flanked by willows
and poplars, were spanned with wooden bridges. Once the ice melted
in spring, the whole countryside suddenly turned green with chenar
trees in full leaf and apricots in blossom. But confined to Kashgar,
Shipton was unable to get out into the enticing mountains he could see
from his terrace. The closest he got to an adventure that first year was
after a birthday picnic outside town, when he floated down the river
back to Kashgar on a half-sized Li-lo accompanied by Lhakpa riding a
motor car inner tube. Worried by their lateness, after three hours a
search party set out, but they met Shipton and Lhakpa returning quite
safe from their trip.

The following summer three Norwegian lads, all aged around twenty,
turned up in Kashgar, each with only one rucksack full of kit. Refugees
from Nazi-occupied Norway, they had made a six-month journey
across Sweden, Finland, Russia, Soviet Tajikistan and eventually
reached northern Sinkiang. In Kashgar they were put in jail, through the
bars of which they could see the Union Jack of the British Consulate.
Shipton negotiated their release and took them in for a week while he
arranged for them to accompany the mail couriers over the Karakoram.
He was thrilled with news of the country which he had grown to love
during his schoolboy holidays with Gustav Sommerfelt. The
Norwegians eventually wrote from India reporting their safe passage,
and affirming that their one object in life was to get their own back on
the Germans. Shipton was sad to see them go, but soon afterwards a
fourth Norwegian arrived. After he dislocated his spine, the others had
been forced to leave him behind in northern Sinkiang, hardly speaking
a word of English. Despite repeated protests from the local Governor,
the Norwegian stayed with Shipton for a month while the Consulate
doctor had a leather corset made to splint his spine for his impending
rough journey over the mountains to India.

Shipton's relations with his fellow consuls remained frosty, apart
from obligatory formal entertaining, when his hosts occasionally
relaxed if well lubricated with vodka. Soon after Russia was attacked by
Germany, he gave a dinner party for Mr Samilovski, the Russian
Consul-General, 'to commiserate with them, or to congratulate them
upon jumping onto the right side of the fence, I'm not sure which,' he

wrote to Pamela. The Russians returned the party and Shipton nursed a hangover for the next twenty-four hours on account of the free-flowing beer, vodka, brandy, liqueur, red wine, white wine and champagne.

After almost a year in Sinkiang, Shipton risked his first trip into the mountains, to Bostan Terek. Not until he was past Opal, thirty-five miles west of Kashgar, did he feel reasonably safe from being hauled back. On the lower hills he enjoyed hunting the abundant ram chikor, birds as big as turkeys. Then he and Lhakpa pitched camp on the edge of a glacier where they spent the bulk of their time. The last part of the ascent to the summit of Bostan Terek, which he did solo, was his hardest climbing in the ten years since doing the West Ridge of Mount Kenya with Tilman.

Shipton enjoyed the approach of winter with 'the weak misty sun, bare trees, ice forming on the rivers, and the duck coming in', though he constantly worried about not being in Europe suffering alongside everyone else. 'I felt rather bad about enjoying myself in the mountains when the war seemed to be working towards a climax,' he wrote to Pamela. 'I have been here over a year. The time has gone amazingly quickly. Living quite alone I find one has to exercise a good deal of self-discipline. I get enough exercise with daily doses of riding and wood chopping. I do rather mind the lack of good talk. The absence of any sex life is not nearly so hard to bear, being right away from all temptation – a fact that has rather surprised me – expeditions were too short and too crowded to be any criterion.'

During this time he started writing again to Diana Channer, serving in the ATS in England. He confessed to his affair with Beatrice Weir and assured her 'that is all dead and buried now', continuing, 'I have had a good many affairs in my life, long and short, happy ones and mistakes. You told me once that you found it almost impossible to avoid having affairs. So we both ought to be able to take a level headed view of the whole thing and not mind saying what we think.'

In fact their long-distance romance revived apace. Shipton's letters, which could take as much as five months to reach Diana from Kashgar, had become increasingly passionate: 'I have never longed for anything more than to be with you now, to hear you talk and laugh and to see your eyes sparkling as they did in Kashmir when they used to fill me with delicious madness. But, Darling, marriage is too serious a thing to undertake on the evidence of that two short weeks together in June 1939, even if they do happen to be the happiest weeks of my life, crowded with so many heavenly, but as you put it "musical comedy" situations. I am sending a cheque for £2 to send me a cable telling me how you are.' He proposed to her, and she replied that she was 'ready for any life ahead'; but she was still uncertain whether they should become engaged before they met again, having only spent two blissful weeks together in Kashmir. 'Ever since that morning, three years ago tomorrow,' he wrote, 'when we started walking in opposite directions at Kalapuri [as he was setting off across the Karakoram], my mind has been on our meeting again.'

Towards the end of his second year, Shipton made the 1,000-mile journey to Urumchi, the capital of Sinkiang Province, to meet Michael Gillett, who had been appointed to take over his post when the term of his contract ended. His other reasons for the journey, apart from his own intrinsic geographical curiosity, were to protest at the persecution of the Indian community (technically British), and to negotiate reopening the trade route over the Karakoram Pass. He travelled in the Consulate's Ford V-8, 30-cwt truck which had been driven from Peking in 1935, and maintained meticulously thereafter by Mir Hamza, a Pathan mechanical wizard. The route followed the oases dotted along the northern rim of the Takla Makan Desert, with the mountains of the Tien Shan standing to the north. This heart of Central Asia, as described in the books of the early travellers, did not fail to thrill Shipton, especially after his virtual confinement in Kashgar for his term of office. Through a gorge they entered the Turfan Depression, which lay 1,000 feet below sea level and soaked up the great rivers flowing out of the Karakoram Range.

Shipton stayed for nearly a month in Urumchi, a hell-hole compared with Kashgar. Starved as he was for conversation, he talked his head off to Gillett and filled his time (which slips away slowly in Central Asia) with official discussions and dinners. After the fifteenth course of his farewell dinner, and the umpteenth glass of Russian brandy, he unsteadily stood up to give his speech. He never got beyond a profound, thrice-repeated opening remark, 'The dawn of civilisation . . .' which, after translation into Russian, was interrupted each time with

gales of applause. 'It was the shortest, and probably the most successful after-dinner speech of my life,' he wrote. 'After that I lost contact
with the proceedings, and when I regained consciousness I was walking
along a garden path on my host's arm.' He returned to Kashgar, halting
for four days to repair the broken-down truck, during which time he
managed a short outing into the mountains of the Tien Shan.

Shipton's two years in Sinkiang were a mixture, on the one hand, of
elation at being in such a remote, exciting land with his affection for
its hardy people; on the other, of loneliness, isolation, hostility and
frustration resulting from virtual imprisonment behind the Consulate
walls.

In his book *Mountains of Tartary* he says by way of apology, 'I have
included one short chapter designed to explain the political background
to my experiences. To those who, like myself, are profoundly bored with
the politics of a remote land, I recommend skipping that chapter.' It is
strange, however, that he took so little interest in the politics of that
pivotal region, and sad that he wrote so little about them. Shipton left
Kashgar on 4 October 1942, and his journey from Sinkiang to India is
enough to make any armchair traveller envious. The distance from
Kashgar to Delhi, as the lammergeier flies, is about 800 miles, a quarter
of the ground he had to cover during the next month on his roundabout journey. He travelled west across the Russian Pamirs into Soviet
Tajikistan, by railway through Tashkent, Samarkand and Bukhara (none
as romantic as their names imply), across the Oxus River; he then hitch-
hiked to Meshed in northern Persia, went by truck to Zahedan on the
Baluchistan border; and finally by train, via Quetta, to Delhi.

Ten days after reaching Delhi, Shipton was back in England in the
arms of Diana Channer. With characteristic honesty, he wrote to
Pamela Freston telling her he was going to be married. 'Sorry to burst
this news on you so suddenly, but my head is in such a whirl. I've never
felt so certain about anything as I do about all this. I do hope you'll like
Diana.'

In the precipitate frenzy born of war, Diana Channer and Eric
Shipton were married in Lyme Regis on 16 December 1942, ten days
after he had returned home from Kashgar. But they only managed a
short honeymoon before being separated; Diana returning to her unit
in the ATS, and continuing to serve as a 'Fanny', Shipton soon to

take up a two-year posting in Persia, now employed by the Foreign Office.

Diana was under no illusions about the man she was marrying, as she said many years later: 'I went into marriage thinking that he must never be bothered by footling little problems like babies. He must always be free to go away whenever he wanted. He was not to be incommoded; I must never be a nuisance.' But Pamela Freston was always a minor thorn in Diana's side: 'When we were first married Pamela so upstaged me that I just crawled away. She was an overwhelming character, very intelligent, stimulating, and interested in Eric's journeys. He wrote to her to the end of his life and was her "possession" to the end.'

Diana said she never truly figured Eric out, but that didn't seem to matter in their first heady days of being in love. She attributed much of her husband's coldness to his mother, whom she met for the first time in a London hotel where she was dying of tropical sprue. Diana described her as 'an ice queen with cold, blue eyes; Eric's eyes, but with no kindness in them. She had an obsession against sex, which Eric crushed down in terror that she would find out about his girlfriends. The first time he kissed a girl he pecked her and flew.'

They snatched moments together during the next couple of months whenever Diana could get away from the army. One day, as Nick Shipton tells of family folklore, his father was wandering alone down Piccadilly wearing a scruffy old army great coat when he was picked up by military police.

'And who might you be, sir?' the police officer asked, presuming him to be a deserter.

'His Majesty's Consul-General in Kashgar,' Shipton replied, without breaking step.

The next phase of Shipton's career from 1943 to 1946 is an enigma. The war for most people was a time of intense experience they never forgot in later life; in his autobiography he disposes of it in three lines. In March 1943 he set out for Persia, leaving Diana in England. From Crewe railway station he wrote to her, 'Saying goodbye to you was the worst moment of my life. That complete inability to talk has only happened to me once before – that time coming down from the North Col in '33.' (He is describing the transient aphasic attack mentioned in an earlier chapter.)

The journey out to Persia was tedious except for a few incidents; one afternoon when they were bombed, and the next night five of their convoy were sunk and an ammunition ship astern of them blew up shattering all the glass in their boat. In Teheran Shipton's official posting was Consular Liaison Officer. He was one of a number of British officials also known as Cereal Liaison Officers, stationed in the provinces doing 'Food Control Work', trying to ensure fair collection and distribution of wheat and other grain, partly imported and partly indigenous, which was in short supply owing to local corruption, and disruption caused by the British and Russian occupation.

Shipton was soon sent to Kermanshah in the northern Zagros Mountains on the border of Persia and Iraq. He spent much time touring the country, along with his assistant, a young Dane named Hansen, with whom he became close friends. In his first month he covered 2,500 miles in a luxurious Buick, which was later replaced by 'a sort of glorified jeep'. His work, which took him through beautiful mountainous country, was most congenial. But he rails on in a letter to Pamela. 'The people are bloody awful. Bribery and corruption are fantastic. Each night the local police let a gang of professional housebreakers out of jail to rob and share with them the profits, at the same time levying a toll from the rich.'

He was billeted in a house with a rather boring messmate, a Colonel Fletcher, who returned one day to find their house on fire and Shipton, oblivious, having lunch. 'I had ordered the servant to hack down the wall behind me so as to get at the fire and put water on it. As there was only one pickaxe I saw no reason to interrupt my lunch, and Fletcher came in to find me seated and eating with smoke billowing up all round me. I must say it must have looked rather funny.'

Occasionally he took the day off to go climbing in the local mountains with some enthusiastic scramblers from the nearby army camp. On one business trip to Cairo to visit his bosses at the Middle East Supply Centre, he missed seeing Bill Tilman by two days. When not working, he kept himself occupied by writing *Upon That Mountain*, and sending chapters to Pamela to edit. Their relationship was as stormy as ever with ongoing arguments. Despite a 'bitter letter' she wrote to him, she remained devoted as his chief literary guide and mentor.

In this bland description of his work, gleaned from the few letters available from that period, it is not obvious whether distributing cereal was his only job. While most informed diplomats disclaim him as a spy, opinion holds that he might have been 'double-hatting', a euphemism (in a strongly euphemistic world) for gathering intelligence. It seems strange that an employee of the Foreign Office, who had already satisfactorily completed one remote assignment in Central Asia, and was considered worthy of being reappointed to the same post three years later should, at the height of the war, be doing something so mundane as distributing grain, important though that was. As one source, familiar with the ways of The Office, said, 'It is clear that Shipton was not, in the accepted sense, a spy. But he was a good and uniquely well-qualified observer and reporter of political and economic information on an unusual area which was of great strategic interest to the Imperial and post-Imperial Government of India and the British Government. In this, he was a lineal descendant of the players in the Great Game.' The fact that Britain and Russia were, during the war, ostensibly allies seems to have been largely irrelevant.

After twenty months in Persia, in December 1944 Shipton was back in England, living at Diana's parents' home at Warminster. He and Diana spent as much of the next four months together as possible whenever she could get leave, and he filled his spare time walking long distances over 'that glorious Shaftesbury-Fonthill country which I love best of all the English country I know'.

He was posted, in March 1945, as an attaché with the British Military Mission to Hungary (having originally thought it would be to Bulgaria) employed by the War Office as an 'agricultural adviser', a job that lasted for just under a year. This period of his life is much better documented than his Persia spell because many of the weekly letters he wrote to Diana have survived. They are affectionate, loving letters from a lonely husband. Diana was expecting a baby, which evidently caused them both alarm and uncertainty about the coming intrusion into their freedom. On another family front, his mother had died in 1943 while he was in Persia, but none of his correspondence shows how this affected him. He and his sister, Marge, sold the flat in Lexham Gardens.

During one of several long delays in Italy on his way to Hungary he climbed Vesuvius, 'crossing lava flows and finally up about 1,500 feet of steep, loose ash to the rim of the crater, a colossal well half a mile across dropping sheer on all sides from a narrow rim. I walked all round the crater and then had a dream of a scree run of 1,000ft to the east.' He spent nearly a month in Bari, unable to wander far, being under orders, and he reiterates a lifelong theme to Diana.

I am terribly bad at having nothing to do in surroundings that I don't like. I quickly start fretting, cursing the waste of time, wishing I had done otherwise than I have done, blaming others for my situation, and becoming thoroughly spoffle and hopeless. Looking back I'm often ashamed to remember some of the times I have felt this way in circumstances that later seem to have provided the best opportunities of my life – when we were held up for six weeks in Urumchi, for example, and on Everest Expeditions even. Afterwards it always seems so incredibly short-sighted – and yet I never seem to learn. It is a manifestation of being spoilt – of having become accustomed to having fun and interest always at hand, an exciting event round each corner; and it requires a great effort of will to force oneself to find worthwhile things to do, compared to Persia when I had a clear cut job to do.

He eventually reached Budapest, the once beautiful city then in wartime chaos and ruin; most of the great bridges across the Danube were down, the lovely waterfront shattered, and the Royal Palace no more than a skeleton. He was soon sent to Debrecen in the east of Hungary near the Romanian border, and housed in an army mess (just the sort of place and company he hated). So he took to wandering in the woods in the flat, dull surrounding country. One thundery evening he was held up by some stray soldiers, 'who relieved me of my watch and money. They contemplated removing my trousers too, but decided against it. Their own were better than mine.' Then came the end of the war in Europe.

He was quite despondent about the job and his inability to get hold of a vehicle. 'To send me here without any transport,' he told Diana, 'is like sending someone on an Everest Expedition without any boots, which in its wildest excesses of fatuity the Everest Committee never quite achieved.' He produced a report on the food and agricultural situation 'from very slender evidence' and was 'finding the ruddy job very frustrating'.

With rare actual mention of the baby, they talk of 'the event', or 'September', or 'the coming delivery', which Diana was evidently dreading. They discussed possible names – Michael for a boy, Susan for a girl. On 21 September 1945 Shipton received a telegram from The Rock, Warminster – 'A SON ARRIVED AT 1 O'C THIS MORNING.'

In October Shipton managed to get himself sent to England, ostensibly to discuss acquiring the transport necessary for doing his job, but more importantly to see Diana and his newborn son. Shipton's reaction to fatherhood is not recorded. But new responsibilities were clearly not going to be allowed to alter his way of life. While at home he wrote to the Alpine Club suggesting they should prepare for the possibility of mounting an Everest expedition in the near future. He insisted that the AC should be solely responsible for the expedition, in other words, that they would bypass the Everest Committee. He went to supper with Geoffrey Winthrop Young, who told him that the AC had indeed decided to ask him to lead the next Everest expedition and he would be free to choose the small team, 'if and when it comes off, but possibly in 1947'. The President of the AC, Leo Amory, put the idea to Lord Wavell, Viceroy of India, who replied on 20 December 1945 about 'the need for caution in any approach made to the Tibetan Government during the Dalai Lama's minority.' Wavell continued, 'I feel your ideas for making an approach to Everest through Tibet in 1947 will have to be abandoned.' Unfortunately, the AC's plans were leaked to the *News Chronicle*, possibly by a guest at the AC dinner, and this news reached the Indian press, causing considerable displeasure to the Viceroy, whose Secretary of State demanded a denial by the club.

Shipton had to return to his job in Hungary, driving his new official car across Europe, through Germany and Austria. His job appeared to improve now that he had some transport, and also with the help of a Hungarian assistant Dubasi Schweng, 'a most intelligent person, tremendously interested in the country, and who speaks English perfectly'. Together they travelled through most of eastern Hungary, inspecting farms and estates, staying in the houses of peasants or once-landed gentry (like the down-at-heel and dispossessed Count and Countess Esterházy, who fed them a meal of boiled potatoes smeared with tomato sauce). But he was still very cagey about what his job actually entailed, and Diana once wrote back, forthrightly asking him. He replied, 'I was doing an agricultural survey. I have covered 2,130 miles since I got back and interviewed 249 farmers, and I've got enough data together for the report, which I've since been sorting out.'

Inflation was rampant in Hungary and the pengoe skyrocketed. Shipton wrote to Diana, 'I must go through the formality of giving you a halfpenny for your Christmas present. I am sorry I didn't send you anything but it seemed hardly worth it when I was expecting to be home so soon after Christmas.' Diana once said that he seemed to lack any regard for conventions like birthdays, the niceties of marriage, presents, and the subtleties of wanting to make people happy, possibly because of his weird mother. He seemed to want to be close to people, but then suddenly he would withdraw. This 'distance' was characteristic of Shipton and the word is often used by people in describing him. However all his letters to her were affectionate, even romantic, though quite restrained for a married man. The more lonely he was, the more vocal his affection.

In May 1946 he was posted to Vienna, doing a tedious job with UNRRA, when a telegram arrived unexpectedly from the Government of India inviting him to take up his old post of Consul-General in Kashgar. Excited, yet thrown into doubt again, he wrote in *Mountains of Tartary,* 'I wondered whether it was fair to ask my wife, for all her love for mountains and strange country, to undertake a prolonged spell of such loneliness and isolation.'

They also had to consider their six-month-old son, Nicky (as he was now called). Kashgar itself was the focus of a revolt of Kirghiz tribesmen who had cut the routes over the passes of the Karakoram to Sinkiang and caused a massacre at Tashkurghan where Shipton had been imprisoned on his outward journey six years before. With rebellion fuelled by Russia in an attempt to destabilise the region, it was obviously still a dangerous area to travel through. Their reluctance to take a small child into so unstable a place is understandable.

However, according to Shipton, his wife would not hear of him turning down the job, and even agreed to accompany him, leaving Nicky in the care of foster parents. Diana's view was, 'The choice was Eric or Nicky. I chose Eric because he would have gone without me and

I didn't want to let him get away with it.' This separation was to have a lasting effect on Nicky, even though he was too young at the time to appreciate its significance.

So Shipton and Diana left England and arrived in India in August 1946, at the height of the post-Independence riots, when no one in the harassed Government wanted to be bothered with an obscure Consul trying to find out how to reach one of their most obscure and distant consulates.

CHAPTER 11

The Great Game

Kashgar and Kunming, 1946–51

ERIC SHIPTON enjoyed his second tour in Kashgar much more than his first. He had the pleasure of introducing Diana to the country, so he was no longer burdened by the loneliness he endured before. The political atmosphere in Sinkiang had lightened and the local people were free to be their natural friendly selves since the suspicion and hostility of the Chinese authorities had lesssened. The travel embargo which had kept him virtually captive had been lifted, so he was able to explore the mountains that he could previously only admire from a distance.

Shipton summoned two of his old servants to Delhi to accompany his party to Kashgar. Amir Ali, a Hunza man, duly appeared at their hotel, but Gyalgen, one of his Everest Sherpas from Darjeeling (brother of Lhakpa Tenzing who had settled happily in Kashgar with his Turki mistress) was delayed by pre-Independence riots in Calcutta. Shipton and Diana travelled to Srinagar, where they had first met seven years before, and revived their houseboat romance on Dal Lake while preparing for their journey across the Karakoram.

Shipton decided to cross the Karakoram Pass, one of the most ancient caravan trade routes of Central Asia by way of Leh, in Ladakh, to Yarkand. This was because Kirghiz tribesmen had revolted on the northern side of the Mintaka Pass, making their usual route from Gilgit to Kashgar very dangerous. Shipton wrote later to Pamela, 'What a fantastic journey! Two passes of over 18,000 feet, three of over 17,000 feet, and three glaciers to negotiate, fifteen consecutive marches without sign of habitation, and nine without any fuel, through some of the most desolate country I've ever seen.' At the end of each stage of the gentle two-week journey over the Zoji La to Kargil and then to Leh, they used rest houses set in luxurious oasis villages. Once into Ladakh the land mirrored Tibet in scenery, architecture, culture and costume. In Leh they stayed at the Residency and met Frank Ludlow, the eminent botanist, who told them of his plans for a forthcoming expedition with George and Betty Sherriff to Tibet and Bhutan.

Shipton received a message from Kashgar to say that bandits, still active beyond the Karakoram Pass, had recently attacked and plundered a caravan of traders. He was sobered by the prospect of meeting desperadoes in that remote country, and of being robbed of the animals which were the party's only means of crossing the wide rivers. Winter was approaching, so the bandits would likely retreat to the lowlands where they could acquire fodder and fuel. For Shipton, the deciding factor in keeping to the Karakoram Pass route was that Dr Binns, the retiring Consulate doctor, his wife and two pre-teenage children had left Yarkand a month before and were probably travelling over the pass towards them, and still in some danger. No news had been heard of them since their departure, and their fate was uncertain.

Shipton decided to move his whole caravan ahead to Panamik, the last inhabited village south of the Karakoram Pass from where, if they had not heard from the Binns family, he could strike north in search of them. In fact, both parties arrived at Panamik together from opposite directions. The Binns children were thrilled with their adventures and recounted excitedly being shot at by Chinese troops on the way.

The personnel of Shipton's caravan, under the leadership of a Turki trader, consisted of change-over Consulate staff – doctor, head clerk, dispenser and his family, Gyalgen and Amir Ali. Several hangers-on attached themselves to the caravan under the misguided impression that the British Consul-General would hold some magic power over any bandits they might encounter. Amongst them were some Chinese soldiers, refugees from the Sarikol region revolt of a year before. They started to climb up into the 'Headache Mountains', so described by an early Chinese traveller. The caravan of heavily laden ponies, donkeys, mules and camels set off surefootedly into the wilderness of moraine rock and glacial ice surrounded by lofty peaks through which they would travel for the next month. 'I had to keep reminding myself,' wrote Shipton, 'that we were not engaged in a desperate attempt to establish a base camp on some high peak to reach some unexplored country, but that we were travelling along a regular trade route on our way to take up a civil service appointment.'

Soon they passed animal corpses lying beside the track in this totally barren land where all food, fuel and animal fodder had to be carried. In the book Diana later wrote about their spell in Kashgar, *The Antique Land*, she wrote, 'The continuous line of bones and bodies acted as a gruesome guide whenever we were uncertain of the route. Never once, until we reached the plains, were we out of sight of skeletons.' It was quite usual for one in ten pack animals to die on each trip over the pass, emphasised by Shipton writing to Pamela later, 'Your letter had been forwarded to Leh and entrusted to a Turki caravan that had been stranded in Gilgit for a year by the wars. They had a bad passage across the Karakoram and lost 50% of their animals due to thirst as everything was frozen solid. There is no fuel of any kind so they were 8 days without water.'

Diana held up well on the tough journey despite the bitter cold, being unable to wash, and long marches of twenty to thirty miles each day. She hated riding and preferred to walk, which was a source of recurring argument with her husband, who said firmly, 'If you come to Asia, you *must* ride.' But Shipton was deeply content sharing with Diana this country he so loved. Once across the Karakoram Pass they descended into the valley of the Yarkand River, which they had to ford as many as thirty times in a single stage. Then they crossed the Kuen Lun Range and descended into the first vegetation they had seen for a month, an oasis of the Tarim Basin where, sitting in the shade of a willow grove, they feasted on grapes and melons.

Mir Hamza met them near Khargalik in the old Ford truck from the
Consulate, and drove them towards the walled city Shipton had left,
with some relief, four years before. 'The market thronged with life and
colour,' he wrote, 'the view from our terraced garden over the tranquil
river to the stillness of the desert hills beyond; the long lines of camels
strung together, moving sedately to the deep clang of bells; the
pigeons tumbling overhead; the mill in the willow grove across the
valley where the boy still blew his horn to announce that his father was
ready to receive fresh supplies of grain; how wonderful to find it all
unchanged.'

Under the new regime life was more relaxed. He and Diana regularly
took their early morning ride or walk outside the confines of the city.
He became keen on shooting, and later joined the Turkis in their
favourite sports of hawking and eagling. On weekends they were able
occasionally to get up into the foothills of the Tien Shan, of which
Diana wrote evocatively in *The Antique Land*, 'The sun was setting. The
stern rock and ice mountains at the head of our valley stood up black
and bold. To the east the dim expanse of the plains was lighted by the
dying sun. Faint lines marked ghostly hills far away. Light, colour, and
shape – all formed into a wide glowing picture.'

One destination that occupied several exploratory trips was an
immense natural arch that Shipton had seen from afar when driving
away from Kashgar in 1942. They tried three times unsuccessfully to
reach the 'elusive arch' from the south but were repeatedly barred by
sinuous passages ending in sheer cliffs or in dark caverns. Eventually
they found a way through canyons from the north and came across the
enormous vault with a span of 200 feet overhanging a chasm 1,000 feet
deep that, as Shipton said, 'has the Rishi Gorge beat'.

Because Sinkiang was enjoying a rare period of peace and easy
access, the Shiptons were able to entertain several interesting visitors.
This was especially important for Diana, who noted, 'It was inevitable
that living alone so much, Eric and I should have grown familiar with
each other's arguments and opinions. We delighted in the stimulus of
new ideas.' A welcome guest was Shipton's old climbing companion,
Bill Tilman, of whose visit he wrote, 'Considering that I was married,
it might have been regarded as a touching tribute to our friendship but
for the unique attraction of the mountains we had to offer.'

Tilman had been on the other side of the Karakoram unsuccessfully attempting to climb Rakaposhi with a Swiss expedition. He then crossed the Mintaka Pass and made a rendezvous with the Shiptons in Tashkurghan. He and Shipton immediately got out maps and started planning which of a dozen mountains they would tackle. 'Our choice was unimaginative, and actuated by second-rate motives,' Shipton wrote in *Mountains of Tartary*. 'We both had a sneaking desire to see how we would react to high altitudes after an interval of nine years. We ignored a lesson we had learnt a dozen years before; that to climb a mountain for its height and fame alone is infinitely less rewarding than to attempt a peak whose form has charmed, or to cast a new light upon an attractive mountain range.'

They decided on the great dome of Muztagh Ata, 24,380 feet, lying to the east of their homeward way to Kashgar, and just south of another giant, Kungur. With them went Diana, Gyalgen, a youth named Roza Beg, and a reluctant yak. Shipton, Tilman and Gyalgen climbed up to their high camp at 20,500 feet (not high enough as it turned out). The next morning they set off in clear weather with a strong wind blowing from the south across the ridge; they later agreed that they had never been so cold before while actually climbing.

Shipton was feeling quite well, apart from being desperately cold, and he persisted in kicking steps up to the summit dome, hoping his feet would warm up when the sun rose. At 24,000 feet they knew they were near the top, so they kept on going over the plateau where it was a question of distance rather than height before they actually reached the summit. Eventually, still not at the highest point, but certainly only a few feet below it, 'with a mixture of relief and bitter reluctance' they agreed to abandon the struggle because of the cold, their fatigue, and rotten snow.

Utterly exhausted, they returned to camp and removed their boots. The toes of Shipton's left foot were frostbitten; Tilman's and Gyalgen's were purple with frostnip; the fingers of all of them remained numb for many days. They had a difficult and painful time retreating down the Chakragil Valley where they relied on picking up local transport and, for lack of anything better, ended up riding some obstreperous yaks. A friendly Kirghiz insisted on wrapping Shipton's frostbitten foot in a poultice of cheese mixed with ash from their yak-dung fire; Shipton added sulphonamide for safety. Diana made the wifely comment, 'It's amazing that with all their experience neither Eric nor Bill knew what to do for frostbite.'

For a couple of months Shipton was on crutches which ruined his exciting plans for further climbing with Tilman. Meanwhile, Diana, who had originally intended to remain in Kashgar for only one year, was so happy she decided to stay for a second winter, although torn by wanting to see her baby son and her ageing parents.

After three weeks Tilman left them, having decided on his route back to Hunza, to make a small detour into Afghanistan across the Wakhjir Pass to see the infant River Oxus. On trying to leave the country he was imprisoned by Afghan border guards and spent about a month in various jails in the Wakhan Corridor. On reaching Gilgit he sent a laconic telegram to Shipton stating, 'NO HARM EXCEPT DIGNITY'.

Among the Shiptons' favourite guests were an American couple, Bob and Vera Ransom, who had travelled overland through China. At the end of the war, in order to escape the conventional drudgery of a San Francisco law office (where a senior partner upbraided him for going downtown hatless), Bob had taken a job in the Philippines defending Japanese charged with war crimes. He was so disgusted by what he called 'mock trials', in which US army judges read comics under their desks during defence submissions, that he quit and he and Vera headed off to Peking.

They travelled by train and postal trucks to reach Urumchi, where they stayed with the US Consul, who advised them to cross the Karakoram to India. He forwarded them to the British Consul-General in Kashgar, remarking, 'These English have a funny language and strange customs.' This fuelled Bob's already strong anti-British prejudice, and he and Vera debated how they could avoid meeting 'the bloody British Consul'. However, they needed his help to acquire Indian visas and so could not avoid him. At the Consulate, scarlet-coated Hunza guards showed them into one of the sumptuous drawing rooms. They were surprised to be welcomed warmly and without decorum by the Consul (on crutches) and his charming wife – the start of a lifelong friendship. At an official Chinese banquet a few days later, tongue-loosed by vodka, Ransom gave Shipton an eloquent treatise on the disagreeable traits of his fellow countrymen; in turn, Shipton tried to persuade him that as a nation the British were no more arrogant, hypocritical or oppressive than any other.

The Ransoms' two-week stay was manna to the Shiptons' culturally arid life, and they would all stay up till the small hours of the morning setting the world to rights. Shipton helped them prepare for their crossing of the Karakoram, arranging for a tailor to make them long fur-lined sheepskin coats, padded suits, fur hats and felt boots. Then with sadness the Shiptons saw the Ransoms off on their six-week journey to India, accompanied by an escort of Hunza guards.

But Shipton's life was not all holiday, as it may appear. He wrote regular monthly reports, marked SECRET, for the Secretary to the Government of India, in the External Affairs Department in New Delhi. These are political documents full of references to the movements around the country of the main players, Russian and Chinese, in the local Great Game. About the Sarikol uprising he writes, 'How far these rebellions were instigated by the Russians is not at all clear, that the rebels received from them very substantial aid in the matter of weapons etc is beyond doubt. The whole place is seething with rumours of further rebellion which would not stand much chance of success against the greatly strengthened Chinese garrisons in South Sinkiang.' He says that local Kirghiz believe that another raid on Sarikol is being planned from Soviet territory, and he gives map references of reported large concentrations of troops and military equipment near the frontier, where spies have crossed to ascertain the strength of the Chinese garrisons. He says that two members of the Soviet Consulate-General recently left two wireless sets, one in Yarkand, the other in Khotan. He also reports that the Kashgar aerodrome is being repaired and the runways enlarged.

'With all eyes on the happenings of the communist armies in Central China, everyone in the Chinese community is nervous about what will happen in Sinkiang,' Shipton writes. 'The Commander of the 42nd Army, General Chao Hsi-kwang warned anti-Chinese agitators that they could not expect the leniency they had hitherto enjoyed, and henceforth anyone indulging in such agitation and subversive talk would be punished severely.' He notes the great increase in Muslim Hajis applying for passports, ostensibly to go on pilgrimage to Mecca, but more likely to get out of the country. Finally he writes, 'It is said that caravans, recently arrived from Ladakh, have brought opium with them to be sold here for Skg. 700,000 dollars per tola.'

During the autumn of 1947 Shipton, accompanied by Diana, made an often-postponed official visit to Urumchi. The journey of 980 miles in the Consulate's old Ford truck took eight days, skirting the Takla Makan Desert to the south and with the Tien Shan mountains to the north. They were made welcome in Urumchi by the American Consul and his wife; the neighbouring British Consulate was a miserable little hovel by contrast to their palace in Kashgar. Diana did not enjoy the three weeks they had to spend in the capital of Sinkiang, which were crammed with official functions. They left Urumchi in a snowstorm, the old truck broke down, and they had to wait for the arrival of the new British Consulate's Chevrolet in which they had a miserably uncomfortable journey home to Kashgar. 'It seemed like a modified version of a return to England after being abroad,' wrote Diana. She left for Britain in April 1948, travelling back to Urumchi, then taking a two-day flight in a Dakota to Shanghai, and so in stages by flying boat to Southampton.

Shipton was under contract until July. His position as Consul was now invidious because, in the wake of Partition, both India and Pakistan laid claim to the Consulate, and he did not know for whom he was working. However, after Diana's departure, another visit from Bill Tilman brightened his outlook and relieved his loneliness. Tilman had travelled across China by bus and they arranged to meet in Urumchi to explore the Bogdo Ola Range to the east. As a climbing expedition it was not a success. Lhakpa and a porter became sick, so Shipton and Tilman had to do all their own carrying. 'We failed because we were not up to it, and far too out of practice on difficult climbing,' he wrote to Pamela. 'We had a beautiful 3 day trek along the main crest of the ridge to the west, pass after pass, each exciting because we didn't know where it would lead; then onto a great hog's back of grassy downland with thousands of miles of Central Asia stretching away on either side of us and views away to the main Tien Shan; then a great plunge down a gorge into pine-filled valleys and clear tumbling rivers, and a swift ride on bor-rowed Khazak horses over golden corn-covered hills to Urumchi.' It was a fitting finish to his time in Sinkiang, which he felt 'had yielded a richer harvest of experience than any other period of my life'.

On his return to England from Kashgar in 1948, Shipton was at yet another crossroads, wondering where his limited qualifications could lead next. Should he emigrate to New Zealand, buy a smallholding in Dorset or Wiltshire, or become a teacher? While he was debating this quandary the Foreign Office offered him a job for which he was well qualified, the post of Consul-General in Kunming, capital of Yunnan, the most southerly province of China. He accepted despite his concerns about taking a young child into so unstable a country where the Communist revolution could take over at any moment.

While on leave, Shipton was invited to talk to the Cambridge University Mountaineering Club. During dinner before the Friday lecture he said to Chris Brasher, the club secretary, 'I've always wanted to be a geologist. Do you think I'd get in here as a mature student?' Brasher thereupon rang the Master of St John's College, James Wordie, the Antarctic explorer, to suggest a meeting between the two distinguished men. It was duly arranged to be at 11 a.m. for coffee the next morning at the Master's Lodge.

Early on Saturday Shipton was round at Brasher's room in St John's, where many aspiring explorers and climbers from the club had gathered to plumb their hero's wisdom. At 10. 50 a.m. the floor of the room was littered with maps and Shipton was directing some keen undergraduate to go 'round there, up that river, and over the pass'.

'Mr Shipton, it's time we left to meet the Master,' Brasher agitated nervously.

'Oh, cancel it,' said Shipton. 'I'm more interested in this.'

Little did he realise then that he would be meeting Wordie again within four years as one of the arbiters of his fate as leader of the 1953 Everest expedition.

The next two years of consular service were much less satisfying and happy than Shipton's second tour in Kashgar, with which it contrasted pointedly. In his later autobiography, *That Untravelled World*, he devotes much space to this rather uneventful period and there appears a strange imbalance in what he considered worth reporting. He gives some minor events – for example, a rather foolhardy caving adventure – undue attention.

The family's journey to Hong Kong in a flying boat took six days with nightly stops, but Shipton resented the lack of opportunity to explore the exotic places through which they passed. Five minutes' walk from their hotel in Hong Kong they discovered Beatrice Weir, now married as Mrs Lumley, living in a flat. Diana got on well with her husband's erstwhile, short-lasting fiancée, who invited Nicky over to play with her younger daughter, Joanna. 'It was an odd situation,' Shipton wrote to Pamela, 'but thanks to Diana a very easy one.'

They flew up to Kunming. 'Oh dear, what a sad contrast the journey was to the glorious approach to Kashgar!' he wrote to Pamela. 'The house added to our gloom. It is like an Indian hotel – cold, marble-floored rooms, bleakly and tastelessly furnished. It's shut in on all sides by other houses with a tiny bit of garden in front. There is some marvellous country nearby to travel in, hilly and very green, with lots of old temples. The town is sited near the northern shore of a twenty-mile-long lake. The great Salween, Mekong, and Yangtse Gorges are all far away and everywhere is infested with bandits and rebel bands and likely to get worse.'

Diana never warmed to Kunming, and things were made worse by the deaths in England of first her elderly mother and then her father, thereby emphasising her distance from home. Soon after they arrived many expatriates, on whom they relied for company, started to pull out in advance of the Communist Red Armies moving down towards Yunnan, one of the last Nationalist Kuomintang-held provinces to fall. 'It's curious waiting for this unknown quantity, the Communists, in such cold blood,' Diana wrote to Pamela, with whom she was now on fairly matey, albeit wary, terms. Inflation pushed prices sky-high so house-keeping became a nightmare, and none of the servants were as good as those she had in Kashgar. Nicky, now aged four, enjoyed his freedom making friends and roaming the bazaar with the gardener's children with whom he spoke fluent Chinese with a Yunnan accent, and vigor-ously sang Communist songs.

Shipton became quite unsettled by a short letter from Bill Tilman, who was enjoying himself on an expedition in Nepal, but saying that even the Himalaya palls a bit after Sinkiang. Shipton subsequently wrote in envy, 'I often think I should have gone back to that way of life, family or no family, and let the "future" take care of itself.' But he bought a horse, and got back into his old habit of riding before breakfast for an hour or two to watch the rain clouds floating about the green hills and in the valleys below him. On one morning ride he discovered a small enclosed basin in the centre of which meandered a river, that disappeared into and reappeared from a limestone hill.

He and Diana frequently went on weekend picnics outside town with the French and American consular families. On one such outing they visited his beautiful secret valley. Several of the party wanted to explore the cavern where a river issued from the mountain flanking the basin, but after entering the first cave they took fright and returned. Shipton and Frank Pile, the Diplomatic Wireless Service operator who kept open radio communications with Singapore, stripped to their shorts and gym shoes and swam on into a narrow defile. With only a small torch for light, they soon became disoriented. On meeting a raging torrent in a transverse tunnel, where they found a small lime-encrusted brass bell wedged in the rock, they decided to turn back. After much stumbling around trying to locate the exit, they found themselves back at the torrent and, yet again, there was the brass bell. They settled down to await rescue, if such were possible, and became very cold – verging on mild hypothermia. Luckily, the two other Consuls had entered the cave to look for them and were shouting loudly to announce their presence. The two errant cavers heard their rescuers' voices, traced them and emerged shivering, humbled, and suitably chastened by their harebrained adventure. Shipton even advertised his folly by writing a detailed article about it later.

Along with a retiring customs officer named West, he decided next to travel west to try to reach the Burma Road, and to make an official visit to the Shan States. On the second day they were ambushed by bandits, who shot at them from a hilltop. After much waving of white handkerchiefs and shouting, Shipton climbed up and met the leader, a polite student with horn-rimmed glasses and red-starred armbands, who apologised for the inconvenience he had caused them and said he was glad they had not hit the jeep. On this point they all agreed, and sat in the sun on the hilltop discussing world politics, especially regarding Mao Tse-tung.

As they crested a high pass into the Mekong Valley, Shipton wrote, 'Dawn was just beginning to break behind us and the moon was sinking low in front of us – always the most glorious combination. It seemed as if all the blue in the world had funnelled into that great valley – as if one were part of the sky and the moon – that the Earth didn't count any more.' Again they heard gunfire and realised they were in the middle of a battle. The captain in charge of the bridge ordered them to turn around; he, with fourteen of his men including one wounded soldier, climbed into their jeep and clung to it like limpets, exhorting Shipton not to wait for any more of their pals. As they started to flee they saw that the suspension bridge they were approaching had been destroyed, and appreciated their luck in not having already crossed it which would have meant going on through Burma and back home via Hong Kong.

On their way back, Shipton and his companion walked for two days through dense forested valleys and ridges, with bamboo and moss-covered rhododendron, grassy alps, clear streams and waterfalls. Then they climbed a 13,000-foot divide to Tali, where by arrangement they met Diana, Nicky and the French Consul-General. Crossing a high pass on the way home they were stopped again by shots and held up by some 'awful-looking ragamuffins' or, as his interpreter called them, 'Bona-fide bandits'.

In the autumn of 1949 tension rose as the cities of Central China fell to the advancing Communist armies. Missionaries and consulates pulled out as soon as they could get the elusive necessary permits. A silent coup d'état occurred in December, and thereafter Kunming was subjected to daily air raids and sporadic bombardment by shell-fire – not a pleasant atmosphere for a family. 'We were suitably scared,' Shipton wrote to Pamela, 'because a few score civilians had been killed or maimed.'

But things seemed to settle down in the New Year of 1950, and they were able to resume their day-long walks over the azalea-covered hills, Shipton often carrying a gun to try shooting pheasants. The mail, their lifeline, was uncertain. 'We've had no air mail since the coup d'état,' wrote Diana; then things improved. 'Letters from home come from time to time, generally 3–6 months old, like shafts of warming sunlight on a cold and dismal day.' Diana was pregnant and still unhappy. 'The shooting of an elderly English missionary on Easter Saturday as he sat in his office has rather unnerved the foreign community,' she wrote to Pamela. 'I try to hide from Eric how much I dislike this place. As he says, if we leave, what next?'

Gradually the new regime tightened its grip on the province of

Yunnan, Chinese friends quietly disappeared, expatriates packed up and left, and freedom of movement was confined to a radius of three miles outside the city of Kunming. In October Diana gave birth to John (and also to her book *The Antique Land*), so getting home became urgent. About the new baby, Shipton wrote to Pamela, 'I still feel somewhat apologetic about bringing him into this grim world, but who knows, he may yet know the feel of a powerful horse between his legs, of standing on an ice ridge in the dawn light with the clouds below him, and of heather against his bare back and sun on his chest with the sound of gulls in his ears – if he does perhaps the rest won't matter.'

On 26 January 1951 Diana set out for England with two small children, really concerned that they might end up in a Communist concentration camp, about which possibility, to her annoyance, Shipton was remarkably cavalier and unsympathetic. But as soon as she was gone he was consumed with guilt and foreboding, and wrote loving weekly letters to her, as he so often did when he was lonely: 'Darling, Darling – Why, Why, Why did we do it? I'd give anything now to be able to reverse our decision of last month. You were so wonderful all the time at this end, no sign of fuss and very little of what you were feeling. I was really proud of you.'

In the company of some departing missionaries, Diana flew to Chungking, where they were held up for several days getting a passage (and a cabin) on a boat down the Yangtse River. She had to change ship at both Wan-hsien and I-chang, at either end of the Yangste Gorges. The next Shipton heard was that she had reached Hankow, and was on a train to Canton. He becomes quite maudlin in his letters, continuing to regret the 'mistake' in letting her go alone with two small children, whom he missed.

On his own in Kunming, he still rode every morning before breakfast out to the lake or up into the hills on Emma or Emil, his two horses. The kite-flying season was busy, with large crowds in the park in full blossom. Consular officers were constantly hassled by the Foreign Affairs bureaucrats demanding that they vacate their houses and move into the British Consulate. Finally Shipton was told he had to get out of his own Consulate, and he worried about 'what to do with all H.M.G.'s furniture etc.'

Diana and the boys reached Hong Kong, safe but exhausted, a

month later. Shipton wrote to her, '*What* a journey – certainly the worst in the world. I can't think how you managed. *Oh*, I wish I'd been with you, both to help and to share the thrill of arriving.' Then when she was back in England, 'I'm not in the least surprised to hear you had some sort of breakdown as a result of the nervous strain of the past two months, but mumps on top of that must have gone near to breaking you in pieces. Darling, please don't worry about expense – take a room at the Ritz for six months if that would help.' In fact she did go into a nursing home for a few days' rest.

To pass the time, Shipton gave an Everest talk to the China Inland Mission. 'It was preceded by a solo by the most mournful-looking woman who sang a song called "I sing because I'm happy".' On instructions from the Foreign Office, he closed down the affairs of the British Consulate and sold all its assets, including the two cars. On 6 May 1951, he started on the same journey as Diana had done three months before, taking the Consulate's wireless transmitting equipment in a vast crate sealed with wire and police rice paper seals that were eaten by rats.

At I-chang he and forty-six of his fellow passengers were confined under armed guard to an inn for twelve days, sharing beds and in oppressive heat. Eventually, he got deck passage on a boat, the *Altmark,* sleeping in a hold 'with hundreds of sprawling Chinese bods'. He arrived in Hong Kong on 1 June and stayed in luxury at the Peninsula Hotel.

CHAPTER 12

Everest from the South

1951

ERIC SHIPTON returned to England from his consular posting in Kunming in June 1951. Diana and their two boys were settled in rural Hampshire and he was looking forward to a spell of domestic peace. As he wrote in *Mount Everest Reconnaissance Expedition 1951*, 'Having so lately emerged from Communist China, the freedom of England and the absence of suspicion, hatred and fear, were sheer delight, and the English summer a rare and treasured experience.'

A fortnight later Shipton went up to London and called on Campbell Secord, whom he knew from his 1939 Karakoram expedition. A Canadian economist by profession, mountaineer by choice (having made two reconnaissances of Rakaposhi), and wartime pilot of Liberator bombers, Secord was convinced of the possibility of climbing Everest from the south.

'Oh, you're back, are you?' said Secord. 'What are you going to do now?'

'I've no plans,' Shipton replied.

'Well, you'd better lead this expedition,' said Secord.

'What expedition?' Shipton asked. Whereupon Secord explained the plan to make a reconnaissance of Everest from the south via Nepal. It was like having a bomb lobbed into his now idyllic, almost settled, life.

Throughout Nepal's governance by hereditary Rana princes during the first half of the twentieth century (the King was kept in his palace out of public view) the country remained cut off from the outside world. The Nepalese, suspicious of Western motives, repeatedly refused entry to foreigners; just a few diplomats were allowed in, but certainly no explorers or climbers. Kathmandu remained tantalisingly isolated behind the barrier of the Mahabarat Hills, which rise steeply from the flat Nepal Terai and the plains of India's Bihar state.

After the Second World War Tibet also remained uncommunicative. The Dalai Lama's horoscope predicted that he would be threatened by foreigners, so doors remained firmly closed to the Roof of the World. Sadly, that prophecy turned out to be true in 1950 when Chinese Communist armies invaded Tibet, claiming it was their dependent territory, subjugating and colonising its people. For three decades this would prevent any serious Western incursion to Everest from the north.

India had been having her own troubles, which eventually led in 1947 to the bloody partition of the country between the Hindu states and their Muslim neighbours with the creation of West and East Pakistan (now Bangladesh). Prospects for approaching Everest from north or south did not look good. However, the Joint Himalayan Committee, an informally revamped Mount Everest Committee made up equally of members of the Alpine Club and the Royal Geographical Society, applied to Nepal for permission for an expedition to Everest; they were refused. In 1948 the British Ambassador in Kathmandu tried the less specific approach and asked the Prime Minister of Nepal if a party of climbers might visit their Himalaya. The climbers had wanted to go to Solu Khumbu, the Sherpa homeland lying at the foot of Everest, flanked by its colossal neighbours Lhotse, Nuptse, and Pumori, and the massive outliers, Gauri Sankar, Cho Oyu, and Makalu. But the Ambassador advised them to ask for somewhere closer to the capital because Solu Khumbu was a politically sensitive border area.

Singha Durbar, the seat of Nepalese Government, granted them per-

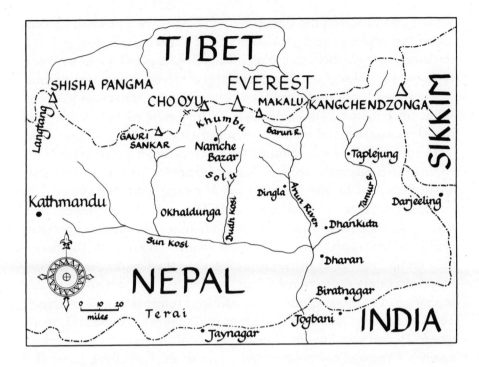

mission to visit the Langtang Himal, a small group of mountains lying immediately north of Kathmandu. Bill Tilman and Peter Lloyd, both then on the Himalayan Committee, asked each other the rhetorical question, 'Someone's got to go; why not us?' So the expedition was afoot. Since the Nepalese Government expected the party to add some serious scientific work to their explorations, Tilman invited Oleg Polunin, a botanist, and J. S. Scott, a geologist to join the expedition. Science was supplemented with surveying by Lloyd, and beetle-collecting by Tilman. They appointed Tenzing Norgay sirdar, or foreman, of the expedition. During their travels they crossed many unnamed passes and reached several high points, including the 19,451 foot summit of Paldor.

Before leaving Nepal, Tilman called to pay his respects to the King, and tentatively asked permission to return the next year to Annapurna Himal in the west of the country; the Himalayan Committee followed this enquiry with an official request. But a favourable reply for 1949 took so long to trickle down the Nepali bureaucracy that Tilman had little time to prepare. His chosen climbing companions were Jimmy

Roberts, an officer in the British Army's Brigade of Gurkhas; Charles Evans, an aspiring neurosurgeon; Emlyn Jones, a solicitor; and Bill Packard, a geographer from New Zealand; Colonel D. G. Lowndes, a botanist, went along too. The expedition explored the country around Manaslu and Himalchuli, and then penetrated the Marsyandi Valley as far as Manangbhot. On Annapurna IV they reached 24,000 feet, just below the summit, before they ran out of steam and had to turn back.

In 1950, the American climber, Oscar Houston, wangled permission to visit Solu Khumbu through some diplomatic friends he had met when President of the International Maritime Law Association – a strange connection with the landlocked Himalaya. Among his cohorts was his son, Charles, who was with Tilman in 1936 on the successful climb of Nanda Devi, and also had been high on K2 in 1938. By chance they met Tilman at an Embassy reception in Kathmandu, and invited him to accompany them on a relaxed 'trekking party' with no particular aspirations to serious climbing. Tilman later referred to it as 'a picnic'. They ambled through Solu Khumbu to Tengboche Monastery, from where Tilman and Charles Houston hurriedly took off by themselves towards Everest. They camped at the foot of the Khumbu Glacier and walked up to the Icefall which pours out of the Western Cwm, but they were not equipped to climb it. In 1921 Mallory had looked down on the Icefall from the Lho La in Tibet, and described it as 'one of the most awful and utterly forbidding scenes ever observed by man'.

Tilman and Houston then climbed some way up Kala Patar on the southern flank of Pumori, and took some photographs but they were too ill to continue. From there they could see the lower part of the Icefall issuing from a mere slot, but a long intervening ridge falling from Nuptse cut off their view into the Western Cwm. Just appearing behind this ridge, and forming the right horizon of the summit cone of the South-West Face of Everest, is the long, steep and rocky South Ridge. Houston concluded that it would be a difficult and dangerous route, but not impossible. Tilman, by contrast, wrote in the *Geographical Journal*, 'The rock of the south ridge looked so steep that we dismissed the hope of there being a route, even supposing the [south] col could be reached.' He correctly surmised that they might not be looking at the ridge which led to the summit from the South Col. Tilman continued, 'Personally, I think the chances are all against finding an easy snow ramp leading from the comparatively low glacier [of the Western Cwm] to this appallingly high col; and the Cwm would be unpleasant and dangerous for an advanced base. Thus although I should not like to write off the south side of Everest without looking into the West Cwm, I think it is safe to say that there is no route comparable in ease and safety, at any rate up to 28,000 feet, to that which we already know so well [on the north side].'

Had they climbed a few hundred feet higher up Kala Patar they would have seen the South Col, with the South Ridge obviously separate from it. But they were both suffering from altitude, having climbed too high too fast. Houston describes himself then. 'I was ataxic, fumbled impossibly loading a camera, fell off a rock I was sitting on, and had a very severe headache.' As a guru of altitude physiology, Houston now recognises these as the classical symptoms of early acute mountain sickness affecting the brain – high altitude cerebral oedema. Tilman acknowledged similar symptoms and swore he would never go high again; and indeed he did not. Those few extra feet eluded them, and thereby the solution to the problem of the southern approach to Everest. Tilman's conclusions were to have a profound influence on the Himalayan Committee which, in 1951, was reluctant initially to support a reconnaissance from the south. Meanwhile, 1,000 miles due east, Eric Shipton, as Consul-General in Kunming, was embroiled in a diplomatic struggle with Communism, and dreaming of the Himalaya.

Independently, Michael Ward, a young trainee surgeon at the London Hospital, then doing National Service attached to the Brigade of Guards, conceived the idea of exploring Everest by way of the Icefall and the Western Cwm. Ward looked at a multitude of photographs in the archives of the Royal Geographical Society, but only a few threw light on the south side of Everest. Mallory took a photo from the Lho La in 1921, but he put the plates in back to front and they were spoiled; Bryant and Shipton took one in 1935 from the col between Lingtren and Pumori, as in 1936 did Edwin Kempson, Ward's teacher and climbing mentor at Marlborough College. All these photos showed the Icefall to be seriously jumbled and dangerous, but none showed round the corner into the upper part of the Western Cwm and the face of Lhotse – the crux of the problem.

The Secretary of the RGS, Hinks, and Milne, the cartographer, had compiled a map of the Everest massif based on Michael Spender's 1935 photogrammetric survey from Tibet, and photos from a 1933 over-flight. Ward then found some photos from the flights in 1945 and 1947 showing the Sout-East Ridge dropping 3,000 feet to the South Col – broad, well covered with snow, and apparently without severe technical difficulties. These photos, together with others, showed the crux of the problem, the slopes leading from the head of the Western Cwm to the South Col. And Tilman's photo from Kala Patar showed a possible route up the ridge to the summit. But this all needed to be examined at close quarters before deciding whether the mountain was climbable from the south – and that meant a reconnaisance through the Icefall.

Ward invited Tom Bourdillon, over six feet in height and built like a second row rugby forward, to join the party. One of Britain's foremost young rock climbers and alpinists, he had just climbed the North Face of the Aiguille du Dru, marking the beginning of a post-war renascence of British climbing, and bringing it nearer to the level of the Continent behind which it had lagged during the war when few Britons climbed, unlike some of their European counterparts. Bourdillon was a rocket scientist, fascinated by the mechanics of oxygen systems, and a strong advocate of the closed circuit apparatus. He spoke slowly, almost hesitantly, appearing to weigh all his words. Shipton wrote of Bourdillon, after his death in the Alps in 1956, 'The searching intimacy of expedition life discovered in him no trace of malice, arrogance or affectation.' Wilfrid Noyce writing in *South Col* likened sharing a tent with Bourdillon to 'being in the company of a bear in a whirlwind', especially when he decided to crawl through the sleeve entrance still wearing his rucksack and crampons.

W. H. 'Bill' Murray had written a classic book, *Mountaineering in Scotland*, while a prisoner-of-war in Germany. With recent experience in the Garhwal Himalaya, Murray was invited unanimously to lead the expedition. 'It is worth recording,' he wrote in the *Alpine Journal*, 'that this is the first instance where the members of an expedition to Everest have chosen themselves, chosen their leader, and initiated the expedition. It is unlikely to happen again.' He was not sanguine about their chances of getting permission through the old men of the Himalayan Committee. After Tilman's gloomy predictions of poor chances from the southern approach, the committee were sceptical. Murray wrote, 'It is one of the few advantages of great experience that a man is apt to discover too many excellent reasons why an adventurous proposition should be impossible; and one of the advantages of inexperience (when high spirits go along with it) that he has an urge to attempt the impossible, which he will then achieve if Providence so disposes.' He evidently had energetic young Michael Ward in mind. However the Himalayan Committee reluctantly applied for permission to the Government of Nepal, and to everyone's surprise this was granted.

Ward consulted Tom Bourdillon's father, a scientist at the Medical Research Council (MRC), over the problems of how low barometric pressure at extreme altitude affected the heart and lungs. Dr Bourdillon directed Ward to a laboratory in the MRC division of Human Physiology to meet Dr Griffith Pugh. There Ward found 'this chap with red hair sitting in a bloody great Victorian bath filled with ice with wires stuck all over him. He was white with hypothermia, shivering uncontrollably, and not feeling at all well.' Ward and the laboratory assistants removed Pugh from the bath (the hallmark of his science always being to perform his own experiments on himself), and wrapped him in a blanket to warm him up. It is hardly surprising that their conversation that day was 'oddly disjointed'. Everest, being 700 feet higher than any other peak, posed unique problems of extreme altitude, which Pugh and Ward discussed in theory over the next weeks, and concluded that they needed to be confirmed in the field.

Then, like a genie, Eric Shipton suddenly appeared from China. Murray, deferring to Shipton's experience, generously stood aside to let him assume leadership of the party. Being such a young group, they needed Shipton's prestige to make the expedition credible; none of them knew him before, but they all welcomed him warmly. As far as Ward was concerned, 'no better person could have been the fourth member'. Now the group consisted of Shipton, Murray, Ward and Bourdillon (Campbell Secord and Alfred Tissières, a Swiss climber, having dropped out). This was just the sort of jaunt Shipton enjoyed and was a master at – low key, low budget, low profile.

But Shipton had reservations about a possible route up Everest from the south because the mountain, like others along the Himalayan range, was far steeper on the southern than on the northern side. Also, as he recounts in his book on the reconnaissance, the approach could not avoid 'the formidable Icefall flowing through a narrow defile which was probably menaced by ice avalanches from the hanging glaciers on the immense precipices above. The West Cwm was a freak of mountain architecture and there was no knowing what we might find there. I put the chances against finding a practicable route at about thirty to one.'

Shipton, having been away from the mountaineering world for so long, with characteristic modesty, was hesitant about his own value to the expedition. But he was swayed to accept for reasons which, typically, had very little to do with the climbing of Everest. For twenty years, ever since he had first known the Sherpas, he had longed to visit their land of Solu Khumbu through which the expedition would travel. 'I had heard so much about it from the Sherpas,' he wrote in *That Untravelled World*, 'indeed during our journeys together in other parts of the Himalaya and Central Asia, whenever we came upon a particularly attractive spot, invariably they would say, "This is just like Solu Khumbu." Almost unknown to Western travellers, it had become, to me at least, a kind of Mecca, an ultimate goal in Himalayan exploration.' So it was that he finally decided, with his wife Diana's encouragement, to accept the invitation to lead the expedition.

They had barely a month to prepare tents, food, climbing equipment, and have everything ready for shipping to India. Being so soon after the war, specialised expedition mountaineering gear was still in short supply. A contract granting exclusive coverage to *The Times* newspaper raised £2,000, the bulk of the total cost of the expedition. The garage of Campbell Secord's mews house in London became the expedition warehouse, and his living room its general office. With a day to go before their equipment was due at the docks nothing was packed, and all was chaos. Shipton sent an SOS to the Women's Voluntary Service asking for emergency help. Within the day, some efficient WVS ladies had everything packed, listed and ready to accompany Murray and Ward by ship.

Two days before Shipton left London the President of the New Zealand Alpine Club sent a cable (with several transmission spelling errors) to the newly formed Himalayan Committee.

ANY POSSIBILITY ONE OR MORE NZ PARTY CONSISTING RIDDIFORD COTTER LOW HILARY PRESENT SUCCESSFULLY CLIMBING GARWAHAL HIMALAYAS BEING INCLUDED FORTHCOMING EVEREST EXPEDITION

PROVIDED CONVENIENT TO THEM STOP DUE RETURN SEPTEMBER STOP
THEY HAVE NOT BEEN APPROACHED SO UNKNOWN WHETHER EXTEN-
SION LEAVE COULD BE ARRANGED STOP EXCELLENT TYPE CLIMBERS
WHO THROUGH BEING ACCLIMATIZED SHOULD PROVE USEFUL
ADJUNCTS REPLY=STEVENSON PRESIDENT NZAC+

Ed Hillary had written a letter of similar content to Scott Russell,
who was on the committee of the Alpine Club. But permits and
finances had already been arranged and the agreed size of Shipton's
party – four persons – was complete, several potential British recruits
already having been rejected. The Swiss had asked for René Dittert to
be included in the reconnaissance and had been turned down by the
Himalayan Committee. So, adding all these facts together, Shipton was
set to refuse the New Zealand application.

However, on the flight to Delhi with Bourdillon, Shipton had time to
reconsider his position, detached from the preceding days of chaotic
preparation. He was going to the south side of Everest with three young
companions, all unknown to him; Murray had completed a recent
season in Garhwal, but Ward and Bourdillon, fine alpine climbers by
repute, had no Himalayan experience. Shipton realised, somewhat
belatedly, that four persons would be too few to achieve any serious
climbing, especially if any one of them got sick or injured. Also they
lacked experience on ice, something the addition of fit and acclimatised
New Zealanders, with reputations as good ice men, might correct.
Then, in a moment of nostalgia, Shipton recalled Dan Bryant, the New
Zealander with whom he had formed a close bond during the 1935
Everest expedition. A tough, cheerful schoolteacher known for brilliant
icemanship, Bryant could never acclimatise above about 20,000 feet,
which rendered him unsuitable for high-altitude Himalayan climbing.
Without consulting his companions (whose expedition it was), Shipton
changed the text of the telegram, eventually sent by the Alpine Club, to:

ANY TWO CAN JOIN US. GET THEIR OWN PERMISSION. BRING THEIR
OWN FOOD AND CATCH US UP.

Shipton wrote in his autobiography about his decision to accept the
New Zealanders:

The correct answer was obvious: I had already turned down several applicants with very strong qualifications on the ground that I wanted to keep the party small; our slender resources of money and equipment were already stretched, and I had no idea where the two climbers were or how to contact them. I soon began to regret this, for, apart from the complications resulting from the last minute inclusion of two new members of the party, still in some remote Himalayan valley and with no permits to enter Nepal, I found it far from easy to explain my totally irrational action to my companions. They could not altogether hide their dismay, though they were too polite to express it.

The words *any two* were to cause conflict among the New Zealanders, emerging euphorically from the Himalaya, having completed an expedition to Mukut Parbat successful beyond their expectations. For them the message, coming from the great Eric Shipton, was 'like Moses receiving the tablets of stone'. So they sat down to decide who the two would be. It became a tussle between the four, threatening the strong bond of friendship forged during the previous months. Now each had to make a case why he should be one of the chosen two.

The Kiwis were then too distant from their own New Zealand Alpine Club to draw on any available funds. Ed Hillary was in a position to go because his brother was looking after their beekeeping business back home. From the outset he regarded himself as one of the chosen. As he wrote in *Nothing Venture, Nothing Win*, 'I pushed conscience aside; the chance to go to Everest outweighed everything else. I was very fit and there were no arguments about my inclusion.' He told the other three to fight it out among themselves as to who would get the second spot – a glimpse of the self-confidence and ruthless tenacity that got him to the top of Everest two years later.

Earle Riddiford, a lawyer in a thriving partnership, although not particularly strong physically, was a powerful character who had shown unwavering drive on Mukut Parbat (which they narrowly failed to climb). His uncle had bequeathed him some money, which the others believed was intended to go towards the costs of the expedition. But the money had not materialised and this became a matter of contention between them.

George Lowe had no financial backing at all, but had gathered together £150 – all the money he had – to go on the trip. He was on leave without pay from a school back home, although prepared to break his contract to return in the autumn. Moreover, he and Ed Hillary had been a close working team throughout their expedition. Edmund Cotter (who, in heavy seas, had walked on his hands along the rail of the ship bringing them to India) quickly withdrew when he noticed the discussion becoming hard-nosed and edgy.

So Riddiford won out, and Cotter and Lowe resigned themselves to returning home to New Zealand. Lowe said that being 'offered the impossible dream of going to Everest with Eric Shipton and then to lose it, was a considerable blow'. Even Hillary admitted, 'Comradeship was forgotten and bitterness crept into the discussion. I can still remember George's accusing face as he watched us depart by bus to the railhead.' Until they discussed it much later, Shipton did not realise the maelstrom he had created with his *any two* telegram, and was appalled when they told him about its divisive effect. He would have been just as happy if all four New Zealanders had turned up.

The expedition assembled just outside the border of Nepal at Jogbani, a railhead village of Bihar state, where Shipton met his old friend Angtharkay, their chosen Sherpa sirdar, who had arrived from Darjeeling, where he owned one of the early successful trekking businesses. He was his unchanged, unsophisticated, charming self, apart from cutting off his long hair, which most Tibetans braid with pink ribbon and wind round the crown of their heads. He had distinguished himself on many high mountains, and was renowned as a 'tiger', the accolade given to outstanding climbing Sherpas since the 'twenties.

They crossed the flat Nepal Terai by truck, passing through Biratnagar to Dharan, a small town lying about a hundred wandering miles almost due south of Everest. It was now the end of August and still the monsoon season when dense cloud sheathed the mountains, a time of deluging rainstorms, rhododendrons and orchids in bloom, and abundant bloodthirsty leeches – a season that any sensible traveller, other than a botanist or a parasitologist, would avoid. Not surprisingly, porters were hard to find, being reluctant to carry eighty-pound loads on slippery, muddy mountain paths. Experience of all attempts from the north told that spring was the only suitable time to tackle Everest, but they knew this was to be only a reconnaissance.

Eventually they set off. Shipton, having had his head shaved, wore mauve Chinese cotton pyjamas, shoes and socks, sunglasses and carried an umbrella. Tom Bourdillon wrote to his wife, Jennifer, 'My respect for Eric grows. He is slow and courteous and with a great deal of reserved confidence. He seems astonishingly casual, never quite sure about how many porters we have or where we are going for the day. But things work out smoothly, and he is utterly calm in the centre of a mob of shouting coolies.'

By dint of double marches the New Zealanders caught up with the party at Dingla. They had encountered several dangerous monsoon-flooded side streams, which they crossed using staffs made from limbed tree branches, a technique with which they were familiar when tramping at home. Hillary and Riddiford, wearing peaked cloth caps, with flaps hanging over the neck like Foreign Legionnaires, bounded up the hill wondering what to expect of the British party. Would they be frightfully formal and decent *pukka sahibs* ? Were they sticklers for shaving every day? Perhaps the Kiwis would have to smarten themselves and clean up their language. Feeling like a couple of naughty schoolboys summoned by the headmaster, they followed a Sherpa through a dark doorway and up some stairs into the upper room of a house.

'Eric Shipton came forward to greet us,' Hillary recalls in *High Adventure*, 'and I felt a sense of relief at his unshaven face and scruffy clothes. I have rarely seen a more disreputable bunch, and my visions of changing for dinner faded away for ever. This was an exciting moment for me. I had read all Shipton's books and followed his tough pioneering expeditions with enormous interest. Now I was not only meeting him but going on an expedition with him too.' Being used to squalid Himalayan travel and also very hungry, the New Zealanders wolfed down a 'horrid meal' of boiled rice and indeterminate green vegetables such as Shipton, who seemed to be more or less unaware of what he ate, enjoyed. Tom Bourdillon, another non-epicure, when once asked his preferences for expedition food, replied, 'The main thing is that there should be some.'

The nightmarish monsoon march from Jogbani to Namche Bazar took nearly four weeks. At first it was so hot they marched in shorts and swam at every stream crossing. Their umbrellas for protection against the sun were soon needed to keep off the incessant rain. A few seconds after Shipton crossed one flimsy bridge, large waves washed it away, forcing them to make a detour of several days. Ed Hillary recounted, 'I have this very vivid memory of Eric sitting in a corner completely content, with an umbrella up over his head, a candle in one hand and reading a book in the other. He could relax under appalling conditions, and all this rain meant nothing to him. But it was a bit hard on his companions!'

The heavily laden porters went on strike because of the dangerously slimy condition of the trail. Clusters of leeches hung like little black sticks from every branch. In one village near their route, fifty people had died in the previous two weeks from an epidemic like bubonic plague. Finally they disturbed a nest of hornets, which attacked several porters, stinging them badly. The monsoon ended suddenly on 20 September, around its customary date.

As they entered the region of Solu Khumbu, Shipton's dreamland for so many years, the mist evaporated and clouds parted, revealing a horizon of snowy peaks. He met scores of friends from pre-war expeditions, and the climbers progressed like triumphant heroes up the valley, being dragged into successive Sherpa houses to drink chang. 'After a while I found it increasingly difficult to recognise anyone,' Shipton confessed, 'and I marched along in a happy alcoholic haze.' In Namche Bazar the festivities continued while the party tried to remain sober enough to sort stores and equipment. Shipton met Sen Tensing, the Foreign Sportsman, companion of many previous Himalayan adventures, from the 1935 Everest reconnaissance onwards.

The climbers walked on for a day to Tengboche Monastery, set on a grassy alpine knoll high above the Dudh Kosi and commanding a view up the long valley that leads towards Everest. In the monastery's sanctuary are two thrones, one for its own Head Lama, the other for the Abbot of Rongbuk, should he cross the Nangpa La to visit. The gong to summon the faithful was an old oxygen cylinder brought over from Tibet after one of the pre-war expeditions. The graceful pinnacle of Ama Dablam, though no giant, dominates the whole valley like a Matterhorn. It stands forward from its neighbours, Kangtega and Tamserku, as does Machhapuchare from the Annapurna Range north of Pokhara. At the head of the valley rises the massive wall of Nuptse with the summit cone of Everest peeping over the ridge; usually a

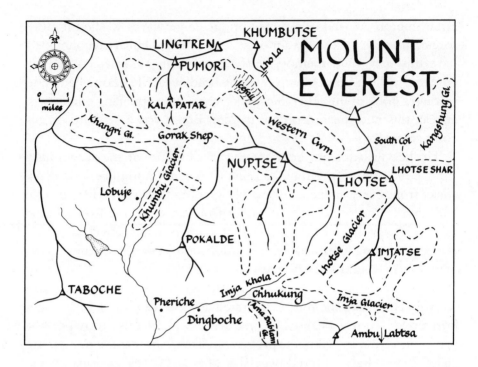

plume of blown snow trails from the very top formed by a vortex of
high wind. It is altogether more steeply impressive than the mellower
view of the North Face of Everest from Rongbuk Monastery. The
climbers all agreed it was one of the most spectacular mountain
prospects any of them had seen.

Beyond Pangboche the path hung suspended above the Imja Khola
until the main valley forked. To the right lay Dingboche, a small yak-
herders' village guarding the closed valley that leads to the back side of
Ama Dablam, Baruntse and Makalu; to the left was Pheriche, a wide,
high grazing pasture walled for yaks, and the highest habitation in the
region. Beyond Pheriche is the lower part of the Khumbu glacial
moraine, a messy jumble of ice and rock with some high detached pinnacles, less dramatic than the forest of tall ice spires found on the East
Rongbuk Glacier.

Shipton chose to pitch their base camp at Gorak Shep, about 18,000
feet high, near the foot of elegant, triangular Pumori. Apart from
himself, all the climbers had infected sores on their legs and feet from

leech bites a month before. Bourdillon, Ward and Murray were also suffering from mild mountain sickness brought on by ascending to high altitude; but Shipton, Hillary and Riddiford, all having climbed high before, were acclimatising well. As on his previous expeditions, Shipton deployed his resources. Bourdillon, Ward and Riddiford hiked across the Khumbu Glacier to study the Icefall close to. Shipton and Hillary climbed a rocky ridge leading to Kala Patar, the subsidiary peak of Pumori; Murray, 1,000 feet lower, struck farther north along Pumori's flank, and thereby got a more complete view of the upper part of the Icefall and into the Western Cwm.

Shipton and Hillary passed the spot from where Tilman and Houston took their photograph of the discouraging steep skyline of the rocky South Ridge. But the higher they climbed, the less did the long foreground ridge falling from Nuptse obstruct their view, and the better they could see the whole approach to Everest. From about 20,000 feet they realised at once that there was a possible route from the foot of the Icefall right to the head of the Western Cwm, and up the headwall face of Lhotse to the open snowy saddle of the South Col, confirming the air photos found by Ward in London. They could not see the ridge to the summit which was just out of sight, obscured by the South Ridge which plunged well forward into the Cwm. This was a significant moment in the history of Everest, which had mesmerised Eric Shipton for nearly two decades, and was shortly to be forever linked with the name of Ed Hillary. Shipton pointed out several features on the north side of the mountain familiar from his four pre-war expeditions – the little bivouac platform at 25,700 feet, Norton's Camp VI, the Yellow and Black Bands, the Second Step and the Great Couloir – names engraved in Everest's past. For Hillary, 'It was one of the most exciting moments I can remember, and we returned to camp bubbling over with the news.'

But their spirits were quickly sobered by studying the Icefall – a frozen cataract, 2,000 feet high, pouring out of the Western Cwm through a narrow slot between the walls of Nuptse and the West Ridge of Everest. Where it hits the valley floor the glacier turns a right angle and flows due south. Shipton drew in pencil a sketch map on the back of Ward's copy of the Milne-Hinks map. Murray, who had seen the lower but more penetrating view into the Cwm, wrote to his friend,

John Tyson, 'If only we can get up the Icefall without exposure to avalanche danger, then the route is a better one than from Tibet where the difficulties on the north side are in the last 1,000 feet.' Meanwhile across the valley Riddiford and Pasang had made good progress more than halfway up the centre of the Icefall.

On the strength of these various discoveries, Shipton decided to enter the Icefall the next day and to try to force a route into the Western Cwm. They threaded their way through a wild labyrinth of ice walls, chasms and towers, rarely able to see more than 200 feet ahead. Justifiably the most dreaded place on Everest, where so many people have died, the ice in the Icefall has a plastic quality and flows at a rate of about two feet a day (which is very fast as glacial movement goes). It breaks up as it flows forward and downward, creating huge towers or seracs. It is like a cut loaf of bread, half of which has fallen over; at the top the slices are in place but riven right across, then they collapse domino-fashion.

Despite abominable fresh snow conditions, Shipton's team climbed through most of the Icefall in a single day, working their way over ground never before trodden. It was bitterly cold until after the sun appeared about 10 a.m., so they had to stop frequently to warm their feet. They reached less than 100 feet below the lip where, with a few whacks of Bourdillon's ice axe, they might have seen into the Western Cwm. But the last steep slope avalanched above a big slumped crevasse. Shipton and Pasang jumped clear, but Riddiford was carried upside down towards the crevasse. Pasang belayed skilfully by jamming his ice axe into the snow, bringing Riddiford to an abrupt halt suspended at the edge of the crevasse – an accident he was lucky to survive.

Shaken and fearful, they all decided to retreat down to base camp and leave the Icefall for a couple of weeks, which might allow time for the new snow to consolidate, both in the Icefall and on the upper slopes of Lhotse leading to the South Col. It might also give Murray, Ward and Bourdillon more time to acclimatise. The most convincing argument against proceeding was Angtharkay's firm no to any Sherpas carrying loads through that dangerous place.

The party now split into two groups. Shipton and Hillary went east up the Imja Khola to seek a pass across to the Barun to access, via Tibet, the Kangshung Glacier which flows away from the vast eastern face of

Everest. Because of the Imja's steep headwalls they turned south and crossed the Ambu Labtsa into the valley of the Hongu, which brought them round the back side of Ama Dablam. Hillary was delighted to be asked to accompany Shipton on the sort of exploring trip for which he was famous, crossing unknown passes and looking into strange country. 'There's no one in the world I'd have preferred to be with on an expedition,' Hillary said. 'Just to live with him and talk with him was a pleasure. It was a marvellous adventure for me. All new country, completely unexplored, and I quickly caught his fervour for such untravelled places.' Shipton at forty-four was still fit and strong and highly competitive even against a tough young man like Hillary. He was content to leave the difficult leading on ice to his younger friend, and together they made a happy team, totally confident in each other's abilities.

They returned to base camp on 19 October, but there was no sign of the rest of the party who had been in the west near Gyachung Kang and Cho Oyu, exploring the approaches to the Nup La, which leads over to the West Rongbuk Glacier. When the others returned a week later they found Shipton and Hillary had moved the camp over to the foot of the Icefall. It is a gloomy place of utter desolation. Immense boulders balance on slender frozen pedestals and dirty moraine rocks are scattered at random on a humpback of ice as though some giant in Tibet has hurled his garbage over the Lho La. From the steep enclosing walls of Lingtren rocks thunder down narrow gullies. Ice cliffs break off from the hanging glaciers of Pumori and hurtle off the mountain face, gathering stones and snow and pushing ahead a white cloud of fine dust that spreads out across the debris cone.

Shipton advocated using the large twelve-man, double-skinned, Arctic dome tent that 'weighed a ton and needed a football field to pitch it in'. But he felt it worth the effort to have the space and comfort, allowing them to make earlier starts without having to get dressed scrabbling around in tiny mountain tents – a detestable morning ritual. In subsequent journeys in Patagonia, an Antarctic pyramid tent became his trademark.

Shipton and Hillary set off again into the Icefall together with Angtharkay and some Sherpas. At first they went easily through it, but soon they found a tremendous change had taken place, owing to the downward flow of the glacier. 'Over a wide area the cliffs and towers that had been there before had been shattered as though by an earth-quake and now lay in a tumbled ruin, and cliffs and seracs were riven by innumerable new cracks which seemed to threaten a further collapse.' A huge block fell close to them causing the ground they stood on to tremble; Shipton and Hillary stood firm, but the Sherpas threw them-selves on the ground in terror. It was just like the aftermath of an atomic explosion with house-sized seracs always in danger of falling on them – truly a game of Russian roulette.

Angtharkay thereupon made up his mind that he was not going through the Icefall with his men, with or without heavy loads. Shipton was also very concerned, not so much for the climbers' personal safety (though, as a leader, that was always one of his priorities), but for that of the laden Sherpas who would have to make several trips through the devastated area. The next day the western party returned, and they all decided to make a final attempt to break through the Icefall into the Western Cwm. Angtharkay and Pasang accompanied them, but made no secret of their apprehension, constantly pointing out the dangers.

They reached a wall at the very top of the Icefall up which Bourdillon cut steps for the others to follow. Soon they were all standing on the lip of the Western Cwm. They could see the long, flat glacier hemmed in by the walls of Everest and Nuptse, with the face of Lhotse at the head of a vast silent amphitheatre. They found their way barred by a vast crevasse, 100 feet wide at its narrowest, that split the glacier from one enclosing wall to the other. To climb down 200 feet into its depths and up the other side would have taken several days of dangerous work, even by Hillary, the best ice climber among them. They did not have enough rope, nor any tree trunks, nor aluminium bridging ladders with which subsequent expeditions equipped themselves. All they could do was stare at the face of Lhotse leading to the South Col in the sure knowledge that a reasonable route lay up it, and most likely from there a way to the summit. By this reconnaissance they had unlocked the secret of Everest from the south.

But some of them felt in retrospect that, despite the dangers of the Icefall at this time of year, they should have returned to base camp and moved everything up to the lip of the Cwm from where they could have made a full scale attempt at getting across the crevasse. Thus they might have reached the foot of the Lhotse Face and had a good look at it from close to. Tom Bourdillon wrote to his wife, 'In the evening we had much discussion. Everyone save Michael Ward and me – and possibly Earle Riddiford – thinking that it was not worth doing any more work in the Icefall. Bill Murray is not going well, no energy or initiative over 13,000 feet.' Ward also was disappointed at not finishing the job properly.

Hillary wrote in *Nothing Venture, Nothing Win*, 'Over the next few days we discussed the problem of the Icefall and there was much talk about 'unjustifiable risk' and 'unsafe for porters'. But I think we all realised that these were attitudes from the past, that nobody was going to get up Everest without taking a few risks, that the Icefall would never be a place for the cautious or the faint-hearted. If we didn't attack it that May, someone else would. The competitive standards of alpine mountaineering were coming to the Himalayas, and we might as well compete or pull out.' Shipton, writing in a supplement to *The Times*, summed up his feelings thus, 'This dragon guarding the Western Cwm is now in restless mood; it is not unreasonable to expect that in the spring he may be found sleeping.'

With the reconnaissance of the Icefall complete (or was it?), Shipton turned his attention to exploring westwards of the Everest massif. They all walked up the Bhote (or Tibetan) Kosi, the western of the two main valleys which join at Namche Bazar, that to the east being the Dudh Kosi (meaning milky with glacial silt), draining from Everest.

At Thami they parted from the New Zealanders who, having been abroad for six months, wanted to hotfoot home; Hillary was anxious about his brother running their honey business alone, and Riddiford had legal clients to attend to. Though both excellent ice climbers, they had joined the expedition as rank outsiders, yet had melded themselves as a crucial force into the team to which they brought vim and pizzazz. During their two-week wander to the south of the Imja Khola, Hillary had formed a special bond of friendship with Shipton, who must have had little cause to regret his impulsive decision, against all logic and diplomatic sense, to invite the two Kiwis to join his party. He must also have known it was not the last he was going to see of them.

Michael Ward, one of Britain's best young climbers, wrote with unusual humility in *In This Short Span*, 'It seemed to me that [the New Zealanders] were much more mature and experienced in their approach to this particular form of mountaineering than the European-trained members of the party who could probably climb technically harder routes, in finer style. In New Zealand much more time is spent on pioneering and, having been three months in the Himalaya already, both Ed and Earle were very well acclimatized and mentally attuned to expedition work.'

The New Zealanders brought an unconventional whiff of fresh air into the Establishment. Ed Hillary tells how one of his tasks in Nepal had been to keep a careful record of all their expenses to be refunded by the Alpine Club. His list included the cost of numerous cups of tea bought from wayside tea shops. On their return they received a note from the Honorary Treasurer (a millionaire, renowned for his eagle-eyed watch over club funds) saying, 'Gentlemen are expected to pay for their own cups of tea.' They advised him by return mail that they were New Zealanders and not 'gentlemen'. They also put in for some taxi fares and got back the reply, 'Have you not heard of public transport?'

The New Zealanders crossed the Tashi Labtsa, a pass of some technical difficulty, and descended the Rolwaling Valley (the first Westerners to do so); thence, with great speed, they reached Kathmandu. Murray and Bourdillon took four days' food and climbed to the Nangpa La, at over 19,000 feet, probably the highest trading pass in the world and a favoured route for Tibetans and Sherpas crossing between Tibet and Solu Khumbu in Nepal. There they found deep channels cut in the ice by the hooves of legions of yaks. They sat beside a cairn of stones impaled with prayer flags and looked north to the ochre hills of Tibet, and at the North-West Face of Cho Oyu. They picked out two feasible routes, the only problem being that they both lay over the border in Tibet – or Communist China, depending on your political viewpoint.

While Angtharkay remained behind to escort Murray and Bourdillon over the pass when they returned from the Nangpa La, Shipton, Ward and Sen Tensing set off up the valley of the Pangbuk Chhu and inspected the Gauri Sankar massif, then they crossed the Menlung La at about 20,000 feet without difficulty, and found themselves on the edge of a huge amphitheatre, dominated by a perfectly triangular, pale granite peak, which they called Menlungtse (gone were Shipton's flamboyant days of naming mountains after his girlfriends). Set by itself in a ring of pastures and glaciers, it reminded Shipton and Sen Tensing

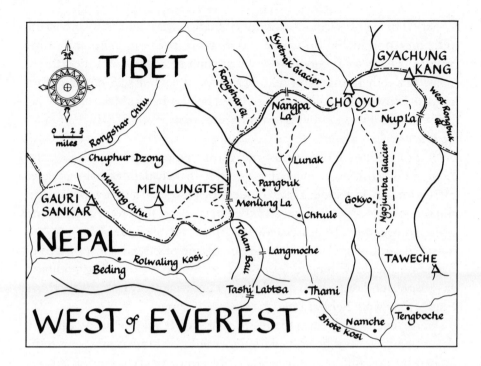

of Nanda Devi in its Sanctuary. The main glacier flowed south-westerly so they had reason to think they were still in Nepal, but on looking north the dun, rusty peaks looked peculiarly like Tibet.

They continued on down the Menlung Glacier and, late in the afternoon, they came upon some tracks in the snow. Shipton described them in his report to *The Times*:

> The tracks were mostly distorted by melting into oval impressions, slightly longer and a good deal broader than those made by our mountain boots. But here and there, where the snow covering the ice was thin, we came upon a well preserved impression of the creature's foot. It showed three 'toes' [actually four] and a broad 'thumb' to the side. What was particularly interesting was that where the tracks crossed a crevasse one could see quite clearly where the creature had jumped and used its toes to secure purchase on the snow on the other side. We followed the tracks for more than a mile down the glacier before we got on to moraine-covered ice.

Sen Tensing proclaimed without hesitation that they belonged to the yeti, or Abominable Snowman. Two years previously he and some Sherpa friends at Tengboche saw just such a creature a stone's throw away. It was half man and half beast, as tall as himself, covered with reddish brown hair; and it had a pointed head, a hairless face and no tail. He was sure it was neither a bear nor a monkey, both of which animals he knew well.

Shipton took photographs of Ward standing beside the tracks. Lower down they were more distinct with sharply defined edges, twelve inches long by five wide; a big rounded toe projected slightly to one side, the second toe was separate, and the lateral three toes were smaller and grouped together. To give an idea of the scale, Shipton photographed his ice axe and Ward's boot beside one of the prints, which appeared to have been made within a day or so. He regarded Sen Tensing's opinion as gospel, and was convinced that whatever creatures made those tracks, they were neither bears nor human beings.

Ward, even now, says the footprints were absolutely as Shipton described them, but he considers they might be human prints with the angled big toe due to a congenital foot abnormality common among Sherpas (one was photographed subsequently by Ed Hillary). Himalayan highlanders (and some mystics) can walk for days barefoot in the snow when herding yaks or hunting wild sheep, without getting frostbite. Alternatively, Ward thinks that several footprints might have been superimposed on each other, as might be made by men walking in single file.

Murray and Bourdillon found the same tracks, and followed them for the better part of two miles until they were forced onto the moraine. Bourdillon, also possessing an analytical scientific mind, wrote home, 'The Abominable Snowman is not a myth. There were about a mile of tracks set 18″ apart and staggered. The pads were 8″×10″ and he probably walked on 2 legs. There were impressions of the front pads where the beast had jumped a crevasse and scrabbled on landing.' He and Murray followed the footprints for quite a way, and were impressed with the creature's good sense of terrain in taking precisely the correct mountaineering route.

They climbed to the southern rim of the valley, at the end of which lay Gauri Sankar (23,440 feet). From there they looked down some fearsome cliffs dropping 7,000 feet into what they assumed to be the Rolwaling Valley. It was a maze of unexplored mountains such as delighted Shipton; Ward was also infected with the exploration fever that characterised all of his older companion's adventures, and he admitted, 'For sheer delight I had yet to come across any activity which gave me more pleasure.'

Debate has fomented ever since over the yeti, which has assumed the notoriety of the Loch Ness monster. Hillary led an expedition in 1960, as have others, to search for evidence of the creature – if such it was. Later he several times questioned Shipton on the matter, only, he says, receiving evasive replies. 'Fond though I was of Eric, and knowing what a cynic he could be, I think there was a strong chance he might have tidied up the track a little, just for a laugh. I told him so many times, but he always denied it.' The zoologists of Hillary's expedition suggested that most of the evidence of the sightings pointed towards the culprit being the Tibetan blue bear. Ward is adamant that the tracks had not been tampered with.

Not long ago Peter Gillman, in the title of his piece for the *Sunday Times Magazine*, denounced Shipton as 'The Most Abominable Hoaxer'. It is difficult to take seriously, being so full of scurrilous invective. He describes Shipton as 'mercurial and disrespectful of authority', 'defiant, non-conformist, restless and embittered'; however, those who knew Shipton found him phlegmatic and dependable, tolerant and unresentful. Gillman postulates that Shipton jokingly fabricated the footprint, which he photographed together with the ice axe; but that, like the Piltdown Skull, the joke got out of hand. So, Gillman affirms, Shipton had to keep up the myth in retaliation against the Establishment that had snubbed him over the leadership of the 1953 expedition. This churlish appraisal of Shipton does little to further the story of the yeti nor to discredit the footprints. Perhaps these tracks will always remain a mystery because we just *want* to believe in them.

Murray, Bourdillon and Angtharkay now rejoined Shipton, Ward and Sen Tensing and they all set off down the valley, which plunged into a deep, forested ravine that joined a much larger gorge further to the west. It was undoubtedly the Rongshar Valley which, certainly, was in Tibet. Shipton knew that Wollaston, the naturalist on the 1921 Everest expedition, had been in the upper Rongshar which he named the Valley of Roses, and he had reached a village with a dzong, or fort, and a monastery at the confluence of the Rongshar and Menlung rivers.

For Shipton the question was whether or not to risk encountering the Chinese (recent invaders and conquerors of Tibet) from whose Communist regime he himself had just escaped. He wrote, 'I could well imagine the zest with which the new Communist rulers would welcome the capture of four British "spies".' Angtharkay was eager to descend to the Rongshar, being the most direct way home to Kathmandu; to him international borders meant nothing because Sherpas traditionally wandered across them regardless while grazing their yaks and sheep. He urged Shipton to ignore any thought of the Chinese authorities far away in Lhasa, because even if they were caught by the local governor, or dzongpen, they could pretend they had unknowingly strayed into Tibet. None of the Sherpas was keen to return to the high pass they had just crossed, and Angtharkay suggested that as the moon was full they could negotiate the Rongshar Gorge by night to avoid being caught. Anyway he was quite confident he could talk – or shout – his way out of any encounter with Tibetans. One of the other Sherpas, who had previously smuggled horses through the Rongshar, knew the way and could guide them down.

With misgivings Shipton agreed, probably swayed by his own expressed thought that 'a passage through this fabulous defile which had never been penetrated by a Western traveller would have made a superb finish to our journey.' They descended the Menlung Valley, where the horse-smuggler suggested they lie up in some woods before the river joined the Rongshar. While they waited for nightfall, some women collecting firewood saw them but appeared to pay little attention.

Stealthily they padded off along a path that ran through the village in the thin light of a full moon, passing under the towering walls of the dzong where Tibetan curs broke into a cacophony. For such experienced risk-takers all the mountaineers were surprisingly nervous. Soon they entered the fissure of the gorge, which was so steep and narrow the moonlight could not penetrate its depths. They proceeded in single file, blindly in inky darkness; high above they could see a silver band, the edge of the ice capping the precipitous opposite wall of the gorge which was now bathed in brilliant moonlight.

They continued through the gorge, which opened out after some hours to a flat area where the Sherpas suggested they stop for a meal. They were all tired and hungry, having been on the go for almost eighteen hours without a restful break, so they lit a fire, brewed tea and all promptly fell asleep. Shipton awoke in broad daylight and roused his companions, cursing himself for not pressing on to safety after their tea stop. He goaded them urgently to get on their way across the frontier, which they later discovered was at a bridge only a couple of miles distant.

As they walked along a flat area beside the river, a sudden uproar caused them to turn around. Seven Tibetans, their pigtails flying out behind them, charged down upon them brandishing swords and uttering wild cries. The Sherpas stood their ground undismayed, while Angtharkay bellowed back at the shouting Tibetans, who were obviously demanding he return to the dzong. Evidently the firewood ladies of the evening before had reported the bearded strangers whose bootmarks, imprinted on the village street, confirmed their story.

Angtharkay told the sahibs to retreat into the forest and leave him to deal with the Tibetans. He returned to the fray and pandemonium continued for half an hour; finally it subsided and Shipton saw money changing hands. Angtharkay returned grinning broadly. 'Everything is settled,' he said, adding apologetically, 'but I'm afraid it cost seven rupees. At first they asked for ten.' Soon they crossed the bridge into Nepal, and reached Kathmandu two weeks later. There Shipton learned the bombshell news that the Swiss had gained permission for Everest the next year, 1952.

Back in England, Shipton wrote a book, mainly of pictures with scanty text, *The Mount Everest Reconnaissance Expedition 1951*, which hardly does justice to the significance of their pristine explorations. In it Shipton sums up the feelings of himself and his companions who had spent precious weeks roaming the southern approaches to Everest, 'This form of mountaineering, the exploration of unknown peaks, glaciers and valleys, the finding and crossing of new passes to connect one area with another, is the most fascinating occupation I know. The variety of experience, the constantly changing scene, the gradual unfolding of the geography of the range are deeply satisfying, for they yield a very real understanding, almost a sense of personal possession, of the country explored.'

Shortly afterwards, he was invited to Sandringham to meet the King and Queen to give an account of his reconnaissance. During the week before, he wandered into the Royal Geographical Society looking characteristically helpless and forlorn.

'I've got no ticket. What shall I do?' he announced to the secretary of Larry Kirwan, the Director.

Thereupon the staff ladies at the RGS mobilised and variously organised him, bought his ticket, hired a dinner jacket from Moss Bros. and bundled him onto the train to Norfolk. Once aboard he discovered he was carrying no money which he would need to pay for the taxi to Sandringham.

'Excuse me,' he diffidently addressed a fellow passenger, 'I have a book of postage stamps. Would you kindly buy them off me for cash?'

Having few clothes, he had filled out his voluminous suitcase with crumpled newspaper, and on entering his palatial bedroom he was embarrassed to come upon one of the footmen unpacking for him.

He wrote to Diana (on royal crested notepaper).

My Darling,

Sorry, I can't resist this one! Dinner was quite terrifying. I sat between the Queen & Queen Mary and could hardly eat anything. Princess M. was there & the D. of E. Not Princess E. When the ladies left I moved round & sat next to the King. Then I was sent off for my photos and everyone stood round a table in the drawing room looking at them and cracking jokes and asking questions for a couple of hours. Then when the Queen had gone to bed I got involved discussing religion with the D. of E. which went on till after one.

CHAPTER 13

Crossroads on Cho Oyu

1952

IN THE AUTUMN of 1951, Eric Shipton, blithely wandering in the Himalayan foothills, was oblivious of the mountaineering political machinery grinding back in Europe, much of it round his persona as the most experienced Everest climber alive. In October, Lucien Devies, President of the Club Alpin Français, wrote to the Alpine Club to say that Maurice Herzog (hero of Annapurna, the only 8,000 metre peak so far climbed) was soon coming over to England to lecture, and wanted to sound out the British reaction to a proposed Anglo-French expedition to Everest. George Finch, for the AC, was magnanimously in favour. Not so Tom Blakeney, the paid Assistant Secretary of the AC, who felt that the British would have nothing to gain by a joint expedition, and the French would be the most difficult of all people to join in such a venture. 'We can no longer use political influence to exclude the French or anyone else,' Blakeney wrote to Scott Russell, 'but I can see no reason why we should help them at our own expense.'

Meanwhile, the Swiss had applied for and, with the help of their compatriot Ella Maillart, the renowned Asian traveller, got permission from the Government of Nepal to attempt Everest in 1952. When Shipton returned in December he was caught off guard by a fever that was endemic in Britain over Everest, about which the public could not hear enough. People were athirst for adventure; Herzog's Annapurna, Heyerdal's *Kon-Tiki*, Thesiger's Empty Quarter, and now Shipton's Everest – again. After a lecture in one of Liverpool's largest halls he had to give three repeat performances and on the last occasion the hall was as full as on the first.

Shipton was the obvious man to lead the British attempt on Everest – their mountain, some Britons would claim. Even Ed Hillary confessed in *Nothing Venture, Nothing Win*, 'The Swiss had been granted permission to attempt Everest so all our ambitious plans could be forgotten. It was strange how we resented this news; as though Everest belonged to us and no one else had any right to it.' How curiously imperial this brash colonial's attitudes had become after three months' close contact with offspring of the British Empire!

The Himalayan Committee sent Basil Goodfellow to Switzerland to try to negotiate a proposed combined expedition with the Swiss, to be led jointly by Shipton and Dr Edouard Wyss-Dunant. The British held an ace, Eric Shipton, who had unequalled experience of Everest, had already charted a route up the mountain with his own eyes, and had himself trodden the crucial ground of the Icefall.

But the Swiss held the trump card – permission for Everest in 1952 with a team of excellent alpine climbers, even if only two had Himalayan experience. They no doubt also recalled René Dittert's rejection and the New Zealanders' inclusion in the Shipton reconnaissance. They politely dispatched Goodfellow back to London with a 'Thanks, but no thanks,' and the smarting Himalayan Committee could only ensure that their own permission was logged for the following year. To entertain the idea of joint leadership of an expedition between two competitive countries seems incredible. The potential prize was too high to expect climbers to subjugate their national ambitions if the chance for the top became theirs. This scenario was highlighted two decades later by the disastrous rivalries that developed on the International Expedition to Everest in 1971. Although individually supreme mountaineers, when it came to possible summiters, inter-national camaraderie shrivelled.

Shipton was twice invited to Zurich by the Swiss in order to brief them, and he made the generous gesture of goodwill, consistent with his nature, of showing his rivals his photographs looking into the Western Cwm and at the Lhotse Face. The Swiss set off for Everest with a strong team under the leadership of Wyss-Dunant; André Roch, Raymond Lambert and René Dittert were legendary alpine guides; Tenzing Norgay, their sirdar, already thirty-eight years old, was veteran of four previous Everest expeditions.

The climbers entered the Icefall, to find its forward flow had changed it radically from the previous year. The easiest route seemed to follow a corridor on the north side underneath the steep ice walls below the West Ridge. Without serious problems they passed quickly through this constant avalanche hazard, which Roch named Suicide Passage. On cresting the lip of the Icefall they found a crevasse completely barring their way from one side of the Western Cwm to the other, as happened to the Shipton party the year before. They made a rope bridge, called a Tyrolean traverse, and thereby carried their stores and equipment across. Then they descended to their base, happy at having opened up a door into the Cwm, like walking through the cupboard to Narnia.

That same day avalanches swept Suicide Passage, both before and after a group of laden porters passed by, but the climbers decided to stick to that route as the quickest way through the Icefall. Now they hurried to place camps at the head of the Cwm, and at the foot of what they named the Geneva Spur. They managed to pitch two tents on the South Col, where the winds were so violent that Lambert spent the night anchored to his ice axe driven into the snow. Because of the danger of being blown away, Tenzing brewed tea still roped up.

Next day Lambert and Tenzing continued climbing to 27,550 feet, where they camped in a small tent without sleeping bags, mattresses or stove. Their only drink came from snow melted over a candle. 'We had a little food,' said Lambert, 'and we had the cold.' While climbing above 23,000 feet, their closed-circuit oxygen system, which was a converted miner's breathing apparatus using a rigid mouthpiece, did not function because their own breathing could not overcome the stiff resistance of the valves. They could use oxygen only at rest, yet they still had to carry the extra weight of the cylinders, which increased their demand for the precious gas.

In the morning Lambert and Tenzing left their camp and climbed through deep snow in worsening weather up a slope of moderate angle until they reached the rocks under the final pyramid at 28,215 feet. This was probably higher than any man had been before (unless Mallory and Irvine had reached the top in 1924). But they were utterly exhausted, so turned round and descended. A second assault party got no higher than the South Col, where they remained for three days before being forced back by hurricane winds and extreme cold. Wyss-Dunant decided to pull everyone off the mountain which, for the next two weeks, enjoyed calm, settled weather.

The Swiss had encountered several major problems; they had come to the mountain too early to take advantage of the pre-monsoon lull in the weather, they had gained little help from their closed-circuit oxygen apparatus, the route up the Geneva Spur was too long and tiring without intermediate camps, their top camp was placed too low for a final assault, and they had engaged too few Sherpa porters to allow for sickness and disability.

The Himalayan Committee invited Shipton to lead a training expedition to nearby Cho Oyu during the Swiss spring attempt. It was an anxious time for those climbers who had already staked a claim in the Icefall the previous year. Hillary summarised his feelings in *High Adventure*, 'I think for the first time I was really admitting to myself quite honestly, that I didn't want the Swiss to climb Everest. Let them get very high – good luck to them in that but not to the summit! I wanted it left for a British party to have a crack at next year.'

Shipton had to muster a strong team that would be the nucleus of a British attempt in 1953, supposing – hopefully – the Swiss would fail in theirs. Not only had he to find good technical ice climbers (who were fairly scarce in the post-war period), but also men who would perform well at altitude. Few had experience of very high mountains, apart from the group who had been with him in 1951, and they were the core of the present party.

During the Cho Oyu expedition Shipton said to Evans and Gregory, 'I don't know anything at all about climbers in this country, so you'd better be the selection committee. Choose a team, take them to the Alps and see how they perform.' Those men were: John Jackson, Jack Tucker, Tony Streather and Michael Ward.

Besides selecting a team, the oxygen problem had to be worked out, and in 1952 the British certainly were not prepared on that score for a serious attempt on Everest; as it turned out, neither were the Swiss. Scientists at the Medical Research Council, under the direction of Griffith Pugh and Tom Bourdillon, together with Peter Lloyd and others at the RAF Institute of Aviation Medicine at Farnborough, got busy to devise the best oxygen delivery system they could – both open- and closed-circuit. It had to be light enough to balance the benefits of oxygen against the weight of the apparatus, a problem which was never solved in the 'thirties. However, they now had the advantage of improved technology and of lightweight alloys developed during the war.

Shipton proposed to the Himalayan Committee four aims for the Cho Oyu expedition: first, to choose a nucleus of men who could climb at, and acclimatise to, great heights; second, to study fluid needs and altitude deterioration scientifically; third, to experiment with oxygen systems that could be relied on to overcome the problems of high altitude; fourth, to test clothing and equipment for use in extremes of cold and wind. They had only six weeks to prepare for such an ambitious programme. With little money available, apart from the residue from the reconnaissance expedition funds, and an advance from *The Times* for dispatches to be sent from Nepal, the expedition had of necessity to be both economical and simple. But being lightly equipped and frugally provisioned was Shipton's style, so he was not bothered by its simplicity. As Hillary put it, 'Eric was not a great one for planning ahead.'

Cho Oyu, at 26,870 feet, lies twenty miles due west of Everest and, like it, straddles Nepal's border with Tibet. Shipton's and Ward's fleeting glimpse of the mountain a year before, when they were exploring in the Bhote Kosi area, had shown a possible route up the south side. It seemed a good peak for the expedition to try because, being near Everest, the weather systems would be similar. The party consisted of ten climbers who all had the right qualifications. 'A party of ten in the Himalaya,' wrote Shipton in the *Geographical Journal*, 'is grossly unwieldy and inconvenient, and I was somewhat appalled at the prospect.' Hillary, Riddiford and Bourdillon had been with him recently on the reconnaissance; Campbell Secord was of that original party but had had to drop out at the last minute; Charles Evans, a Liverpool neuro-surgeon, had proved his ability in the high thin air on Annapurna IV with Tilman in 1950; George Lowe, Hillary's climbing partner in Garhwal, was a strong New Zealand ice man; Alfred Gregory and Ray Colledge were two Lake District climbers with wide guiding experience in the Alps. With these men Shipton had the makings of a strong climbing team.

Griffith Pugh, a physiologist at the Medical Research Council laboratories, was included rather casually by Shipton, who had met him once before in Persia in 1944. Shipton never really told the other members of the expedition about the intended physiological research, needle jabs, breathing tubes and all, to which they would have to submit. Ward had stretched the goodwill of the army the year before, and the RAMC would not give him leave a second time in six months to go on a climbing jaunt. Murray was not included because of his poor performance at altitude, and his meagre technical skill on glacier ice.

On one of Shipton's visits to Zurich to show the Swiss his photos of Everest, he had promised them to take a different route to Solu Khumbu, and to arrive in Namche Bazar after them, so as not to compete for porters. At Jaynagar, Shipton hired an elephant and some buffalo wagons to carry some of their gear across the Terai. The march was much more pleasant and trouble-free than the year before, although several of the Europeans got sick from drinking unboiled water, made necessary by becoming separated for a day from their porters (and the elephant) who travelled up the opposite side of the river. They climbed into the hills towards Okhaldunga, and then on to the Dudh Kosi Valley which led them to Namche Bazar.

Cho Oyu was an ideal peak for a trial run for the 1953 Everest aspirants. They pitched their base camp at Lunak at the head of the Bhote Kosi, and quickly got busy. Evans and Gregory climbed a ridge running down from Cho Oyu, and reported that the projected route up the South Face was too steep and too long. This was a serious blow, but Hillary and Lowe climbed two 21,000 foot peaks from where they could see a good route up the north side of the mountain in Tibet.

The most promising approach from the north was up the Kyetrak Glacier, which lay across the Nangpa La, the main trading pass leading into Tibet. This border question immediately posed problems for Shipton, who had great reservations about trespassing into Tibet for fear of creating an incident between China and Nepal that might jeopardise a British expedition's chances of Everest in 1953. The Sherpas told him that the Chinese had already moved a garrison into Tingri, a town you would eventually reach by keeping on walking down the Kyetrak Glacier. Besides which, Shipton knew that if they were picked up by the Chinese they would be imprisoned as spies, himself especially after his consulship in Kunming, while his reconnaissance party's close call in the Rongshar the year before was a discouraging memory. These doubts caused the climbers to sit around camp endlessly discussing the border crossing question, which made for a bad start because they all became unsettled and at odds with each other. Shipton and Bourdillon were strongly against crossing into Tibet; Hillary felt that Chinese soldiers would hardly be patrolling above 17,000 feet, and anyway he could outrun them; Riddiford was irritated by what he perceived as Shipton's vacillation.

However, they came to a compromise. A small group of four climbers – Hillary, Lowe, Evans and Bourdillon – would set their advanced camp on the Nepalese side of the border and make a reconnaissance across the Nangpa La. They would place no camps on the Kyetrak Glacier, but would set one camp high on the mountain. In the event they pitched a camp at 21,000 feet on the North-West Ridge of Cho Oyu, from where Hillary and Lowe planned to have a look at the summit. But nothing seemed to be in the expedition's favour; several of the climbers were sick, bad weather harassed them, their food was unappetising, and climbing was not of prime importance.

At about 22,500 feet Hillary and Lowe emerged under a series of ice cliffs stretching right across the face and surmounted by fractured ice fingers. As Hillary wrote in the *New Zealand Alpine Journal*, 'Unless we were prepared to take the risk of cutting steps on steep ice for several hours underneath the active cliffs above we could go no further. We had therefore no hesitation in declaring the route quite unjustifiable.' This version of events varies considerably from his account in *Nothing Venture, Nothing Win*, 'I ended up cutting some steps towards it with half the party shouting out not to be a fool but to come down. So down I went; we seemed to have lost the spirit to attempt such a place.

Afterwards I had a terrible sense of shame that we had given up so easily.'

The above paragraph is important because much of the ammunition for Shipton's later axing was based on the 'failure' to climb Cho Oyu. It is also conveniently forgotten that the *ascent* of Cho Oyu was not itself the prime objective of the expedition, which, as Charles Evans wrote in the *Alpine Journal*, was 'mainly a trial of men and materials for a British Everest expedition in 1953'. In an interview with *Mountain Magazine* several years later, Ed Hillary referred to the Cho Oyu expedition as 'one of the biggest cock-ups of all time', which was a bit hard on his leader.

While the climbers were on Cho Oyu, at base camp Riddiford, who was not acclimatising well and was suffering from sciatica, had a confrontation with Shipton. As a barrister, Riddiford was used to arguing but he became irritated by the perpetual discourses of Shipton, who used them as a way of talking himself through a problem. As George Lowe said, 'If someone argued white, Eric would argue black in order to see what would come out of it, and the game itself sometimes became more important than the question. If you didn't understand that, you could quickly become frustrated, as did Earle, falling for the bait of this sort of mental ping-pong every time, and interpreting it as Shipton dilly-dallying.'

Likewise, on the walk in Shipton had entered into a lengthy debate with Cam Secord on the future of the Alpine Club, along the lines of, 'Should the AC be perpetuated? I think we should let it die.' Secord got caught up in this argument, and for several frustrating days tangled with Shipton who would repeatedly swap sides as soon as he appeared to be winning, just for the fun of it and to keep the debate going. For the others this sort of dialectic was harmless and had the advantage of taking their mind off the travails of marching.

But according to Lowe, Secord, an ex-bomber pilot, saw Shipton as 'this to-be-or-not-to-be, Hamlet-like character holding the skull', and would say, 'This is no bloody good, Eric. You can't fly an airplane by having a debate.' Hillary, on the other hand, as Lowe continued, 'was good at cutting through the bullshit on the important questions. He would say, "Hey, Eric, stop buggering about. As leader what do you think we should do?" If Hillary suggested going off to look at some peak or other, Shipton would reply, "Good idea, Ed. Get on with it."'

Shipton once told Lowe, 'One part of me wants to climb Everest but another part doesn't. Somehow I'd prefer not to sully the top, but to leave it untouched.' Lowe could see this poetic side of Shipton's character, and yet he knew his driving side. 'When Eric saw somebody like Riddiford who was 90% drive and 10% poetry he was left with the terrible thought that perhaps those were the people who were going to inherit the world.'

Riddiford was not so accommodating or compliant. He went round each of the two-man tents trying to drum up support to cross the Nangpa La and to hell with Eric Shipton. But none of Riddiford's colleagues responded to this hint of mutiny, and next day he walked off down the valley complaining of his sore back. This was a real challenge to the leadership of Shipton, who responded in his magnanimous way, 'Maybe Earle is the sort of chap we want to climb Everest – so determined, dedicated, thrusting, bloody-minded.' But Riddiford had reached an impasse, and withdrew from the expedition.

The party now split into three self-contained units. Shipton, Gregory and Evans went up the Bhote Kosi, hoping to explore the complicated knot of country at its head and to find another pass into the Menlung basin. Not succeeding in this, they crossed the Tashi Labtsa and turned immediately north into the Tolam Bau, a narrow-walled basin at the head of which they found an ice plateau that was the hub of the geography of the region. Pugh, along with Bourdillon, Secord and Colledge, set a physiology research camp on the Menlung La at 20,000 feet, intending to test flow rates of oxygen required by the open- and closed-circuit systems so as to increase climbing rates at extreme altitude.

Michael Ward still feels that basically Shipton's heart was never in the *science* of climbing Mount Everest, and that he neither understood science nor trusted scientists, although he regarded them as an evil necessity both for funding and for high climbing. He felt that taking a non-climbing physiologist on an expedition just meant another mouth to feed and someone who might also become a liability in the mountains (in fact, Pugh was neither). 'A physiological expedition to Meade's Col on Kamet, by all means,' Shipton said, 'but not to Everest. Everest is a job of its own.'

Moreover, Ward thinks too that in 1953 John Hunt did not want to understand the science because it conflicted with his religious views of Everest. On the mountain he disagreed with the medical team, especially about the importance of placing an intermediate camp between the South Col and the top which could act as a safe haven for the first assault party of Evans and Bourdillon for their summit attempt (and was a considerable help to the second party of Hillary and Tenzing). In his book *The Ascent of Everest*, Hunt condescends, 'At the very least it could be said that the inclusion of a physiologist was justified as an insurance against failure.' But understanding the science of living and working at high altitude (defined as heights above 8,000 feet, or 2,500 metres) is vital to understanding the whole saga of attempts to climb Everest, which were so often foiled by lack of knowledge of the physiology of oxygen at high altitude, a recurring quandary for the pre-war expeditions.

Pugh was a medical doctor first; later he became a research scientist at the Medical Research Council's Division of Human Physiology, studying the effects of extreme environments on man. In his Oxford University days Pugh climbed in the Alps, and became an Olympic class downhill and cross-country skier. During the Second World War he instructed at the Mountain Warfare Training Centre in the Lebanon, and did research on selecting mountain troops, fitness tests, load-carrying and nutrition. After the war he concentrated his formidable energy and brain power on physiological research. So Pugh was the obvious person to head the scientific team of the Cho Oyu expedition. He was a man of strong and outspoken opinion. Hillary was once on the receiving end of a Pugh tongue-lashing, which he likened to God summing up on Judgment Day, and remembers being present on separate occasions when both Shipton and, later, Hunt suffered the same treatment. Pugh believed in pragmatic science with research done out in the field far from the comfort and convenience of a laboratory. But he strongly believed that researchers themselves must be as physically and technically competent as those guinea pigs they were testing, and also be prepared to undergo all the tests themselves. So he always insisted on being part of the team.

At a physiology camp set up just below the Menlung La, Pugh exercised his subjects, Bourdillon, Secord and Colledge on a prepared track with a gradient rising 350 feet, and under identical climatic conditions.

He confirmed many already established facts. Acclimatisation proceeds at different rates in different people. Some are never troubled by altitude, provided they ascend slowly enough, while others for no obvious physical reason never acclimatise properly, however long they remain high, even at relatively low altitudes. Others, like Shipton, who have done well at altitude before are likely to do well again. After about three months at very high altitude, say above 20,000 feet, the physical condition of the climbers steadily deteriorates and they sleep and work poorly, and lose appetite and weight. Retreat to the valleys for a long holiday is the only solution.

In the 'twenties and 'thirties George Finch predominantly advocated using supplementary oxygen on Everest through an open system, where bottled oxygen enriches the air the climber breathes. He dismissed the closed system of rebreathing the oxygen after extracting the carbon dioxide residue with soda lime as 'only of use in enabling budding medicos and postgraduate students to tell us how well up they are in text book chemistry'. Finch's question – do the advantages of oxygen counterbalance the disadvantages of the extra weight and equipment? – was fundamental to Pugh's enquiries on the Menlung La. In 1924 Norton had described dramatically the misery of climbing without supplemental oxygen at 28,000 feet, 'Our pace was wretched. My ambition was to do twenty consecutive paces uphill without a pause, to rest and pant, elbow on bended knee; yet I never remember achieving it – thirteen was nearer the mark. Every five to ten minutes we had to sit down for a minute or two; we must have looked a sorry couple.' Pugh, in a *Geographical Journal* supplement, likened this situation to 'a runner doing 100 yard sprints indefinitely for six hours at a stretch – a feat no athlete could endure at sea level, let alone at high altitude.'

Pugh showed emphatically that, using the open-circuit apparatus, a flow rate of four litres per minute was necessary to boost a climber's performance, whereas the pre-war expeditions, and the Swiss in 1952, had all used flow rates of two litres per minute. This four litre flow of oxygen would effectively lower the climbers' altitude by several thousand feet, compensating for the weight of the oxygen apparatus, and increasing their rate of climb, but some acclimatisation would still be essential. The trouble with the open-circuit system is that nine-tenths of the oxygen is wasted, whereas in a closed-circuit the balance is reused. But the open-circuit is virtually fail-safe, whereas a closed-circuit depends on valves, a well-fitting mask, and soda lime to remove carbon dioxide – all of which are potential causes of trouble. Pugh also showed that using oxygen at night allowed people to sleep better and to feel less fatigued next day, as Finch had shown in 1922 on Everest. He later compared the performance of the Swiss on Everest with the British on Cho Oyu, and reckoned the Swiss were fitter and better acclimatised, but the valves of their oxygen system failed. Also they allowed themselves to become debilitated by being severely dehydrated through not drinking enough.

Pugh's rules for the use of supplemental oxygen with an open-circuit were: four litres per minute on ascent, two litres per minute on descent, and one litre per minute during sleep. The added oxygen reduces the need to overbreathe in order to extract enough oxygen from the oxygen-depleted air on high. Also, at 28,000 feet, so much body heat is lost from the lungs that oxygen helps to maintain the body temperature, which is in extreme jeopardy at −40°C. Pugh's other physiological work on the Menlung La showed that climbers need at least 3,000 calories per day of high carbohydrate food (a surprisingly low estimate considering Amundsen catered for 4,500 calories as a sledging ration to the South Pole), and to drink three litres of fluid per day to avoid dehydration. He also tested clothing, boots, gloves, tents and stoves.

So even if the climbing part of the Cho Oyu expedition was no great success – in fact 'a balls-up' as Alf Gregory described it – the scientific results were of great moment. Michael Ward says adamantly, 'If Pugh had *not* done his work in 1951 at the Medical Research Council, and in 1952 on the Menlung La, we would *not* have climbed Everest in 1953. Pugh was the only indispensable person in that party. We'd still have got up Everest, even with Eric Shipton, because the physiology was right.'

Pugh felt quite bitterly towards Shipton's lack of interest in his programme, which was specifically designed to help get climbers to the summit of Everest, and also about the expedition's sloppy attitude to basic sanitation, to which he attributed the high rate of bowel upsets and chest infections. On his return to England he gave a scathing report to the Himalayan Committee – one of several nails in Shipton's 1953 leadership coffin.

Hillary and Lowe were very discouraged by their party's frustrations on Cho Oyu. After all, this was the élite group from which next year's team would be chosen, and a much lesser mountain than Everest had turned them back. Shipton, realising their discontent, agreed that they should go off by themselves to try circumnavigating the Everest massif, a plan they had formulated on the approach march. He had stuck to his principles about not aggravating the Chinese by crossing the border to climb Cho Oyu, and yet here he was letting two Kiwis – Brits as far as the Chinese would be concerned – scamper into Tibet to within sight of Rongbuk Monastery, which the Sherpas knew was occupied by Chinese troops. But this little sortie by two very fit climbers, at a height no soldiers ever went, was quite different from allowing a team of ten to cross the Nangpa La trade route, as Riddiford had urged. Could it be that for Shipton anything in exploration was fair game, whereas just climbing mountains had restraints?

Anyway, Hillary and Lowe set off towards the foot of the Nup La, the pass between Gyachung Kang and Pumori on the further side of which lay the West Rongbuk Glacier. Hillary, the assured climbing leader among them, was supremely confident of his own strength and ability. Lowe, the garrulous natural jester, was strong and lithe and deft with an ice axe, despite a left elbow deformed and weakened by a fracture when a boy. The previous year Bourdillon, Ward, Riddiford and Murray had tried to climb the Nup La. Murray described it in *The Story of Everest* as 'a formidable icefall, a tottering mass of séracs, which were big and broad and grew as thick as trees in a forest, and cliffs, every ledge between being piled with débris.' They only made it halfway to the top of the pass.

Hillary and Lowe explored every approach, finally battling for four days up an icefall lying further to the north. Eventually they crested the Nup La and, leaving all but essential gear, they raced down the West Rongbuk Glacier carrying heavy loads. Being exceptionally fit, they galloped round to the East Rongbuk Glacier catching a glimpse of Rongbuk Monastery ten miles away. They tried, and failed (having left their crampons on the Nup La to save weight), to climb Changtse, towering over Everest's North Col, which Shipton had attempted twice before the war.

This carefree, exciting jaunt cheered them, and Hillary said, 'I felt I could now shrug off my feelings about Cho Oyu.' With a Herculean push they recrossed the Nup La in thick monsoon snow and made a scary descent of the glacier with avalanches thundering around them. Wishing to find out how the Swiss had fared, they crossed towards Everest base camp, which they found deserted. They met a Tibetan man on the way and asked him about the Swiss; unable to speak their language he placed his hand on his shoulder, then pointed to his head and shook it, indicating a negative. They raced on down the valley where they met Shipton and Evans, who also had heard the news of the Swiss failure, heroic though it was.

First, Shipton sent a message (drafted by Bourdillon and representing the views of all the party) from Tengboche to the Himalayan Committee saying they should go ahead with plans for Everest in 1953. This 'Tengboche document' urged speedy action for next year's expedition, a drastic overhaul of the whole overly amateur organisation, the need for a full time secretary, better training, and the importance of the oxygen work. Then Shipton sat down and wrote a 2,000 word dispatch for *The Times*.

But to the east the Barun Valley beckoned Shipton with its unexplored glaciers flowing down from Makalu. He invited Hillary and Lowe to join Charles Evans and himself on a trip, departing the next day. The Kiwis had sent all their gear down the valley, so they had practically no clothes and only a tossed-together heap of food to embark on a fairly major exploration. But they reckoned it would be worth it. So the Cho Oyu expedition members went their separate ways. Pugh, Gregory, Secord and Bourdillon returned to Britain; Colledge to New Zealand, whither Riddiford had already departed.

This was a milestone for Eric Shipton, a crossroads where he took the wrong turn because the desire to go another step further over passes to the east with a bunch of his closest friends was too strong to resist. He knew in his head that he should have hurried home to England to begin the multitude of preparations that another British Everest expedition would entail; but his heart prevailed.

A holiday air pervaded the small group as it headed east into the Hongu over the Ambu Labtsa, a pass Shipton and Hillary had crossed the previous year. 'With the cares of a large expedition off his shoulders,' wrote Hillary, 'Shipton was a new man and revelled in the type of expedition in which he excelled.' Evans had gone on ahead and crossed

into the Barun Valley, where he found yaks grazing, indicating that there must be a way down the valley, which dropped from 17,000 to 4,000 feet in twenty-five miles, suggesting a deep gorge ahead. Having hauled double loads of food over the Ambu Labtsa, enough to last three weeks, Shipton, Hillary and Lowe met Evans beside one of the five lakes, Panch Pokhari, in the Hongu basin. Then they all crossed a pass to the Barun Glacier, climbing three peaks of over 21,000 feet on the way, and camped below the huge western face of Makalu.

They had stopped discussing who would be in the party to climb Everest the next year, a common topic up till then. They just presumed it would be the four of them together with Bourdillon and Gregory. But Shipton was growing uneasy about his decision to wander off into virgin country at this critical time, and he started one of his tortuous debates, positing the question – should he go on or go back?

'It's too bloody late, Eric,' pragmatic Hillary replied, 'you can't go back on your own.' And that settled the matter for the moment, but not for long.

Lowe recounted how Shipton used the loads they had been hauling to debate the whole question of lightweight versus heavyweight expeditions. Six people would be perfect; eight or ten was too big. But what happens if someone falls sick? And so round and round they went, even getting into a heated discussion about the possibility of having oxygen in pills rather than bottles.

Charles Evans, the strong, quiet one, the wise surgeon, also espoused Shipton's philosophy of just travelling with one Sherpa and picking up food along the way. He had become specially close to Shipton and from Namche wrote in a letter to a friend, 'Eric I like more and more. He is a small party man alright, rather vague & doesn't give much for all this complex arrangement and large organization. I'd like a trip alone with him.' Shipton in turn admired Evans's efficient, modest qualities. These were summed up a year later by Wilfrid Noyce in *South Col*, 'Of all the friends I have, he is the one to whom I would least like to tell a lie. Thus he is one with whom humbug, sham and false sentiment receive shortest shrift.' Evans sympathised with Shipton and took a silent, amused view of his dilemma. Hillary and Lowe laughed at the whole debate, and thought Shipton was really saying, 'I don't want to lead a great heavyweight expedition to Everest – and yet I do want to lead it.'

As Lowe recounts, Shipton awoke one night restless with self-doubt. He got up and poured all the grape-nuts, of which, being a fad of his, they had a surfeit, from round five-pound tins into one huge flour sack. 'It's utterly ridiculous carrying all these tins,' he raved almost berserk as he piled them in a great heap, 'I've made my chorten now; it's an obeisance to the gods.' The Sherpas grabbed the sack of grape-nuts and tied it to the load of a porter who was carrying the paraffin; so for the rest of the trip they had a mélange of grape-nuts in paraffin.

They all walked up towards the head of the glacier, and camped under Pethangtse, which they hoped to climb. From a saddle on the Tibetan watershed they looked over the Kangshung Glacier under Everest's colossal East Face, which Howard-Bury had reached from the north side in 1921 on the very first British expedition. Then the weather broke, as did the monsoon, covering all with a thick mantle of snow.

They descended to a yak pasture where grew carpets of azaleas, primulas and cowslips. There they saw two men roofing a hut, so

Shipton told the Sherpas to go ahead and explain to the men about these bearded, scrawny giants – just like yeti – who had descended out of the mountains. But the Sherpas, unable to contain their ever-present fancy for a joke, rushed down the hill uttering catcalls and piercing whistles. The terrified men fled in panic down the valley at such speed that none of the climbers could head them off. Shipton was furious with the Sherpas for their brutish behaviour because he thought it might spread alarm further down the valley where they hoped to find a guide to take them through the gorge.

Nearly out of food, the Sherpas climbed some trees to gather fungi. Then they met a man who, after a day and a half of cajoling, reluctantly sold them a scrawny old ram. They devoured the tough meat, which bucked them up no end. Then they entered dense rhododendron, fir, and birch forest and from then on, as George Lowe put it, 'Eric got fire up his arse, as though the furies had started to chase him.' He drove and drove, day after day, walking for longer and longer days in order to get out to the railhead.

'What's the hurry, Eric?' asked Hillary. 'You don't like civilised living anyway.'

But Shipton was by now convinced he had made the wrong decision, though he covered it by bemoaning his lot.

'What have I got to go back to?' he bleated. 'Nobody wants me. I've got no job; you've got professions. When I go to a cocktail party a woman says to me, "How nice to see you Mr Shipton, and when are you leaving on your next expedition?"'

Hillary and Lowe were concerned because he became quite depressed for two or three days. One said to the other, 'Poor Eric; is the old bugger breaking down?' Shipton appeared to be appealing to them to prop him up and in need of mothering, despite being over a decade older than both of them. But after a few days his spirits perked up.

Charles Evans, intrepid as ever, parted from them at a log bridge in the Arun Valley and headed east with two Sherpas across the Lumba Sumba Himal towards Taplejung, and thence to Darjeeling. 'Unfortunately, none of the other three of us was able to spare the time to accompany him on this interesting journey,' Shipton wrote in the *Geographical Journal*. 'I was under some obligation to return as soon as possible to assist with the preparations for the 1953 Everest expedition.'

The other three hammered on down the Arun Valley, buying chickens and rice as they went. After three days Hillary and Lowe fashioned
a couple of driftwood paddles and made a raft of their air mattresses
lashed together with staves in order to float down the river and thereby
avoid some of the tedium of the march. Early next morning Shipton
continued on the trail above the river, while the Kiwis launched their
frail craft. Shortly they heard the roar of rapids, which became ever
more deafening as the water ahead dipped out of sight.

'Stick to the raft no matter what happens,' shouted Hillary, as he
recounted in the *New Zealand Alpine Journal.* 'Hang on! Here we go!'

The river washed them towards a 200 foot high cliff, which jutted out
like the prow of a ship. This created a great standing wave, which cush-
ioned the raft against the cliff and then sucked it back into the vortex.
Round and round they went in a huge whirlpool full of circulating
flotsam. After six revolutions Hillary yelled to Lowe, 'Obviously we can't
go on like this forever. How long can we last on a bar of chocolate?'

Watching from above, Shipton realised that the British Everest
expedition itself was in grave danger of having a couple of vacancies
for star performers. He slid down a shallow gulley on the end of a
climbing rope secured by the Sherpas above. From the ledge he threw
a second rope, which Lowe caught and hauled himself and Hillary onto
a wet bank into which they dug their fingers and scrambled out.
Undeterred by this narrow escape from the whirlpool, they launched
the raft again and floated on until a series of cataracts halted their
passage.

In less than a week, the three of them, together with the Sherpas, all
filthy, and wearing tattered mountain clothes and heavy climbing boots,
reached Jogbani railhead in the middle of the night. The stationmaster,
thinking they were a bunch of dacoits, told them there were no seats
available. They got aboard, however, and once the train departed they
tried to get into a 2nd class carriage to avoid having to sleep on the floor.
Shipton knocked on the carriage door, but there was no response
because the door was locked from the inside to prevent bandits getting
in.

At this point he lost his temper and kicked the door open. As Hillary
recounted, 'Eric was a very peaceful man but he occasionally had these
violent outbursts of anger.' Lowe was astonished at the change in their

friend and leader who, a week before, could not make up his mind about anything. They all piled inside and found a terrified group of Indian travellers who had to put up with the smell of them for the rest of the journey. Once settled into the compartment they ate 160 bananas and countless mangoes within twenty-four hours – with the inevitable consequences.

On return to Kathmandu the Swiss immediately sought permission to try Everest again in the autumn of 1952. The Nepalese Government consulted of the British, who consented provided the autumn expedition had the same personnel as in the spring. Tony Hagen, a much respected Swiss working for the International Red Cross, described how the British Ambassador, Sir Christopher Summerhayes, came to his office quite upset by an article in the *Times of India* naming the participants of the Swiss autumn team, which comprised only two European members of the spring expedition – the new leader Dr Gabriel Chevalley and Raymond Lambert – the other five being new. Summerhayes asked Hagen to intervene with the Swiss to prevent this clear breach of a gentleman's agreement, but the latter was diplomatically not in a position to do so, and the expedition went ahead.

From the start nothing went well for the second Swiss attempt. The weather was so bad during the approach march that two porters died of hypothermia. Chevalley fell ill and seemed to lose impetus as leader, which torpedoed morale. The Icefall was in better condition and they had carried tree trunks for bridging crevasses, an innovation that, with aluminium ladders, has been successfully used ever since. They abandoned the closed-circuit oxygen system in favour of the more reliable open-circuit, but for that they needed many more gas bottles. Because of Tenzing's sterling performance in the spring, they invited him, besides being sirdar, to join the climbing team. Once on the Lhotse Face, a freak block of ice fell from a serac into the couloir below the Geneva Spur killing Mingma Dorje, a Sherpa tiger, and dislodging a rope of three Sherpas who fell 600 feet into the basin with only minor injury. The climbers carried on to just above the South Col, but a freezing gale turned them back. This time they were a couple of weeks too late to catch the lull at the end of the monsoon. The Swiss had taken their two chances on Everest in 1952 and failed. Now it was the turn of the British.

By way of preparation for this the Cho Oyu expedition had been both unsuccessful and controversial, which probably accounts for the fact that Shipton allocates only half a page to it in his autobiography.

CHAPTER 14

Thruster John
The Everest Leadership Crisis, 1952–53

Wʜɪʟᴇ ᴛʜᴇ ǫᴜᴀʀᴛᴇᴛ of Shipton, Evans, Hillary and Lowe were exploring the Barun Glacier in East Nepal, back in London Campbell Secord
wrote to the Himalayan Committee complaining about Shipton's leadership of the Cho Oyu expedition; Riddiford and Pugh expressed
similar sentiments. As a result, during July, August and September of
1952, debate over the leadership of the forthcoming 1953 Everest
expedition pervaded the halls of the Royal Geographical Society and
the Alpine Club, flowed from the pens and buzzed down the telephone
wires of the various people involved.

The Himalayan Committee chairman in 1952 was Claude Elliott,
President of the Alpine Club, a modest alpinist, Provost of Eton
College and an unassuming man with a shy, hesitant manner. For the
RGS was the Director, Larry Kirwan; Claremont Skrine, an old Central
Asia hand and former Consul-General in Kashgar (two decades before
Eric Shipton); Donald George Lowndes, an ex-colonel in the Royal

Garhwal Rifles and a Himalayan plant hunter with Tilman around Annapurna in 1950; and James Wordie, a notable polar explorer and President of the RGS. For the Alpine Club there was the Honorary Secretary, Basil Goodfellow, a seasoned administrator, and a senior executive in Imperial Chemical Industries; Harry Tobin, a colonel in the Bombay Pioneers, co-founder of the Himalayan Club, and twice transport officer for Bavarian attempts on Kangchenjunga. The AC youngsters were pre-war Everesters Lawrence Wager and Peter Lloyd. Tom Blakeney officially recorded the minutes as the salaried Assistant Secretary of the Alpine Club (where the meetings of the Himalayan Committee took place).

In the middle of 1952 the situation concerning Everest was critical. The Swiss had failed in May, and the Britons waited hoping they would get no higher in the autumn. The Royal Nepal Government had given permits to the British for 1953, to the French for 1954, and to the Swiss again for 1955. With a young Queen awaiting her coronation, Britain hoped to usher in a New Elizabethan Age with a success on Everest.

Responding to Secord's letter of complaint, on 4 July 1952 the Himalayan Committee invited a report from Secord, Gregory and Pugh; Riddiford, possibly the most vocal malcontent, was in New Zealand. They claimed that the organisation of the equipment was too haphazard, and that rife ill health and poor acclimatisation were due to lack of hygiene (although no one explained the causal relationship between the two). They recommended that climbers be barred from Sherpa houses, and Sherpa cooks be closely supervised. Pugh urged that priority be given to developing a closed-circuit oxygen system, and suggested a team shakedown in the Alps in January 1953, and in the Himalaya in March, when climbers should spend longer acclimatising above 15,000 feet.

On the main issue – the leadership of Shipton himself – they claimed he had shown 'inadequate drive' in failing to press the assault of Cho Oyu. The Himalayan Committee discussed possible alternatives to Shipton, 'if his own fitness made this necessary', but did not specify whether this referred to his fitness to lead, or his physical state (he had never been fitter in his life). So the Committee was allowing itself to be swayed to consider seeking a replacement for Shipton, without waiting for his return a couple of weeks thence to hear what he, or others in his

party, had to say about the Cho Oyu expedition. But it was on dangerous ground because Shipton had become something of a national
figure, his books were applauded, his lectures a sell-out, not to mention
that he was widely respected and admired for his mountaineering and
exploring skills, particularly by Evans, Bourdillon, Hillary and Lowe, the
acknowledged nucleus of the 1953 team.

Soldiers, Jimmy Roberts, Charles Wylie and John Hunt, featured high
on the Committee's list of seven possible alternative leaders because, as
recorded in the minutes, 'preference was expressed for military officers
on the grounds that they could most readily be released and could be
expected to have organising capacity.' Gurkha Officers Roberts and
Wylie, both experienced climbers, had been out of the country during,
and immediately after, the war. Hunt, a distinguished colonel in the 60th
Rifles, was almost unknown to British climbers, though he had ten
alpine seasons to his credit and two forays into the Himalaya, one in
1935 when he reached 24,500 feet on Peak 36 in the Karakoram, later
renamed Saltoro Kangri, and in 1937 when he climbed the south-west
summit of Nepal Peak (23,350 feet) on the western border of Sikkim,
after having been turned down for Everest 'on medical grounds' in
1936. But he was a friend of the Himalayan Committee's Honorary
Secretary, Basil Goodfellow, who considered him a 'terrific thruster'
after a recent busy alpine season together; indeed he was the only
member of the Committee to have met Hunt. Another contender was
Secord, who suggested himself as a possible leader, but no one took
serious notice because he was renowned for his laziness (Hillary
asserted that he never saw a rope on him during his whole time on Cho
Oyu).

Goodfellow expressed a general feeling of alarm over Everest.
'We've got this one chance, and if we don't get it right we've had it.
And dammit, it's our mountain.' So he wrote to his friend Hunt, serving
with the 1st British Corps in Germany, recounting the Himalayan
Committee's doubts about Shipton's organisational ability and commitment to the job of leader. Both Chairman Elliott and Goodfellow told
Hunt, apparently jumping the gun on the Committee, that they would
like him to become the organising secretary of the expedition, and to
go as a climbing member on the mountain. Later Elliott invited him to
be deputy leader to Shipton ('prematurely as it later transpired', Hunt

admits); Goodfellow, in a letter dated 10 July 1952, even held out considerable hope of Hunt becoming the actual leader. 'Most people feel a new leader is required and your name stands out.'

On 23 July, Hunt wrote to Goodfellow saying he would be overjoyed to grasp the chance to join, and perhaps lead, the expedition; and he thought the army would release him willingly. This led to frequent correspondence (shown by Elliott to Brocklebank, one of his Eton housemasters) from Hunt urging Goodfellow to give him an official answer so he could ask the army for leave of absence. Elliott was now concerned about what he saw as Hunt's pushiness, but conceded that perhaps a pushy man, a thruster, was what was needed to get up Everest. In his autobiography, *Life is Meeting*, Hunt wrote, 'I nearly jumped over the moon. I knew nothing of the background to this sudden change of fortune: of the difficult and devious discussions, and the vacillations of the Himalayan Committee which had led to this invitation. I doubt whether, if it had not been for our [his and Goodfellow's] climbs together that summer, I would have been asked in 1952 to go to Everest.'

On 28 July 1952, Shipton was invited to attend a hurriedly summoned meeting of the Himalayan Committee to give his account of the Cho Oyu expedition, and to discuss plans for the organisation of next year's venture. Present were Elliott, Skrine, Lowndes, Tobin, and Kirwan; Goodfellow and Lloyd were on holiday in the Alps (a strange absence when matters of 'national importance' were afoot); Shipton, Gregory and Pugh attended by invitation. Shipton noted later that none of the Himalayan Committee members present had been on Everest, or on any major high altitude Himalayan climbing expedition, and many were quite elderly.

On the agenda, after Shipton's report on the Cho Oyu expedition, was 'Leadership of the 1953 Everest Expedition'. In *That Untravelled World* Shipton wrote:

It was clear that the Committee assumed that I would lead the expedition. I had, however, given a good deal of thought to the matter, and felt it right to voice certain possible objections. Having been to Everest five times, I undoubtedly had a great deal more experience of the mountain and of climbing at extreme altitudes than anyone else [Frank Smythe had died in 1949]; also, in the past year I had been closely connected, practically and emotionally, with the new aspect of the venture. On the other hand, long involvement with an unsolved problem can easily produce rigidity of outlook, a slow response to new ideas, and it is often the case that a man with fewer inhibitions is better equipped to tackle it than one with greater experience. I had more reason than most to take a realistic view of the big element of luck involved, and this was not conducive to bounding optimism. Was it not time, perhaps, to hand over to a younger man with a fresh outlook? Moreover, Everest had become the focus of greatly inflated publicity and of keen international competition, and there were many who regarded success in the coming attempt to be of high national importance. My well-known dislike of large expeditions and my abhorrence of a competitive element in mountaineering might well seem out of place in the present situation.

The Himalayan Committee minutes of that meeting read:

After Mr Shipton had expressed his personal views concerning his own future concerning the Everest Expedition, he together with Mr Gregory and Dr Pugh left the meeting. The Committee then discussed the question of leadership together with the possibility of an alternative leader to Mr Shipton. The names of Hunt and Roberts were considered. After some discussion the Committee concluded that Shipton's presence on the expedition was very valuable as an overall leader, and considered that a leader of assault or deputy leader should be chosen for the final attack on the summit.

Shipton, on rejoining the meeting, accepted the Committee's 'unanimous view' that he should be leader of the expedition (which he already was), and also the suggestion of appointing a deputy leader (a term he preferred to assault leader), for which position he proposed Charles Evans. He also named climbers he wanted on his team – Hillary, Lowe, Ayres (New Zealand's unequalled ice climber and Hillary's mentor), Gregory and Bourdillon – stressing that they should be between twenty-five and thirty-five years old. The Committee concurred with Shipton's suggestions, despite their preconceived ideas of who should be his deputy. They decided to set up an oxygen sub-committee under Pugh and Bourdillon to get to work immediately on an oxygen system, the main source of failure of the Swiss.

So the 28 July meeting ended with a compromise that pleased no one. The Himalayan Committee retained Shipton as leader, agreed on some form of deputy (but no one was sure what or who), and for the moment there were no hurt feelings. This hotchpotch of a meeting, described by Blakeney as a 'disaster', resulted from the Committee not having the courage to come out and tell Shipton in plain terms that they wanted to have at hand an alternative leader. After the meeting Blakeney, the minute keeper, overheard Shipton remarking to Lowndes that 'it would take a fanatic to get up Everest'. Then Shipton disappeared off to Norway for a couple of weeks which, on top of his tardy return from Nepal, was a tactless move.

The day following the meeting, Chairman Claude Elliott wrote to Hunt telling him of the Himalayan Committee's decision to offer Shipton the leadership on the understanding that he had a deputy leader. 'It is, I think, on the cards (though here I speak beyond my brief and only for myself) that you may be asked to be organiser as well as a member of the climbing party.' The name of Evans, Shipton's pro-posed deputy, was not mentioned, despite the fact that he was a strong climber, a good organiser, got on well with the Sherpas, and understood the science of high altitude. No one seemed to realise that Hunt was merely three years younger than Shipton. On 7 August Elliott wrote to Kirwan, 'I hope that S. will invite Hunt and that H. will accept. I am more convinced that a thruster like him is needed, but as TGL [Longstaff] says, much would have to depend on Evans' tact.' Lowndes told Elliott that Longstaff was in favour of Hunt as leader, which swayed Elliott considerably, even though he himself did not like TGL. One of Shipton's most fervent friends and supporters, Tom Brocklebank, strongly disclaimed this view of Longstaff's position on the issue, and protested to Elliott in his study at Eton where they reviewed the correspondence on at least three occasions.

Kirwan replied to Elliott on 9 August, 'I am sure that we should have [Hunt] whether we get Wylie or not, but I am equally sure that the proper title and position would be as deputy leader instead of Evans. This would be justified on the grounds of his age and general experience. I am perfectly sure that Evans would fall in with this. Shipton's position as leader above Hunt is equally well justified by long experience of Everest itself (which Hunt has not) and by his more extensive experience generally.' In fact, at this time Evans withdrew his name because of commitments to his surgical work. Over the next few days the definition of the role of deputy leader, and various names for the job, were tossed around between Elliott, Kirwan, and Goodfellow.

Goodfellow, with the authority of the selection subcommittee, wrote on 12 August to Hunt, still in Germany, agreeing with the appointment of Shipton as leader, but offering Hunt the job of organising secretary (to start as soon as possible), and to be a member of the expedition. He asked Hunt to come over to meet Shipton, adding that Shipton was not yet ready to appoint Hunt as deputy leader. Lloyd also wrote to Hunt on the same day, saying he hoped he would take on Everest because he felt Shipton had been there too often and was sick of it. Kirwan added the only light-hearted comment in the whole of this episode. 'I've had to send a rude letter to Eric about the state of our photographic and survey equipment returned from Cho Oyu, packed with crampons.' Then he added, 'During the preparatory period doubtless we won't see Eric at all!'

On 22 August Hunt came over from Germany to meet Shipton at the RGS alone. Shipton regarded this as an interview for the job of organising secretary, not just a meeting to discuss deputy leadership, which was Hunt's belief. They studied photos of the Western Cwm and the Khumbu Icefall. Shipton said that in 1951 the left-hand side had looked much easier, but it was swept by avalanches from the West Shoulder of Everest; the right (Nuptse) side at least was safer from avalanches. He asked Hunt which way he would choose; Hunt replied to the effect that if he went to Everest he would take the bit between his teeth and follow the left-hand route.

About this meeting, Shipton wrote in *That Untravelled World,* 'We had a frank discussion, and John told me he did not feel able to accept the position unless he were made deputy leader. While I understood his point of view as a high-ranking Army officer, I could not, of course, agree to his terms, since I had already nominated Charles Evans as my deputy. Also, it was clear to both of us, and admitted, that our approach to the enterprise, both practical and temperamental, was so fundamentally different that we would not easily work together. We parted, however, on friendly terms.'

Hunt's *Life is Meeting* (which title itself holds some irony) records, 'It was a sadly disillusioning encounter. No doubt I was over-keen and showed it. As I saw it something more was at stake than simply climbing a mountain.' Unsaid were the words 'national prestige', a concept anathema to Shipton. Before returning to Germany in very low spirits, Hunt told Goodfellow at the Alpine Club that the meeting was a failure. This should have been no surprise to anyone considering the disparate personalities, backgrounds, and philosophies of Shipton and Hunt.

Meanwhile, strong opposition to Shipton was being organised by the Old Men – Tobin, Lowndes, Skrine and Wordie – who told Blakeney that Hunt should replace Shipton as leader. Wylie was now appointed as organising secretary, and began work at the RGS on 1 September under Shipton's direction, with the administrative assistance of Ann Debenham.

On the morning of 11 September 1952 the Himalayan Committee met again at the Alpine Club; present were Elliott, Wordie, Skrine, Lowndes, Tobin, Goodfellow, and Finch, standing in for an absent Lloyd to represent oxygen interests. The meeting was held at short notice and without any prior warning to Kirwan and Wager, both ardent Shiptonians, away on holiday. Shipton and Wylie attended by invitation.

According to Blakeney, the official recorder, the minutes written in the Minute Book of this momentous meeting differed significantly from those first drafted. In fact, he claimed, Claude Elliott had completely rewritten them so they represent poorly what was actually discussed. This information comes from Blakeney's memorandum written in 1967, of which Peter Lloyd said, 'The clearest record of what happened at these meetings, even though he was not in the inner councils, comes from Blakeney's record.' It is a meticulous, if somewhat personally interpreted, account of these historic events.

Item 2 on the agenda asked Shipton to produce written reports on the Cho Oyu expedition so the selection subcommittee could review members of the party for 1953. Item 3 was 'Everest 1953'. Shipton and Wylie were thereupon asked to wait in the ante-room, where the walls were hung with mountain paintings and memorabilia lay on the lintel of the fireplace. To pass the time they studied the portraits of ex-

Presidents of the Alpine Club hanging on the walls leading downstairs to the library. 'So we started by being kicked out,' said Wylie. 'I went to the meeting with no idea that John Hunt, or any others, had been, or were being, considered as leader.'

Each man on the Committee spoke his piece. Tobin opened with a salvo demanding a more forceful and dynamic person to organise and lead on the mountain, urging the case for Hunt with mutterings about 'responsibility to the Nation and Commonwealth'. Skrine agreed with Tobin about Shipton's 'lack of interest and drive', but thought his name might be useful, especially in dealings with the Sherpas. Lowndes recalled the 28 July meeting when Shipton expressed diffidence about being the right man to lead it, and his remark about needing to be a fanatic to get to the top. Wordie (according to Kirwan, 'a good friend but a bad enemy, much addicted to clandestine manoeuvres') pushed the case for Hunt saying he had always felt Shipton unsuited to be leader, but that he could be useful as an adviser. Finch urged having a leader with a strong grip on the party and rejected 'divided responsibility'; he agreed with Wordie about keeping Shipton on in an 'advisory capacity'. Lloyd made no bones about wanting Hunt with full powers throughout. Elliott wavered because he disliked revoking the decision reached by the Committee on 28 July, but accepted the current views that Hunt must be brought in as leader.

After long discussion they agreed to put the following proposition to Shipton: 'That the Himalayan Committee feel it is necessary to recognise that the Everest Expedition is of national importance and it is therefore necessary to strengthen the party by associating a man of dynamic personality, drive and enthusiasm with the leadership. They therefore propose that Shipton be co-leader with Hunt up to Base Camp, and Hunt be sole leader thence forward.'

The Committee voted unanimously in favour of Hunt. Then most of the members withdrew, leaving only Elliott, Goodfellow and Wordie to break the news to Shipton, thereby hoping to spare him embarrassment. Summoned back, Shipton listened to what they had to say, and then stated that he was not prepared to appoint Hunt as deputy leader, though he conceded that Hunt might become secretary-organiser, and a climbing member of the expedition. He felt that deputy leadership should be decided later, perhaps in the field. However, he said he was prepared to resign if the Committee thought it in the best interests of the expedition, but he could not remain in a party with Hunt as leader because of their conflicting philosophy and temperament.

After five minutes Shipton withdrew to join Wylie in the ante-room.

'What do you think of the offer of dual leadership?' he asked Wylie.

'It's ridiculous, you can't have two leaders,' Wylie replied, spontaneously reacting to, as he put it, 'this totally new idea'.

While Shipton was out of the room yet more discussion took place, leaving Elliott feeling very uncomfortable. The Committee agreed unanimously to accept Shipton's resignation and to offer the leadership to Hunt. After what seemed to Wylie 'an interminable time', Goodfellow appeared and recalled Shipton into the inner sanctum. Elliott maundered on about the leadership, so Shipton was unclear what he was getting at.

'Am I to understand that Hunt is to be offered the leadership?' Shipton eventually had to ask him.

'Yes,' Elliott replied.

Shipton took his leave; 'absolutely shattered', he returned with Wylie to the RGS at Kensington Gore. It dawned on him that a great deal of back-door diplomacy, of which he was totally unaware, must have taken place since the last meeting, and he could not follow the influences that had caused the Committee's turnabout. He went home and said tersely to Diana, 'I've been given the sack.' She was as upset as he was.

Jack Longland, who by chance was in the lobby of the Alpine Club that fateful day, met Claude Elliott, who said to him, 'That's the most awkward decision I've had to make in my whole life.' When the gentle Elliott returned to Eton, Tom Brocklebank remonstrated with him in the Provost's Lodge, and produced a letter from Tom Longstaff (who was out of active mountaineering politics by then) to Eric Shipton saying how much he regretted his having been turfed out, and how a rumour, that he (TGL) had a hand in it, was false.

On the very same day, 11 September, Hunt received a telegram from Elliott inviting him to lead the British Expedition to Mount Everest in the spring of 1953 – his moment in history.

Two weeks later, on 24 September, the Himalayan Committee reviewed the traumatic events of the previous meeting and dealt with several written protests. Tom Bourdillon, Lawrence Wager and Larry

Kirwan spoke in person, and conveyed feelings in favour of Shipton from Jack Longland, Charles Evans and other members of the 1951 and 1952 expeditions. They regretted the way the matter had been handled and were unwilling to endorse the Committee's decisions.

The Himalayan Committee, as a sop, invited Shipton to join them as an adviser. Shipton replied to Claude Elliott, politely refusing the offer, and saying that he regarded committees as having have only three functions: sponsorship for gaining political permission, the appointment of the leader, and handling of funds. 'Of all other matters, emphatically the choice of personnel, I believe the leader should take complete charge.'

Hillary expressed the view that 'Everest without Shipton won't be the same.' He was very touched by a letter from Shipton, shortly after his sacking, which read, 'Ed, I want you to give your full loyalty to John Hunt and to give him every assistance in making a success of the expedition.' However, most of them agreed that, since Hunt had now been offered and had accepted the leadership, the latest decision must stand. But Bourdillon wrote a letter asking to be released from the expedition, despite Shipton's urging him to stay.

Hunt arrived in England in early October to take charge of the expedition, with Wylie as organising secretary. He wrote in *Life Is Meeting*, 'Fortunately I had had no part in the process by which the painful decisions were made, but I felt very sorry indeed for Shipton. He took the blow to his pride with dignity and without fuss.'

In *That Untravelled World*, Shipton said:

The influences which caused the Committee's volte-face are still obscure. Assuming both the need and the desirability for a large heavily organised expedition, their ultimate decision was right. My taste for simplicity would certainly have influenced my conduct of the enterprise. Moreover, partly because of this disposition, I am neither an efficient organiser of complicated projects nor a good leader of cohorts. [The original MS reads – But it was a pity the Committee found it necessary to resort to subterfuge and clandestine lobbying to achieve their ends.] Even so, the chagrin I felt at my sudden dismissal [abdication in original MS] was a cathartic experience which did nothing to increase my self-esteem. I had often deplored the exaggerated publicity accorded to Everest expeditions and the consequent distortion of values. Yet, when it came to the point, I was far from pleased to withdraw from the despised lime-light; nor could I fool myself that it was only the manner of my rejection that I minded.

In November 1952, while the Swiss were mounting their second attempt Shipton wrote a letter to James Wordie, President of the RGS, summarising the whole sorry 1953 leadership affair:

Dunsbury,
Hillbrow,
Liss, Hants.

Dear President,

I would like to thank the Council of the Royal Geographical Society for their expression of regret that I will not be leading the Mount Everest Expedition next spring, conveyed to me by your letter of 28th October.

While I do not wish in any way to question the correctness of the Himalayan Committee's ultimate decision upon this question, it would, I believe, be wrong for me to pretend that I condone the manner in which the matter was handled.

It will be recalled that when the Himalayan Committee met on 28th. July, shortly after my return from India, to consider the plans for the 1953 Expedition, I asked the Committee not to assume that I would lead the Expedition merely because of my record. I urged, rather, that very careful consideration should be given to the question before a decision was reached; that my obvious qualifications, such as my unique experience of the problems of climbing at extreme altitudes, and of Mount Everest in particular, and the prestige which I enjoy among the Sherpas, should not be allowed to blind the Committee to possible potential weaknesses which were more difficult to assess; such, for example, as my realistic estimate, due to past failures, of the chances of success, and my belief that fanaticism and nationalism should not form the basis of a moun-taineering enterprise. I left the committee room while the matter was being discussed, and when I returned I was invited, in very pressing terms, to undertake the leadership of the Expedition. To this I gladly agreed.

The next meeting of the Himalayan Committee was on 11th. September. I was invited to attend. In the six weeks which elapsed between the two meetings I had not received the slightest hint, either privately or officially, that the Committee as a whole, or any member of it, wished to reconsider the decision regarding the leadership of the Expedition. The chief item on the agenda for the meeting was the appointment of a deputy leader. When, early in the proceedings, this matter came up for discussion, I was asked to withdraw from the room. This surprised me, for I had always regarded the appointment of a deputy leader as the prerogative of the leader, and it can hardly be denied that it is at least his concern. However, I complied without comment. After more than an hour I was recalled, and informed that the Committee proposed to appoint Colonel Hunt co-leader. Whether this fantastic proposal was intended to be taken at its face value I cannot say; it seemed to me incredible that it should be, and obvious that the Committee wished to reconsider their former decision. I therefore invited them to do so. After further discussion, at which I was not present, I was again recalled to be informed of the Committee's decision to appoint Colonel Hunt leader of the Expedition.

That the Committee, on maturer consideration of what I had said at the first meeting, or of other factors unknown to me, should wish to reverse their decision is understandable and would have my full sympathy. To do so without consulting me, without keeping me informed of the trend of shifting opinion or of the private discussions which must have preceded their volte face, without, even in the event, informing me of their reasons for it, to do so without troubling to ascertain the views of several absent members of the Committee or of those of my colleagues on the recent expeditions, many of whom, with the Committee's approval, I had invited to join the next expedition, was an action that cannot escape censure. I find such conduct the more incomprehensible in view of my attitude at the first committee meeting, which surely demanded reciprocal candour and merited some confidence in my disinterested concern for the welfare of the Expedition.

I would like to make it clear that neither these events nor the opinion of them which I have ventured to express alters in any way my sense of gratitude for the sympathetic help and courtesy which, during the past twenty years, I have invariably received from both the Council and the Staff of the Royal Geographical Society. For this reason, and also because there has been a great deal of uninformed gossip regarding the change of leadership, I would be grateful if you would circulate this letter to the members of the Council.

      Yours sincerely,

        Eric Shipton

John Hunt's first job was to get all the members of the expedition on side, and to this end he tried to meet personally as many of them as he could. He travelled up to Liverpool specially to talk to Charles Evans and Alf Gregory, his message being that anything that had happened before was history. He would now choose the team, but would not be taking anyone from New Zealand because he had not met them and did not know them (which sounded like the end of Hillary and Lowe). But Evans and Gregory persuaded Hunt to change his mind, although he was adamant about not taking Ayres (Shipton's appointee).

Even at this late stage the Himalayan Committee were still considering the proposal, first made in February 1952 by Henry Hall, President of the American Alpine Club, that two of their members should join the expedition. But with Houston and Bates taking perhaps four or five of the possible choices to K2, Hall was unsure who remained 'with the right stuff'. Eventually, in November, Hall was told, 'We regret the time factor makes it impossible to include any of your men in the party.'

The 1953 Everest expedition ran with military precision that validated the doubts of those who sought, and got, a change in leadership. The team, the core of it being climbers handpicked by Shipton, was strong; the weather, barring high winds, was good; there were no major setbacks and everything went like clockwork. That John Hunt did an excellent job, once in the driver's seat, is beyond doubt. Certainly his place in the annals is assured. Hillary concluded, 'If there had to be a thruster, you couldn't have done better than having John Hunt.'

One can speculate how history would have viewed Eric Shipton had the British failed on Everest in 1953. In the post-mortem Shipton supporters would have crowed that military-style leadership was not the panacea of success so many had prescribed; that Shipton's vast experience on the mountain would have been indispensable in the event of tricky weather and snow conditions; that the loyalty of his small powerful band would have carried them through without the encumbrance of a big expedition.

Could Shipton have foreseen the outcome of the events of those three months in late summer of 1952? Furthermore, could he have done anything to avoid being usurped, had he done so? Everyone has an opinion, but hindsight generally agrees with Larry Kirwan, who concluded, 'If ever there was a case of the right thing done in the wrong way, this was it.' Roger Chorley, a subsequent President both of the Alpine Club and the RGS, sees the Himalayan Committee's conundrum through the eyes of a pragmatist. 'It was a boardroom decision. In the world of corporate takeovers you say, "Tough luck, but we'll ditch the bloke we've got and get the right bloke."'

Several people intimately involved with the saga have answered the question: 'With Eric Shipton as leader would your team have climbed Everest?' Most think they would. 'I absolutely do,' Ed Hillary answered forty-four years later. 'I'm quite definite, and I'm sure George Lowe is too, that with Eric's leadership, bumbling though it might have been at times, we would still have done it. We were a very tight group and had a very great affection for, and loyalty to, Eric and respect for his abilities. We really weren't worried by his dislike of big expeditions. Of course we had tons of organising ability ourselves. We had just organised Mukut Parbat, and Charles Evans organised Kangchenjunga two years later.' Alf Gregory also said they would have got up anyway; Charles Wylie was sure that their strong team would have 'carried the thing by force of character'; Michael Ward thought they would have made it because they had 'got the science right' which was more critical to success than the leadership; Jack Longland's opinion was that a Shipton-Evans team might well have succeeded; Raymond Greene thought they had such an excellent team that they'd certainly have got up.

But the French had permission for 1954, and the Swiss for 1955; so 1953 was probably Britain's last chance to be first on the summit of

Everest. Many people felt that national prestige could not be compromised by taking chances, and that John Hunt was the nearest they could foresee to a leader who could guarantee success; he was the man for the job and, in the event, so he proved to be.

At 5 a.m. on the morning of 2 June 1953, outside Buckingham Palace a ripple ran through the crowd waiting to see their new Queen crowned, 'Everest has been climbed . . . Everest has been climbed.' Then the newspapers followed with banner headlines, the most unforgettable of which, in the *Daily Express*, was 'All this, and Everest too.' The triumphant team and their respected leader thoroughly deserved the universal acclaim of that moment, and of all that has followed them down the decades ever since. But if one man might have felt salt rubbed into his open wound, Eric Shipton did not show it, but remained dignified and unstinting in his praise of the returning climbers. He went to London Airport to congratulate them; Ed Hillary remembers, 'We were welcomed like conquering heroes. Even Eric Shipton was there – thrusting into my hands a bunch of the bananas, which I have always enjoyed, and I ate them all on the way up to London.'

Shipton himself wrote a summary of his own philosophy in an article for the *Sunday Express*:

In the highlands of Central Asia, whose mountains I know best, there are scores of peaks exceeding 25,000ft in height. In mountaineering it is unwise to prophesy, but it would not surprise me to be told that even the next generation will not live to see the last of these giants climbed. Kangchenjunga is a far tougher proposition than either Everest or K2, and it is probable that it will continue to defy the assaults of mountaineers for many, many years. On great portions of the maps of the southern Andes of Patagonia there are blank spaces with the word 'Inesplorado' written across them.

The climbing of Mount Everest will, I believe, open a new era of mountaineering in the Himalayas. Mountaineers wishing to climb and explore in the Himalayas will be forced to do so on their own initiative, and on modest resources. They will discover how incredibly small those resources can be, while still providing all their needs. Above all, they will find in the simplicity of their approach the true enjoyment of their endeavour.

When Eric Shipton stepped from the Alpine Club's premises into South Audley Street on 11 September 1952 he was walking from the sunshine of acclaim into the shadow of obscurity as far as the general public were concerned. Those interested in the history of alpinism and mountain exploration know better, and realise that after a spell in the doldrums, his journeys in Patagonia were a final chapter confirming his worthy place as one of the world's great explorers of the twentieth century. But for him it was yet a long and bitter road to recovery.

CHAPTER 15

The Lakeland Warden

Eskdale and Shropshire, 1953–57

In 1953 Eric Shipton again found himself out of a job. He cast around widely, and somewhat desperately, applying to become British Consul in Tonga's Friendly Islands, and in Punta Arenas, Patagonia (for which jobs he was well qualified after Kashgar and Kunming). Jan Morris, when working for *The Times*, remembers Shipton coming to the office of the editor to ask if there was a job going as foreign correspondent, 'anywhere in South America, preferably in the mountains'.

Suddenly the Wardenship of the Outward Bound Mountain School (OBMS) in Eskdale, Cumberland, came vacant when its incumbent, Adam Arnold-Brown, resigned to follow a career in industry. Kurt Hahn, founder of Gordonstoun School, started the Outward Bound Sea School at Aberdovey in Wales during the Second World War, having observed that many fit and able young merchant sailors drowned after shipwreck for lack of basic survival skills and mental toughness. His philosophy of providing character training for young people through the challenges of the outdoors, had caught alight, matured, and moved into the mountains by way of the Outward Bound Mountain School. Shipton applied, and was appointed in May 1953, largely on his name. Alf Gregory, who had also applied and was considered a strong candidate, withdrew in deference and loyalty to his old leader, now jobless.

Shipton, Diana and the two boys, Nicky aged eight and John aged three, took up residence at Eskdale Green in the vast, grey granite, towered and turreted mansion set on a high terrace overlooking a small lake surrounded by rhododendron bushes and pine trees. Away in the distance at the head of Eskdale stood the elegant triangle of Harter Fell, coloured still in the brown shades of dead bracken and highlit by golden gorse. Scattered around the grounds of the Victorian baronial house that was their home were storerooms for equipment and stables and outhouses serving as dormitories for the students.

The period of Shipton's life at Outward Bound is considered by some as arid, empty and unachieving – perhaps because of its unfortunate finish. However, the people who worked at the school during his wardenship saw it quite differently. John Lagoe, who became his chief instructor and subsequently Warden, thought Shipton had a profound impact on the Outward Bound Mountain School, and said, 'By 1953 a change was needed, it wanted a man with a name and a reputation to question the received wisdom of Outward Bound passed down from Kurt Hahn, and to make the first dent in the Kahn mythology.' Shipton had this, and did it; and the Board of Outward Bound listened to him because he was who he was.

Before he arrived, the emphasis of the courses was on winning badges, performing well at athletics, and achieving in competition. But Shipton wanted boys to have a real experience in the mountains. As Warden he encouraged the instructors to develop mountain schemes to fit that experience, culminating in a final scheme when the boys would be out on the hills for five days on their own. To George Trevelyan's words, 'without spirit of adventure in young men civilisation must wilt and wither,' Shipton added, 'and the adventure must be *real*.'

Although good in small groups out on the hills, he was uncomfortable communicating with eighty boys together; however, he related well to most of the instructors who respected his wisdom and experience.

He usually gave an uplifting talk on the first evening of the course, exhorting the boys (who were trembling in anticipation) to 'find your star and follow it.' This was followed by Frank Dowlen, a gangly clownish instructor, demonstrating various rock climbing techniques on the bookshelves of the library, and mantel-shelfing onto a ledge under the beam at the end of the common room.

Shipton was constantly streamlining the courses to make the most use of the time available. One of his favourite projects was the 'Quest'. Starting any time after supper, boys from each patrol had to get as far away from the school as possible, and return by 6 p.m. next day with proof of arrival at their ultimate destination. Each boy took rations for twenty-four hours, and could carry with him not more than one shilling. Two boys got to within thirty miles of Glasgow, and one reached Liverpool but returned three hours late so was disqualified. In another course he encouraged a similar challenge, but as a team effort along with instructors. One patrol, with instructors Dick Marsh and Vernon Walker, hitch-hiked to Fort William, bivouacked twice on a traverse of Ben Nevis, and hitch-hiked back from Kinlochleven by the evening of the fifth day. No one took more than five shillings.

June was the month in which Mount Everest was climbed, and inevitably one of mixed emotions for Shipton. He expressed his feelings unreservedly in a letter to Pamela Freston:

> To you (and to no one else except Diana) I can confess to pangs of regret over 'spilt milk', though I doubt if there is anyone alive who in the circumstances would not feel them. I am quite sure that the effort to overcome them and to achieve a sense of real values is very good for one. One certainly has to delve pretty deep! Of course I'm really delighted that it was Ed Hillary who pulled it off – he is a grand mountaineer and a delightful person: he is one of the few I know who has the strength of character to withstand the avalanche of public acclamation that is coming to him. And *nothing* could have been more fitting than that Tenzing should have been there to represent the Sherpas.

In a generous gesture, Shipton invited the entire successful Everest team to spend a weekend at Eskdale in order to relax and get away from the press brouhaha. The Eskdale miniature railway, nicknamed the Ratty, laid on a special train to bring them to the school from Ravenglass on the coast.

One afternoon four of the Everest party, with four of the school staff, set off down the River Esk in flood. The first boat, a Canadian canoe carrying Lowe, Band, Marsh (chief instructor) and Shipton, came to grief early. In the capsize Lowe lost his false teeth, which prevented him from speaking at the Lord Mayor's luncheon the following day. The second, a kayak containing Hillary and others, capsized twice further downriver, but they managed to continue the journey to Ravenglass. The third, with Bourdillon on board, got through unscathed. In his monthly report to the Outward Bound Board, Shipton noted laconically, 'There is obviously no question of allowing boys to canoe down the Esk when the river is in spate.'

John Lagoe tells the sequel to this story. A local fisherman, having heard about Lowe's loss on the radio, turned up at the front door of the school with a set of false teeth he had found on the bank five miles downriver after the flooded Esk subsided. Lowe was back in New Zealand by then, so they were sent to the RGS for forwarding.

From the start of his wardenship Shipton questioned the 'instructor-pushed' mountain schemes. He thought the boys themselves should accept more responsibility, so experiments with 'boys on their own' began in the autumn of 1953. That winter vicious Lakeland storms caused some near-misses. Frank Dowlen described how some boys were bivouacking on the top of Scafell Pike in mid-December. 'One tent was completely buried in snow so they had to tunnel through from another tent to get the lads out. But they all survived and got down safely.' John Tyson, another instructor, brought a hypothermic boy down from Pavey Ark to the Old Dungeon Ghyll Hotel where Sid Cross, the publican and local mountain rescuer, gave him a hot bath and so much first aid brandy that, when he came to, he had all the symptoms of a hangover. These adventures were knife-edge balancing as far as a respectable outfit like Outward Bound was concerned.

Administration was not Shipton's forte, but he paid great attention to detail in the boys' reports. The instructors would try to write a perfect piece of prose, and Shipton would just 'turn it around, tidy it up a little and reshape it', adding his own comments where appropriate. But he could buckle down and have all eighty to ninety reports done in a day and then Margaret Mossop, the secretary, would type them. Dick Marsh, the chief instructor, was a strong shadow Warden. Shipton gave him a free hand, and spent much time in his own office writing a new book longhand in pencil. Marsh was an impetuous character, bubbling with enthusiasm, and impatient with Shipton's laid-back approach. Consequently they were often at odds. At staff meetings Marsh was pragmatic and impulsive; Shipton snuffled a lot in a shy hesitant manner, trying to select shades of meaning before reaching a conclusion.

Shipton was happier out on the fells observing the boys and instructors, oblivious of the rain and contentedly chewing on raw onion. What little gear he carried was stuffed into his pocketless 'Ship-sack'. The instructors expected him to be Himalaya-fit and to go bounding off uphill, but to their surprise and education, he walked in perfect balance at a slow, steady pace he could keep up for hours on end. In his report on Course 36 he noted, 'Disappointing results of the 5-day scheme, not nearly enough attention has been given to the exercise and development of individual enterprise and responsibility, the lesser the supervision the smoother things run and the higher the standard of actual achievement. The boys are faced too rarely with the necessity of making difficult decisions in unpleasant, complex or lonely circumstances.'

Six months later Shipton reported, 'There is no doubt that our chief problem is to find time for more comprehensive and thorough mountain training; to make boys really confident and competent to move about difficult country for long periods in any weather and to look after themselves with a minimum of equipment by night and day, so that in the final week they can tackle with assurance and enjoyment the most searching test we can devise.' Because winter conditions that year precluded serious rock climbing, he had to consider whether, with its inordinate demands on instructor power, it should be removed from the syllabus. This was a revolutionary concept for the Warden of an Outward Bound *Mountain* School. However, as John Tyson said, he was always on the lookout for 'long mountaineering Moderates'.

Christmas parties at OBMS were legendary. One year the instructors performed the pantomime *Cinderella*; a hideous red shoe taking the place of a glass slipper. Diana Shipton (a natural mimic who became keen on amateur dramatics in Kashgar) and Frank Dowlen were the two teeth-blackened Ugly Sisters; Shipton was Buttons. Fairy Godmother Vince Veevers, a stoic, silent Lakesman, jumped down from a bookcase waving his magic wand but landed so heavily he almost stunned himself and thereafter wandered around speechless. At one point in the evening everyone was milling about in the Warden's sitting room having drinks, when a cousin of Diana's, who hadn't seen her for some time, suddenly turned up unannounced at the school and thought he had come to a madhouse. But it only confirms what another instructor, John Earle, said about Shipton. 'He inspired his staff to run exciting and imaginative courses, and also brought fun and laughter to the Outward Bound with his enormous sense of the ridiculous.'

Pamela Freston came to visit the Shiptons at Eskdale in November 1953. Eight months later Shipton wrote to her:

I continue to find it interesting. We have now got the courses much more 'streamlined' and I think there is a vast improvement. The whole atmosphere of the place is quite changed. Looking back to the period when you were here I can hardly believe the abject pettiness of the issues we discussed with such heat. We still argue in conferences, of course, but there is no longer that awful undercurrent of personal pride and touchiness; we are all agreed on the main issues and as a result discussion is clear and objective. There is no need to look far for the cause of the change. John Lagoe is splendid as Chief Instructor.

This happy state of equilibrium was not to last, however. In the middle of 1954 the staff noticed trouble brewing in the Shiptons' marriage. Diana was seeing a lot of David Drummond, a dashing, handsome, athletic instructor. Shipton started giving Susan Denholm-Young, the bursar's wife, rides in his car to her parents' home near Leeds on other side of Ilkley, Otley and Skipton Moors – known by the instructors as the 'Skipton Deviation'. Patrick Denholm-Young, the bursar, was a straightforward army officer (known in his regiment as 'Dunem Wrong').

Shipton was certainly quite indiscreet, ranging from being seen with his lady friend in Leeds, to being observed at 2 a.m. climbing through a bedroom window in Eskdale village (not the first time a drain pipe had featured in his philandering). The staff made great efforts to encourage Bill Tilman to invite David Drummond to join the crew of his thirty-ton ketch, *Mischief*, sailing to Patagonia. With Drummond off the map for a year, they hoped the romance might cool. He signed on, but the rest of the crew mutinied off Gibraltar because the only food on board was hard tack biscuit. So, a fortnight after his farewell party, Drummond turned up back at OBMS to everyone's disappointment, except, one assumes, Diana's.

Denholm-Young, the one left out of the triangle, brought the matter to a head in late 1954 by causing a scene. According to the Shipton sons' family legend, he chased their father round the kitchen table brandishing a knife, shouting,' You're a shit, Shipton.' The latter thought this quite unnecessarily theatrical. The Outward Bound Board met in crisis, decided summarily to sack Shipton, and called John Lagoe back from holiday to take over immediately as Acting Warden.

Shipton summarised the situation:

> I could not see myself as a leader of youth, for though I like people individually and certainly have a capacity for enthusiasm, I felt I was too much of an introvert to impart it to large numbers of boys. However, I found that this could be safely left to a carefully chosen staff of instructors, and my chief function was to guide the design of the courses into imaginative channels. In this I believe I was reasonably successful until, at the end of 1954, the conduct of my private life made my position no longer tenable and I was discharged.

Many instructors felt that the two marriages could have been salvaged if this crisis had been handled better by the Board which demanded a steep price for dalliance, as Shipton was meant to be setting a flawless example in a school of high moral principle where adultery did not feature. Moreover, there had been no sign of serious problems in their marriage up till then, despite the stresses of their escape from Kunming. Shipton's letters to Diana right through the Cho Oyu expedition, only a year before, were as loving as ever. However, the turbulent months of late 1952 must have taken an emotional toll of them both. Many people, including the Vicar of Eskdale and the local lady of the manor, wrote letters pleading with them to come to their senses. But sadly to no avail, and they went their separate ways.

After his sacking, Shipton moved with Susan Denholm-Young to Shropshire, where they lived in a cottage on the farm of her sympathetic cousin, Robert Cross. She became deeply distressed after the Eskdale marital roundabout, and Shipton felt remorseful over the whole stupid affair which had virtually scuttled his career. 'Tormented by self-reproach at having made such a monumental mess of things,' he wrote, 'I felt a strong urge to escape into obscurity.'

He also felt responsible for Susan, but did not know how to extricate himself from an affair he could see was going nowhere. Thinking he was going to have to marry her, eventually he suggested giving her the family house in Liss as a way of buying himself out of the situation. Then he announced that they should neither meet nor correspond, and he was planning to go off to the Antarctic for two years – but he did not do so. A few months later the devastated Susan, after some very acrimonious contact with Shipton, returned to her forgiving husband with whom she made plans for putting their marriage together again. Meanwhile Diana got her divorce, and married David Drummond, while Shipton floundered in deep melancholy at the mess he had made of his life. His salvation was in starting work on Robert Cross's farm where the heavy physical labour, on which he had always thrived, helped lift his spirits and also put a roof over his head.

He wrote to Pamela, his constant confidante during the whole of his marriage turmoil.

I spend my time fencing fields, driving cattle about on mysterious missions, I 'muck out' pigs (I muck out my own house once a week just to set an example), chop trees, hump sacks about, mix balanced diets, chase lambs, and so on. I'm now alone with Sid (the other farm hand); we get along well as we rarely speak. Compared with him, Bill Tilman is a chatterbox. He gives the appearance of regarding me as a harmless nitwit who can be counted on for light entertainment every now and then by hitting my thumb with the hammer. I live in a room, uncarpeted and devoid of furniture except for a bed, a chair, a table and a sort of coal stove. There is no bed-making as I use a sleeping bag.

Robert Cross had recently returned from Argentina where he had emigrated intending to farm there for the rest of his life. But President Peron's hostility to the British made it impracticable. The beauty of the Andes, where Cross had journeyed on muleback, had made a deep impression on him, which he communicated to Shipton. His talk rekindled memories for Shipton of his schoolboy reading when he discovered mountains through the pages of Whymper's *Travels Amongst the Great Andes of the Equator*. It was a part of the world he had already shown a readiness to visit when enquiring after consulships.

Around this time he also heard from his old friend, Bill Tilman, who had sailed his boat *Mischief* round Cape Horn and up through the Chilean Archipelago and thereby reached the Southern Patagonian Ice Cap, which he crossed with two companions.

From the age of thirteen, after his father died, Cross had spent much time with his childhood friends, Geoffrey and Phyllis Wint, who lived at The Haye, a manor house near Bridgnorth in Shropshire. The Wints gave him their front door key and the freedom of their house. Geoffrey Wint, an amiable, humorous countryman, and one of the best amateur point-to-point steeplechase jockeys of his day, farmed a large acreage. When Cross returned from South America he bought from the Wints, The New House, Chelmarsh, a rundown farm which he had always dreamed of owning, and began to work it single-handed in 1952.

Living in Cross's cottage, Shipton led an ascetic life, feeding on kippers, cornflakes, potato soup and stew, that he would brew once a week and top up as it became depleted. On rare visits to London he took biltong with him to eat for lunch in Hyde Park. He worked half the day for Cross on the farm or in the newly planted woods, and wrote for the other half. Cross was then about twenty-nine years old, two decades younger than Shipton, and yet the two men formed a strong friendship. Leaning on their pitchforks they would engage in lengthy philosophical discussions that often ended in uproarious laughter – just what Shipton needed to purge his gloom. Sid, the young tractor driver, would look on with wry amusement.

The farm overlooked the upper reaches of the River Severn, and included grazing meadows from which Cross took crops of hay. A busy one-track railway ran across the land, and sometimes Shipton would act as signaller to tell Sid when the line was safe to drive the tractor across.

ES and Diana
picnicking near
Kashgar

ES and Tilman
having tea

The Consul-General with his secretary (in the gari)

The British Consulate   ES on the Consulate steps

Everest Reconnaissance 1951 – (from left to right) ES, Michael Ward, Bill Murray, Tom Bourdillon

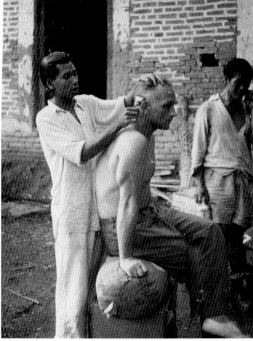

ES being shorn at Jogbani at the start of the 1951 Everest reconnaissance expedition

Tilman's photo taken from below the top of Kala Patar, showing the steep, rocky South Ridge. Not high enough to see the South Col, cut off by the ridge of Nuptse in the foreground.

Photo taken from Kala Patar (about 300 ft higher than the photo above), showing the South Col and the start of the S-E Ridge set behind and separate from South Ridge.

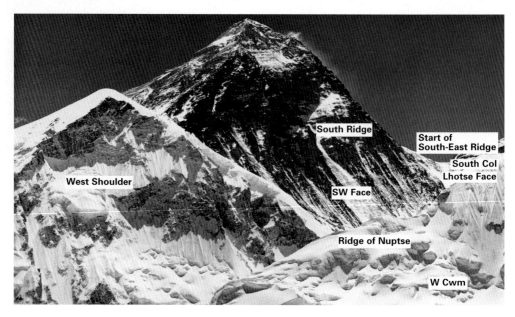

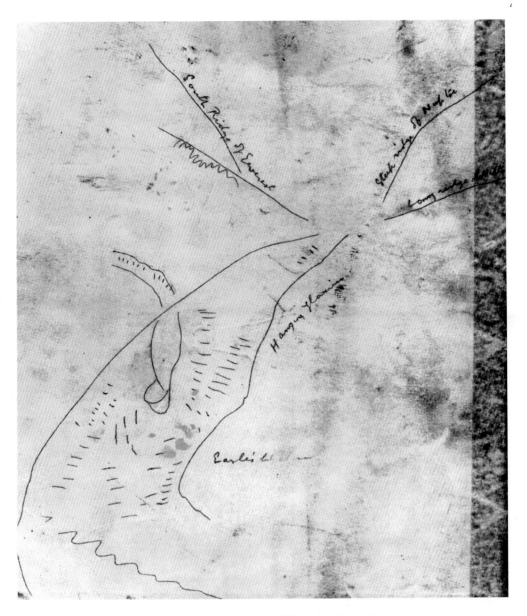

The first pencil sketch of the Western Cwm from a
20,000 ft buttress on Pumori, drawn on 30 September
1951 by ES on the back of a photostat copy of the
1933 Milne-Hinks map.

Members of the Cho
Oyu expedition.
Standing (left to right):
R.G. Colledge, E. Hillary,
ES, L.G.C. Pugh,
H.E. Riddiford,
G. Lowe. Sitting:
C.H. Secord, A. Gregory,
R.C. Evans,
T. Bourdillon

ES signing on Sherpas
for Cho Oyu

The pyramid tent at the base of the Marinelli Glacier, Tierra del Fuego, 1962

ES in Patagonia

ES approaching Mount Burney

But his signals were often far from clear and the tractor had one or two narrow escapes with approaching trains. Shipton was also prone to near-disasters on the farm. On one occasion, Cross and his wife went out to dinner leaving him in charge of their house. Cross, in bow-tie and dinner jacket, returned to find a herd of cattle in his flower garden, and Shipton engrossed in a book, quite unaware. Another time it was a sow. One day they were walking across the farmyard deep in conversation when a rat suddenly ran out of an old barn. Cross threw a hammer at the rat, which darted towards them and ran straight up the trouser leg of Shipton, who stood wide-eyed with amazement until they both collapsed laughing.

At first Shipton did not mix socially with the county Shropshire folk because he was still extricating himself from his own melancholy. But when word got around that the famous mountain explorer was living in the neighbourhood, he became quite a catch at dinner parties of the local landed gentry. At one such, Robert Cross witnessed a rich American hostess, who lived in an elegant mansion nearby, look across the table deeply into Shipton's blue eyes and say, 'Marrakesh. I can see by the stars your psychic spiritual background.' She later discovered, to Shipton's chagrin, that he thought psychic matters bogus.

During all this time Shipton kept up a friendly correspondence with his ex-wife, for example, 'Dearest Diana, As I said in London the other day, my aloofness is on purpose. It must be like that for a bit and I don't *feel* it. The best 12½ years certainly haven't been obliterated for me.' He amicably discussed their 'finances', and matters concerning the boys, who came regularly to stay with him in Shropshire. He also continued to meet Diana, who said, 'Eric went on drifting in and out of David's and my life without any thought that it might be upsetting for us. Because I wanted to see him, he came.' Throughout, he was totally charitable towards her, once writing, 'I think you have faced your various trials most wonderfully,' and he laid no blame on her for the break-up, although he might well have done so.

After they had gone their separate ways, Shipton was involved in a sort of *ménage à trois* with two other lady friends in London. All three agreed they should draw the liaison to a close for a trial period of six months. But according to his son, Nick, Shipton forgot about the arrangement and turned up to tea the next day.

Meanwhile Shipton moved into the stables of John Reed, a local landowner and friend of the Crosses; for several years he stayed there writing and making occasional forays into society. One of these was to go up to London to receive a CBE from the Queen. Recommendation for the honours list had been discussed for some time in alpine circles, 'based on his contribution to the Everest success and not on his mountain exploits in general'. Moreover, Noel Odell thought a knighthood would have been appropriate.

Around this time Shipton also became friendly with the Wints. Geoffrey Wint, an alcoholic, was now sliding steadily downhill, but devotedly tended by his wife, Phyllis, who covered up for him and denied the real state of affairs until he died in 1959. Shipton gave moral support to her during this trying time, and their friendship deepened. He eventually moved from Reed's cottage into The Haye, the start of a common-law marriage, liaison, partnership, love affair – call it what you will (Phyllis never had her doubts) – that flourished, with occasional distractions, for the next twenty years until he died. Phyllis was shy, independent and, to the unknowing, rather distant. Shipton always kept up the pretence of being homeless, all the while ensconced in Phyllis Wint's manor house in Shropshire, or in her comfortable basement flat in Tite Street, Chelsea, across from the Royal Hospital and within a stone's throw of the Thames Embankment. It was also just down the same street as fellow explorer, Wilfred Thesiger, whom he used to meet occasionally. 'I'm a nomad,' Shipton would tell anyone who asked for his address, 'I don't live anywhere. Just write to me c/o The Royal Geographical Society.'

In 1957 an enterprising group of students from the Imperial College of Science, London, none of whom had experience of the Himalaya, invited Shipton to lead their expedition to the Karakoram, and to suggest a destination. He chose the Siachen Glacier, the largest in Asia, which lies due east of K2 and Gasherbrum. He was fifty, and this was his first venture out of the doldrums in which he had languished for the past four years.

The party of six was chosen by what one of them called 'the novel method of self-selection'. The boat carrying their luggage was delayed, giving them a late start from Skardu. Then they had the usual trouble with Balti porters, who this time stole some expedition equipment.

Shipton notes, 'Friendship with the porters should be developed gradually, and overfamiliarity with them in the early stages of an expedition leads to a lot of trouble.' Nevertheless, he had an intuitive understanding of native people and was disinclined to upset their way of life.

But once back in the heart of his much-loved mountains – the Shaksgam, Hunza, Shimshal and the Karakoram trade routes – he found, as he expected, that the country had lost none of its enchantment. It had, he wrote, 'a sense of strangeness, a kind of celestial loneliness, which is unique in my experience'. The expedition's plans were too ambitious for the short seven weeks allowed by a university vacation; the weather turned bad towards the end of August and daily snow for three weeks hampered travel on the glaciers. So they achieved only a fraction of what they set out to do. But the Siachen area came fully up to Shipton's expectations. 'For my part I am deeply grateful for the opportunity to add this superb region to my knowledge of the Karakoram.'

CHAPTER 16

Essays in Masochism

Patagonia, 1958–66

STORMBOUND on the Siachen Glacier in the Karakoram, Shipton had shared a tent with a young Tasmanian, Geoff Bratt. Talk inevitably veered to other remote faraway places, and by the end of the expedition the two men were laying plans for visiting Patagonia, a turn of events that would shape Shipton's next decade. Patagonia, the foot of South America below latitude 40° South, encompasses both the wide pampas of Argentina and the bottom end of string-bean Chile. The frontier between the two is the Andes mountain range where spectacular peaks protrude out of two ice caps from which glaciers flow east and west through dense, wet forests. The tempestuous Pacific coast of Chile is dotted with a 1,000-mile-long archipelago of uninhabited islands and deep fjords that reach right into the heart of the mountains. Argentine Patagonia is a prairie country of grassy scrubland that rises through gentle foothills to high mountains interspersed with large, spidery-shaped lakes.

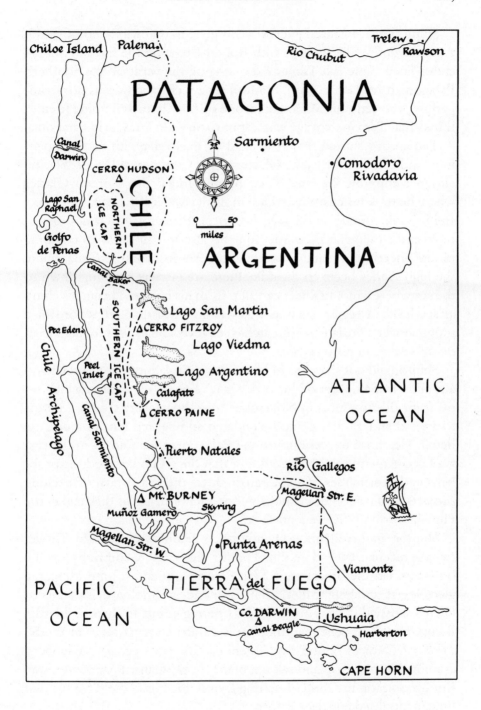

Shipton had nurtured a tentative interest in that windy tip of South America during discussions with Robert Cross on the farm in Shropshire. Then came Bill Tilman's crossing of the waist of the Southern Patagonian Ice Cap in 1957. Shipton always claimed he was non-competitive, yet Cedomir Marangunic, one of his Chilean climbing friends, thinks that Tilman's voyage was a spur to Shipton's travels in Patagonia.

Tilman had started from the head of Peel Inlet with two companions, and climbed the Calvo Glacier to the Continental Divide, placing eleven camps on the way. Then he descended the Moreno Glacier where he took his customary bath in the icy waters of Lago Argentino. In his book, *Mischief in Patagonia* he writes, 'Proverbially it is not easy to blow and swallow at the same time. So also it is not easy to combine mountaineering and sailing. On the southernmost coast of Chile, where the high Andes begin to dwindle, there are glaciers reaching down to the sea where a mountaineer can step from his boat and begin his climb at sea level. A region such as this has an irresistible attraction for a mountaineer who, late in life, catches sea fever and aspires to making an ocean voyage in his own boat.'

Shipton did not share his old friend's nautical conversion and had no ambition to be master of his own vessel. For his expedition which set off from Buenos Aires in November 1958, boats were strictly a means to an end and, if they could be deflated and packed flat, so much the better. He chose to reconnoitre the Patagonian Ice Cap from the east via Lago Argentino; 'I had no doubt that once I understood the problems and possibilities of exploratory travel there, a swarm of exciting projects would soon be clamouring for attention, just as they had in the Himalaya twenty-five years before.'

Shipton gathered his companions as haphazardly as did Tilman (whose recent crew had mutinied on the high seas). Geoff Bratt was the only climber; the others were Peter James, a botanist; John Mercer, a glaciologist; and Peter Miles, a naturalist and entomologist. This mix of talents satisfied the scientific bodies offering grants to finance the trip. Being on a tight schedule, they took a third class passage on the SS *Highland Chieftain* bound for Argentina. Its 350 steerage passengers, crammed into one squalid saloon, made for permanent pandemonium. But for Shipton the thrill of setting foot in the New World for his first time, neutralised any discomfort.

From Buenos Aires they travelled south 2,000 miles overland to Calafate on the shore of Lago Argentino. Like most Patagonian villages, the houses were roofed with corrugated iron and sheathed in tin painted bright colours. The streets were clean of garbage, which never had long to settle before being moved on by the constant howling wind. Calafate also gives its name to a scrubby thorn bush with a small yellow flower and blue berries, eating which, local legend tells, will ensure a visitor's return to Patagonia. For Shipton it worked.

The weather on the lake was habitually stormy, and Estancia La Cristina, their destination at the head of the most distant north-western arm, had been isolated for three months because of high seas. Mr and Mrs Masters, an octogenarian couple who farmed sheep there, invited Shipton to make his base at their ranch, whither he and his companions took a ride in the government launch on a rare calm day. Over his ham radio the Masters's son, Herbert, kept contact with Calafate and the rest of the globe.

After ten days in this lovely place where many sorts of waterfowl congregated in reedy lagoons – black-necked swans, steamer ducks, widgeon and teal, pink flamingos, and Caiquen geese – they moved on to Onelli Bay. Onelli lay at the head of another tortuous arm of the lake, from where they hoped to gain access to the Cordillera Darwin. The ubiquitous windswept southern beech tree, *Nothofagus antarctica*, reached right down to the water's edge. In the forest roamed wild horses and cattle, the legacy of an attempt by the Masters to farm there. A network of trampled tracks made for easier human passage.

Shipton had brought a rubber dinghy from England to help them penetrate the furthest reaches of the lakes. Soon after launching, their outboard motor hit an ice floe, was wrenched from its bracket, and sank in deep water, never to be retrieved. Rowing became exhausting in the heavily laden and cumbersome inflatable, so they beached and unloaded it. While they were returning to ferry more gear, the front face of the Onelli Glacier calved and a house-sized chunk of ice slid into the water. The tidal wave it created spread out across the lake, and the swell nearly carried away their stashed gear. Thereby the hazards of boating quickly impressed Shipton, who had little mechanical bent.

In the *Nothofagus* forest they saw flocks of green parrots, wrens, woodpeckers and hummingbirds. Penetrating it was relatively easy

where the trees were large (up to eighty feet high), but higher up a
tangled, twisted lattice of dwarf *Nothofagus* predominated. They moved
onto a rock ridge, and then to a snow slope where the surface was composed, as he describes in *Land of Tempest*, 'of balls of ice like marbles,
which slipped like quicksilver beneath our feet and threatened to carry
us down on a rolling mass over the brink of the precipice below'. They
reached the Continental Divide at 6,500 feet (which tallies with Tilman's
highest recorded camp a few miles away to the south), and then surmounted an ice cliff running across the face of the mountain, 'overhung
by a cornice decorated with icicles, and separated from the snow below
by a bergschrund like a moat beneath a castle wall'.

In the course of this exploit Geoff Bratt slipped and drove one of
the sharp points of his crampon into his calf; but he carried on unperturbed after wrapping the deep flesh wound in a silk scarf. They reached
the summit of their mountain at 8,100 feet, then turned and descended,
very tired but safe, to Onelli Bay for a pre-arranged rendezvous with the
launch. 'It was the hardest day I've had on a mountain for a great many
years,' Shipton wrote to Pamela Freston.

The party had settled down and were steadily achieving their
scientific aims. Peter Miles, the entomologist (or 'bugger' as he called
himself) weighed about seventeen stone, was very tough, but looked
'the wrong shape for an expedition'. Peter James, the botanist from the
British Museum, had already collected nearly 1,000 species. John
Mercer's peculiarities were 'restlessness and enormous energy, and an
angry attitude to the injustices of the world and a way of answering
one's questions (usually in the negative) some twenty minutes after one
has asked them'.

Shipton was keen to visit an area west of Lago Viedma (the next lake
north of Lago Argentino) to investigate a mysterious volcano, Volcàn
Viedma, said to be erupting through an ice sheet some thousands of
feet thick. Dr Frederick Reichert's expedition of 1933 reported seeing
'a volcanic cone, 3,000 metres high, arising from the glacier from which
clouds of steam were issuing'.

On the drive round to Lago Viedma they encountered ostrich-like
rheas and large herds of guanaco, long-necked animals like llamas. By
way of rough dirt roads they reached Estancia Rio Tunel at the north-
west corner of the lake. There they managed to hire a pony to carry

their gear through a gorge and up the further valley that opened onto a mix of gentle pasture and forest. This was dominated by the graceful spires of Cerro Fitzroy and Cerro Torre, which had been the centre of furious controversy only the year before over whether the Italians had made the first ascent. It was to become the focus of much climbing activity in the decades to come.

They soon encountered a glacier barring the valley, so the pony could go no further. Shipton, a skilled horseman after his riding experience in Central Asia, folded a canvas bag as a makeshift saddle and cantered off back down the valley to return the animal to its owner. While descending a steep slope the improvised girth slipped, and he fell head first down the slope. As he recounts in *Land of Tempest*, 'The friendly animal stopped and eyed me pityingly as I scrambled back and recovered the "saddle" from under his belly. After that I bore in mind the Tibetan dictum, "If your horse can't carry you uphill he is no horse; if you don't lead him downhill you are no man," and we reached the estancia with no further mishap just in time for supper.'

Returning to his companions, Shipton climbed to the Paso del Viento, which led onto the glacier from where they could easily identify the Volcàn Viedma as a long black island in a sea of ice. Three miles short of the glacier they found pumice of recent origin scattered over a wide area. But their excitement was short-lived because a storm broke. Bad weather lasted for a week, and eased for only a few hours, but it was sufficient to allow them to explore the supposed 'Volcàn'. However, they found no sign whatever of any volcanic or thermal activity, either contemporary or ancient. A tornado resurged and, literally, blew Shipton off his feet. When it subsided they descended in freezing, drenching rain, conditions that were to become very familiar in their subsequent travels in Patagonia.

Returning to Lago Argentino, they made for one of its southern fingers, the Seno Mayo, that cuts deep into the Andes. The head is only about six miles from the most northerly finger of Calvo Fjord, near Tilman's starting point on the Pacific side of the range.

In wind and driving rain they tried to cross the two-mile-wide barrier formed by the Mayo Glacier crossing the valley at right angles. But they were barred by 'ice broken and twisted into a chaotic mass of ridges and spires, intersected by a labyrinth of deep crevasses', as Shipton wrote to Pamela. 'These glaciers behave quite differently from any I've seen before, and the wind is worse than anything I remember on Everest. An unpleasant feature of it is that it is *just not* freezing so one gets absolutely soaked.'

Near their exposed camp they found an overhanging cliff roofing dry mossy ground, screened from the weather by undergrowth and tall trees. With plenty of dry firewood at hand, they settled down in comfort – an unusual luxury for Patagonia. After another unsuccessful attempt to cross the glacier they decided to use the dinghy to ferry themselves and their loads through the ice pack round the end of the glacier tongue.

On land they had to fight through tangled undergrowth, which was misery for Shipton but delight to Bratt, who was used to bushwhacking through similar forest in his native Tasmania. After some more boating adventures in which they were swept over the waves, 'like a leaf with no control over its direction', they were nearly capsized by violent gusts of wind. Finally they climbed to the head of the Mayo Glacier, which was a satisfactory finish to this first season of reconnaissance.

Shipton then spent a few days on the Beagle Channel of Tierra del Fuego, as guest of the Bridges family at the Estancia Harberton, where he subsequently made many happy visits. Thomas Bridges, originally a missionary at Ushuaia, branched away from religion and started a ranch at Harberton in 1886. Aided by his sons, they used a dozen offshore islands to graze their sheep and cattle without need of fencing. Bridges built a mutual trust with the primitive indigenous Yaghan canoe Indians, and compiled a 32,000-word dictionary of their language. Lucas, the eldest son, similarly made contact with the even more reclusive Ona tribe, who inhabited the forests of the interior of Tierra del Fuego. His classic book, *Uttermost Part of the Earth*, tells of the family's travails in farming this rugged land and of founding another estancia at Viamonte on the north-east coast of the island.

The aim of Shipton's second journey to Patagonia in the austral summer of 1959–60 was to find the mysterious Volcàn Viedma. Being serious about his quest, he went to Grenoble to ask the advice of Dr Lliboutry, the distinguished French glaciologist, who was not sanguine about his chances of finding the volcano, mainly on account of the appalling weather (of which, by now, Shipton was well aware).

His crew was almost entirely new, apart from Peter Miles, the naturalist, and his wife. Jack Ewer, a tested mountaineer with experience in Antarctica, had studied air photos of the ice cap, and found definite volcanic activity near the top of Cordon Lautaro, lying on the ice cap almost due west of Lago San Martin, the obvious point of approach. This lake is a maze of interconnecting fjords, which, on the Argentine side, like its three neighbours, drain into the Pacific. Peter Bruchhausen also had Antarctic experience.

They started their voyage from Estancia El Condor on Maipu Fjord, from where, on an unusually calm day, they had a clear view of the O'Higgins Glacier, named after the Chilean revolutionary who joined forces with the Argentinian General San Martin. 'Suddenly I noticed,' wrote Shipton in *Land of Tempest*, 'that one of the white clouds, far away in the background, seemed, unlike its neighbours, to be in a state of considerable agitation. Three times we saw it shoot swiftly upwards to form a great mushroom-topped column.' What good fortune that the volcano chose that very moment to erupt!

Although the party had been active for only two weeks, one person, who had asked to join, decided to quit after he began to realise that the trip was going to be a lot tougher than he had bargained for. During Shipton's career he was rarely at odds with his expedition colleagues (unlike Tilman with his crews), but this time he wrote frankly, 'In an undertaking of this kind, when conditions must inevitably subject people's tempers to a good deal of strain, the mutual compatibility of the members of the party is a matter of vital importance. It was already clear that [we] did not see eye to eye on some fundamental issues, and it was better that we should part company while it was still possible to do so.'

For this journey Shipton had the loan of a bigger rubber boat, a Zodiac, and two 4 h.p. Seagull outboard motors, with which they transported their gear to the head of the south arm, or Brazo Sur, of Lago San Martin. The next two weeks was a period of hard work, relaying loads up the glacier to make a food dump on the ice cap from where they could fan out on exploratory forays. The O'Higgins Glacier was shrinking and receding fast – five miles in thirty years – which caused contorted ice formations and deep crevasses. Shipton fell into one, dislocating his shoulder, which popped back into place during a rescue by his companions.

Eventually after a lot of hard work they pitched their fifth camp on the ice cap in view of the Cordon Pio XI and its highest peak, Lautaro. In the *Alpine Journal* he wrote, 'About 300 feet below the summit, the ice slope on the northern side was gashed by a black fissure, from which there flowed a steady stream of vapour, mounting vertically for several hundred feet, then to be carried away by a southerly air current.' This was their elusive volcano. The next day as they were skiing across the plateau they saw ash erupt from it, blackening the snow over a large area of mountainside.

Peter Bruchhausen developed a painful, inflamed cyst on the top of his foot severely crippling him, especially when skiing, so he reluctantly decided to go down. The others made a food dump near the foot of the volcano beside a nunatak, or rocky outcrop, that was to be their base camp. But the weather broke and two weeks of almost continuous snow, storm and wind confined them to their tents. Finally both the petrol stoves, chosen by Shipton instead of their accustomed Primuses, failed; even Ewer, inured to the rigours of Antarctica, admitted that life on the open plateau, with damaged tents and no means of cooking or melting snow, might well prove intolerable. So they collected rock samples close by the nunatak and returned to the lake, leaving the sledges behind but taking the skis, which they cursed all the way especially when negotiating the forest.

In the middle of the remote, stormy Lago San Martin they spied another boat and went to meet it. On board were four dishevelled young climbers from the University of Santiago, Eduardo García and Cedomir Marangunic among them; the latter recounts their meeting. After a few minutes of polite exchanges Shipton asked, 'Where are you going?'

'To climb Mount O'Higgins,' they replied, awestruck by talking to the world famous explorer himself, and self-conscious of their ragged clothes and shabby equipment.

'You'll never do it,' said Shipton. In fact, spurred by this put-down, they went on to prove him wrong by making the first ascent of the mountain. But Shipton was not to forget this meeting.

This second expedition was disappointing because, although Shipton had proved the existence of the mysterious volcano, they had covered little new ground over the ice cap. But the experience of travel gained on these first two trips prepared him to tackle the challenge of further journeys. On his return through Bariloche he had an emotional meeting with an aunt he had never met before. Mrs Stewart Shipton was his father's brother's widow, known throughout Argentina as 'La Gaucha'; and, as recounted to Pamela, she 'clucked around him like a hen with her lost chick'. Sadly, this tantalising vignette is all we know about La Gaucha.

When he returned to England, Shipton received an invitation from Ed Hillary to join him on an expedition to search for the yeti. 'In a way it is tempting to go on a trip which is so well endowed with cash,' he wrote to Pamela, 'and not have the job of finding money, etc. and also I'd like to be with Ed. It would be exciting to see it as I have been pondering the possibilities of an expedition there.' But he turned down the offer in favour of Patagonia.

From his experience of the previous two southern summers, Shipton now felt ready to undertake a major journey that cried out to be completed – the lengthwise traverse of the Southern Patagonian Ice Cap. Tilman had crossed the waist of the ice cap from the Chilean side, as several others had tried before him, but the crossways distance was a mere twenty-five miles. Travelling along the north-south axis of the ice cap would involve a journey of about 150 miles. By starting in the north they would, with luck, have the prevailing wind on their backs. They would be travelling from uninhabited country towards civilisation and ground they had already trodden, which would be good for morale and safety. The idea of covering the whole region 'in one magnificent sweep' had an irresistible appeal to Shipton.

On his way home the previous year, he had stopped in Santiago to discuss the plan with an enthusiastic Jack Ewer. They agreed that the party should comprise four mountaineers, and decided to invite two of the young Chileans they had met in the middle of Lago San Martin. Eduardo García and Cedomir Marangunic had evidently formed a 'deeply agreeable' impression on Shipton, so they all met together to discuss the plan. Both Chileans had climbed widely in the Andes and were acquainted with Patagonian weather, so they knew what to expect on such an adventure. They decided to start at the Ventisquero (more euphonious than plain 'Glacier') Jorge Montt at the head of the Canal Baker, which thrusts deep into the Andes just south of the Golfo de Penas.

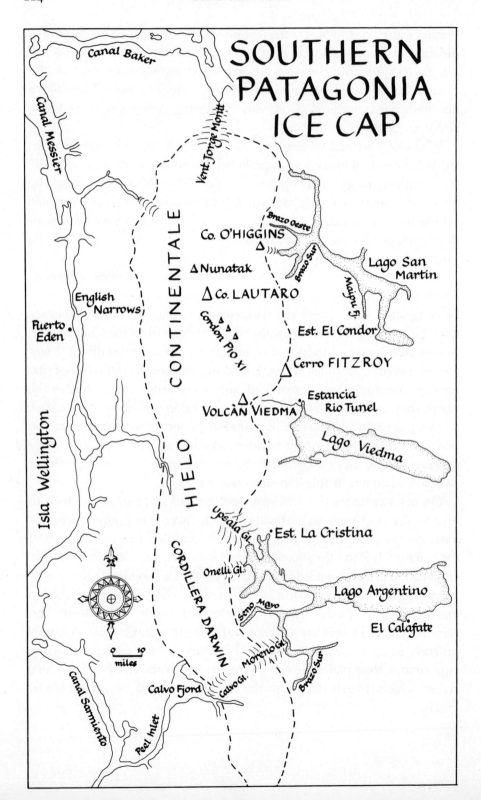

From his two earlier forays onto the ice cap, Shipton realised that lightweight Himalayan equipment was useless in the wet climate and savage gales of Patagonia. Relying on Ewer's Antarctic sledging experience, they opted for the old-fashioned, double-skinned Pyramid tent. Four ten-foot poles held it up free of guy ropes, snow skirts obviated the use of pegs to hold it down, and the ground sheet was sewn in place. Dry, it weighed fifty-five pounds; wet (its usual state), almost double.

No clothing material would ensure keeping them dry from the incessant rain and wet snow outside, and from condensation of sweat inside. But Shipton had outer garments made of the best available cloth. He also persuaded a company to fabricate one large, punt-shaped fibreglass sledge suitable for hauling their 750 pounds of gear, yet collapsible for carrying through forest; Ewer designed his own one-man sledge. They decided to use snowshoes, made for them by Slazenger, the tennis racquet manufacturer, because they had found skis awkward to carry in dense forest. Shipton admits that taking snowshoes instead of skis was a mistake; they were more difficult to use, they did not give as much support over crevasses, and the wearers sank into the soggy snow because they had to lean so far forward when hauling. His preliminary researches cannot have been extensive because certainly short, fishscale, no-wax skis were then available in Norway, and cheap snowshoes were common in Canada.

Lightweight nutritious food was essential because Shipton and his friends would carry and haul their own stuff. He planned a ration, weighing 32½ ounces, of 4,500 calories per man per day, composed of sugar, oats, wholemeal biscuit, dehydrated meat, butter, cheese, milk powder, rum fudge, soup powder and potato powder. Each day's ration was vacuum-packed, to save weight and to keep it dry.

The party foregathered in Punta Arenas, which Shipton described as 'a film version of a Klondyke gold rush town, emerging from the grip of the long Arctic winter' (an image that he must have conjured from his memory of Charlie Chaplin since he had then never been north of the 49th parallel). He had previously made friendly overtures to the Chilean Navy, or Armada, which offered to take the party from Punta Arenas on the Magellan Strait, to the Canal Baker, 600 miles northwards through the Chilean archipelago. Unfortunately the expedition baggage had been delayed by a dock strike in England and was still travelling down the west coast of Chile when the navy vessel was about to depart.

Prospects for getting the expedition off the ground seemed bleak until, by means of amateur ham radio, they managed to raise Captain Thomas of the MV *Salaverry*, which, with their cargo on board, was then approaching the Angostura Ingles, the aptly named English Narrows. The Captain had always been interested in the Everest expeditions and said he was keen to help them but he had no idea where their stuff was. However, he would 'do his damnedest' to find it, provided it was not buried too deep. True to his word, he extracted their crates from among the 2,000 tons of cargo in the hold, repacked them into twenty-seven smaller packages, and dropped them off at Puerto Eden, the only settlement in the entire archipelago.

Meanwhile Shipton was trying to assemble his crew, and to extricate himself from a farewell lunch arranged for them at Cedomir Marangunic's family home in Punta Arenas. Eventually, an hour late, they presented themselves at the naval dockyard and were taken out to the waiting frigate *Covadonga*.

The Chilean Navy Captain greeted them in perfect English, 'It is a pity, Mr Shipton, that you could not keep the timetable we'd arranged. We may have a small navy but we take it seriously.' Shipton wished a trapdoor would have opened and swallowed him up. He apologised and the matter was quickly forgotten in the warmth of their welcome on board. Soon the *Covadonga* was steaming through the Magellan Strait towards the Sarmiento Channel. So, after a shaky start, the expedition was under way. As Shipton wrote in *Land of Tempest*, 'I could wish for nothing better than to be here on this ship at the start of a 600-mile voyage through the narrow channels of one of the most fantastic archipelagos on earth, bound for the best of all mountaineering adventures, a journey through an unexplored range. Life occasionally provides moments of complete happiness; this, for me, was one.'

They passed the *Salaverry* during the night in mid-channel and sent a message of thanks to Captain Thomas. Their baggage awaited them at Puerto Eden, a community of the last remaining Alacaluf Canoe Indians, whom Shipton described as 'savage-looking people clad in skin or ragged cloth garments, some with long matted hair falling over their faces and shoulders. They squatted motionless in their boats, gazing up at the frigate with expressionless mongoloid faces. Some of the boats contained piles of enormous mussels.' Then, after transferring their baggage on board, they steamed through the narrow channels, bordered by numerous uninhabited islands with *Nothofagus* forest growing down to the water's edge, and rising to mountain peaks that disappeared into glowering clouds.

In the luxury of the boat, as in the calm before a storm, Shipton had a chance to get a measure of García and Marangunic, virtually complete strangers with whom he was about to embark on an arduous two-month journey.

But the choice of companions for an exploration is in any case something of a lottery [he wrote in *Land of Tempest*], and my experience has taught me to mistrust my judgment in the matter. Normal acquaintance with a man, however close, is a poor guide to whether he will be suitable or even a tolerable companion on an expedition. Faults that may normally seem utterly trivial often become nagging irritations in the enforced intimacy of an expedition; characteristics that may never appear in ordinary life can be distressingly or splendidly revealed in conditions of hardship, danger and physical or nervous strain. Some men who will rise magnificently to a crisis, may wilt under the stress of enforced inactivity. Then there is the diverse interplay of characters upon one another. A man may find himself with two companions, both of whom he likes very much, but who cannot tolerate each other. One of my most successful and delightful expedition partnerships was with a man who, I had been warned, was generally regarded as quite impossible to travel with [Michael Spender]. The argument of those who believe that an 'arranged' marriage had at least as much chance of success as one based upon a love affair, seems to be applicable here.

They were put ashore at the head of Canal Baker near the front of the Ventisquero Jorge Montt. 'Left on that lonely shore,' wrote Shipton, '150 miles of rugged travel ahead, the way to the Plateau unknown and no ready means of retreat – it was a stimulating situation; and I was glad to find my enjoyment of it was as keen as ever. My companions were no less delighted.'

They unpacked their stores and equipment, separating the necessities from surplus stuff which could be left behind. This incurred some heated debate over what items were absolutely necessary. Shipton's abiding and guiding precept seemed to the Chileans to be 'If in doubt, chuck it away' – shades of the chorten of tins he made on his way over to the Barun after the attempt on Cho Oyu?

Throughout the expedition the Chileans persisted in addressing their senior companions with the prefix Mister. As Cedomir Marangunic recounted with a laugh, 'Whenever anything was mislaid we would invariably say, "Mr Sheepton chuck it away my spoon/ glove/ (or whatever)." We usually started with enough stuff, but he always forgot most of his equipment along the way, and at the end of the trip there was nothing left.'

Ewer had a detailed plan for reaching the ice cap by clambering through the forest, but the tough young Chileans thought it better to ascend the icefall. Shipton listened to the discussion and said nothing; they put it to the vote and the glacier route won. Next day he said he had thought Ewer's proposal was crazy.

'Why didn't you say so at the time?' Marangunic asked.

'Because I wanted to hear your arguments,' Shipton replied.

From the start he became firm friends with the Chileans; one spoke English well, but understood little, and the other understood but did not speak much. 'I liked him very much, and I felt very comfortable with him,' said Marangunic. 'We liked to do lightweight expeditions and had similar styles of mountaineering. At fifty-five he was still in good shape, although he was not as strong as Eduardo and me, who were in our twenties. He always carried what he could. An Argentinian party, used to large groups of people, disliked him very much because of his expedition style.'

Shipton had estimated that the crossing would take fifty-five days so, adding an extra five days for safety, they had to transport 750 pounds of food, fuel and equipment up the glacier in relays. Each man was allowed only twenty pounds of personal gear; Shipton, in addition to the essentials, took '1 lb tobacco, 2 pipes, and 2 books (*Madame de Pompadour* and *Cakes and Ale*).'

Down in the valley the sledge came in useful as a boat for crossing a river, which gave them more excitement than they bargained for when

García capsized and had to swim in the icy water. Shipton stepped into a hole and sprained his right ankle, which took several days for the swelling to subside and to heal. With it strapped, he could hobble along carrying only a light pack. The actively receding glacier left a wide strip of bare country through which they could progress easily, allowing them to avoid the contorted lower section of the glacier and some of the dense forest belt. For a week the going was fairly straightforward but thereafter they were forced onto the glacier, where a thick mantle of winter snow still covered most of the crevasses.

Once they reached the flat snow plateau, they started hauling the sledges but this was much harder work than they expected because the runners dug into the soggy snow, and their snowshoes did the same. With practice their technique improved, but they were able to haul for only ten to fifteen minutes without a rest break. Ewer dragged his own sledge, which was generally more efficient in relation to its size than the big one, and often with more than his share of the load. The other three were harnessed to the large sledge.

Then occurred an incident that could have spelled disaster and the end of their trip. In the tent Shipton had just removed his sodden boots and socks, and was sitting on his sleeping bag beside the stove, preparing to make tea, as was his wont. Suddenly the pot tilted, pouring boiling water over his feet and scalding them, the left worse than the right; blisters formed quickly. Such a misfortune could happen to anyone in the crowded confines of a tent with few flat surfaces on which to balance a stove. Shipton was so incapacitated he had to be hauled sitting in the sledge for a couple of days, and he was unable to help relaying any loads for a week. It is surprising that his foot healed so quickly, and extremely lucky that it did not become infected, which would have forced the whole expedition to retreat.

So far the weather had been mainly wet; after a short clear spell the wind started with fury. Now they were on the plateau at 5,000 feet above the sea and heading almost due south. For ten days, blinded by spindrift, they marched by compass, still hauling over 500 pounds. The wind blowing from their backs helped, but it precluded relaying loads as they could not have returned battling the force head-on. Their days followed an unvarying pattern. Waking by means of his own in-built alarm clock, Shipton would rouse his companions on the dot of 3.30 a.m. and start to boil water while they still lay in their sleeping bags. Breakfast consisted of porridge oats, sugar and powdered milk, followed by tea. Climbing into cold, wet clothes, that never seemed to dry even by hanging them in the apex of the tent, took at least an hour. Digging the tent and sledges from under drifted snow, using ice axes because they had neglected to bring shovels (a serious omission), took another three hours. They rarely managed to start walking by 7.30 a.m.

They hauled in harness and trace till midday, with occasional halts for rum fudge; then, provided the wind was not too strong, they stopped for half an hour for lunch – biscuits, butter and cheese. They usually quit sledging at 3 p.m. and, depending on the wind, took at least an hour to pitch camp. Then the Pyramid tent came into its own. To erect it they would lay it flat on the ground, having laid out the sledges, snowshoes and spare gear as a windbreak. With the apex pointing into the wind, entrance uppermost, they secured the snowskirts with long aluminium pegs, and weighed them down with gear and snow or rocks to prevent the tent blowing away. Shipton would belay the windward guy rope round an ice axe; Ewer would control the apex while García and Marangunic crawled inside the flapping canvas to peg down the corners. When all was ready they inserted the poles and raised the whole tent.

Afterwards they prepared supper, and once they got settled, Shipton usually read for an hour or two, or wrote his diary. He always made the tea – English-fashion – but, according to Marangunic, cooking supper consisted of 'just dropping stuff into a pot'. The 'stuff' was a meat bar thickened with potato powder, together with a repeat of the breakfast menu. But as Shipton observed, 'The more lavishly an expedition is victualled, the greater the variety of choice supplied, the more people complain about the food.'

Marangunic remembers Shipton having a huge fund of limericks, a different one every day. García would write them in his diary – his 'English lesson' – and later recite them (the bawdier the better), often misquoted in a thick Spanish accent. After a while he had compiled such a copious anthology that, Shipton wrote, 'Jack Ewer and I were astonished at our own resourcefulness.' Shipton was quite reserved about his private life, and never harked back to reminiscences about his previous mountaineering expeditions, as climbers confined to tents tend to do.

But he was always planning new trips, always thinking how to reduce equipment (even how to share an ice axe).

Early on he had said, 'To travel successfully in the mountains of Patagonia one must make up one's mind as far as possible to ignore the weather, and we resolved to make this our basic principle.' But it is difficult, even for those accustomed to the discomforts of mountaineering, to imagine the labour and tedium of sledge-hauling, the misery of always being wet and cold, and the uncertainty of never being really sure of one's position. However, Shipton set little store by these concerns. 'Now that we were actually there coping with the weather, we gradually gained confidence in our ability not only to survive the worst that it could do but also to travel securely; and with this confidence came a positive exultation in the violence of the elements.'

Once on the ice cap, the snowstorms were heavy and continuous, and rain was rare. Although snow severely reduced visibility, it had the advantage of safely covering most of the crevasses. On a rare clear moment they found themselves surrounded by granite spires (with no signs of volcanic rocks), but then the weather closed in and for nearly four days they saw nothing at all. They were now four weeks out, had covered more than half the projected distance, and were approaching ground Shipton had already trodden in previous years. After weeks of almost blind travel, navigating by compass, they found the rocky outcrop of the nunatak and, with some difficulty, their old depot. From it they salvaged twenty meat bars and a two-pound tin of butter, which they scoffed within a day.

A rare dispute arose over the position the stove should occupy in the tent; Shipton wanted it in the entrance corridor so he could get at it in the morning to make tea, and yet be within reach of snow to melt; Ewer objected, saying it should stand in the middle of the floor in order to dry clothes hung in the peak (where they never did dry). But this position squeezed Shipton and Marangunic against the wet, sagging tent walls, and increased the danger of 'fire and flood'. It behoved them to resolve the conflict speedily. Shipton's view was that 'Primus stoves, like horses, are peculiarly sensitive to emotional atmosphere, and to succeed with them one must be thoroughly relaxed. On the whole, however, considering our constricted living-quarters there were remarkable few quarrels and I have rarely travelled with a set of more congenial companions.' This was his second trip with Ewer, whom he regarded as tough, intelligent, thoughtful and always full of optimism. 'This is splendid,' Ewer would say, as he climbed into a wet sleeping bag; his one fault was his know-all attitude. García was an indefatigable clown, but also a very good mountaineer; Marangunic maintained a silent, unruffled calm and a quiet humour.

On the second half of the journey they encountered some severe blizzards, but their technique for dealing with the atrocious weather, and their mental attitude towards it, was now so refined that it barely bothered them. Shipton noted, 'I remember looking forward keenly to the next day's march, hoping that snow conditions would be better, wondering what we might see. I certainly experienced none of the boredom and frustration I remember during the attempts to climb Everest.'

They were able to travel more quickly now because their sledges were lighter, and they were on the home stretch, with time and food in hand. Occasional brief clearings in the omnipresent cloud and mist gave them expansive views of the high peaks sprouting from the ice cap. At one point they found themselves in a corridor abreast of the cathedral spires of the Fitzroy Range. They even climbed a couple of smaller peaks and were rewarded, as Shipton reported in the *Alpine Journal*, with views of 'an exotic statuary of ice composed of a delicate pattern of crystal flowers; huge mushrooms and jutting gargoyles sculptured in rime by the saturated wind'.

Eventually they started descending the Upsala Glacier in the customary wind, mist and driving sleet. When the ice became too rough, they regretfully abandoned the sledges and shouldered the loads, which Shipton complained 'were still uncomfortably heavy because of Cedomir's rock samples'. What he did not know was that, along the way, García and Marangunic were collecting climbing gear he had jettisoned – pitons, karabiners, rope etc. – none of which was readily available in Chile. Finally, after fifty-two days of traversing the ice cap, they reached the valley and walked along a path through gentle woodland, 'stopping often to lie on banks of moss and leaves, gazing up at the trees, listening entranced to the song of birds and tasting the nectar of earth-scented air'. And so to the 'fleshpots' of Estancia la Cristina – Mrs Masters's home cooking, strawberries and cream, and clean sheets.

They had crossed one of the wildest mountain regions on earth entirely without outside help during the worst summer weather the Masters could remember in sixty years at the estancia. 'It was a very difficult journey,' Cedomir Marangunic said modestly. 'Eric never paid attention to his personal comfort, whether he was wet or dry. I didn't care much either, so we got on well together. You could *feel* his happiness in Patagonia. He liked the simple life and once he told me, "If I had another life I'd like to be a Yaghan Indian; just take a pot and matches and go fishing."'

Reading this account of their journey in home comfort, it is hard truly to imagine how adrenaline and endorphins alter one's view of grim situations such as Scott, Shackleton, and other polar explorers (for this is what Shipton's crew virtually were) must have experienced. It is also hard to understand how they put up with the unremitting discomfort of being constantly cold and wet from blizzard and hurricane winds, marching by compass for days on end, unsure of their whereabouts, hauling dead-weight sledges, and eating a frugal diet.

For Shipton in his mid-fifties, the traverse of the Southern Patagonian Ice Cap was probably the toughest trip he had ever done, or would ever do again; he concluded in *Land of Tempest*, 'It had been an experience as completely satisfying as any I have known.' That is profound indeed from a man with a lifetime's experience of penetrating wild places of the globe. With this journey achieved, you might think he would have called it a day and turned to new fields of adventure, perhaps somewhat less demanding. But as Cedomir Marangunic remarked, 'He was always thinking ahead of what to do next, planning new trips. He was quite willing to do strange things or to follow any crazy proposition. I'd say, "There's a peak; let's climb it." He'd reply, "Let's go then."'

Shipton would return, between his masochistic forays into wildest Patagonia, to Shropshire where he enjoyed the comfort of Phyllis Wint's undemanding affection at The Haye, or at Tite Street, Chelsea. This domestic arrangement suited them both, because he had the freedom to come and go as he pleased, yet still claiming to be a homeless nomad. While in Shropshire he cultivated vegetables with passion, delight and increasing success. Phyllis Wint's family were quite bemused by their unconventional relationship, nevertheless she got on with her own life regardless of their opinion. This was a love affair of later life that had all the tenderness of youth without its consuming passion and jealousy. 'He always got into dreadful muddles with women because he wanted to please everybody,' said Phyllis Wint. 'He liked to keep all his friends, and especially his women friends, in separate compartments so nobody knew who anybody else was. I suppose he was very weak in some ways, but I knew he was never going to leave me.'

By now Shipton had given up the liaisons that he had been loath to drop even after he moved in with Phyllis. 'He was very considerate to me,' she said, 'and certainly he wasn't self-centred. After his expeditions we'd always meet at a certain place on a certain day – Punta Arenas, or Bahia Blanca, in Patagonia, for example. He was always there, and he never failed to send me a letter to confirm it. It was very romantic really.' In fact Shipton had almost taken over Phyllis Wint's household. 'We couldn't have a TV because he said it smacked of ostentation,' she remarked. 'And yet he'd happily buy an air ticket to South America and back. He was a bit of a snob, really; always talking about the Lower Orders.' It is not clear exactly where the money came from to finance these trips; some from his royalties, some from investments left to him by his mother – and then there was his austere lifestyle (where shopping for a meal he always budgeted at 50 pence per head).

Next he began to plan a trip into the Cordillera Darwin in the unexplored heart of Tierra del Fuego and known for its evil weather. He described it in *Tierra del Fuego: the Fatal Lodestone* as, 'Almost completely surrounded by sea, lashed by the ferocious gales that rage around Cape Horn, guarded by a massive rampart of forest which, nurtured by incessant rain, has a strangely tropical appearance, the mountains had such a reputation for inaccessibility that no one had ventured into the interior of the range.' The Darwin Range is as large as the greater part of the Central Alps of Europe; the highest peak is 8,500 feet measured straight out of the sea. If you think of well-known photographs of Mount Everest from Rongbuk, or of K2 from Concordia, you can only see about 10,000 feet of mountain because the base from where they are taken is at 18,000 feet already; therefore describing mountains as 'Himalayan in size' can be quite deceptive. Mount St Elias in Alaska, for instance, rises 18,000 feet, all totally visible, from the sea.

For the first time ever, he went into serious training in Shropshire. From a local farmer he borrowed sacks of pignuts, weighing seventy

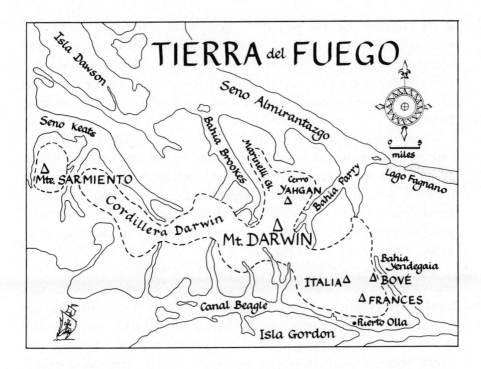

pounds in total, and climbed up and down Clee Hill on Lord Boyne's estate close to The Haye. Feeling rather self-conscious, he avoided footpaths and kept to the woods. On one of his furtive excursions a gamekeeper apprehended him and demanded to know what was in his sack. His feeble explanation linking pignuts with the mountains of Tierra del Fuego did little to allay the angry bailiff's suspicions.

On this adventure his staunch Chilean friends, Eduardo García and Cedomir Marangunic were joined by Francisco ('Pancho') Vivanco; unfortunately Jack Ewer was otherwise engaged. They expected much steeper ground than on the ice cap, so they took short skis instead of sledges, their faithful Pyramid tent, and a radio that never worked.

Shipton had so charmed the Chilean Navy, that again they agreed to transport the party to their starting point, as they also did on several subsequent occasions. A naval patrol ship put them ashore at the mouth of Brooke's Bay, leading south off Seno Almirantazgo which cuts deeply into Tierra del Fuego from the Magellan Strait. About to depart, the ship's crew leaned over the rail to say farewell to Shipton in the

Zodiac loaded with 800 pounds of gear, enough for eight weeks. For ten minutes he yanked unsuccessfully on the starter cord of the 10 h.p. outboard motor, then he noticed that the petrol feed pipe was connected the wrong way round. 'He was hopeless with motors,' said Marangunic, 'absolutely hopeless. And not much better at handling boats.'

They motored to the head of the fjord surrounded by a cirque of calving glaciers and mountains rising abruptly to 7,500 feet, and found a lagoon where hundreds of ducks swam and dolphins played. A rocky ramp left behind by the shrinking Marinelli Glacier provided them with an easy stairway to bypass the forest, and the worst of the broken lower icefalls. They reached the heart of the range in only six days and made a base camp up on the ice plateau.

Their aims were threefold: first, to climb Mount Darwin; second, to reach the Beagle Channel so Marangunic could complete a geological transect; and third, to climb a beautiful spire they named Cerro Yaghan. By fortune of a few perfect days in between horrendous storms, they achieved all these objectives. On one occasion after a blizzard the twelve-foot aerial mast belonging to the useless radio just poked through the new snow guiding their safe return to base camp. Finally, during a huge storm the Pyramid tent was driven four feet down into the snow, a pack weighing fifty pounds was blown 200 feet away into a crevasse (from where it was later recovered), and each of them in turn was hurled to the ground by the wind.

Having satisfactorily completed their tasks in the mountains, they returned to the sea shore where they enjoyed a week's holiday while awaiting the return of the ship. Then they cruised slowly down the fjord, 'camping in little bays, basking in the sun, diving into the icy water of deep tidal pools to fish for edible crabs, eating enormous quantities of mussels and sea urchins, and lying beside camp fires under a starlit sky,' he wrote to Pamela Freston. 'Wonderful country, particularly the fjords, full of porpoises, sea lions and ducks, and flanked by forest and huge glacier cirques.' For Shipton it was an excellent trip and achieved everything they had hoped for.

Soon after returning to Punta Arenas, Shipton set off again with Cedomir Marangunic, along with Marangunic's sister and her husband, to explore Mount Burney, which lies on the Munoz Gamero peninsula south of Puerto Natales. Marangunic claims that this trip was one of their best together. From Estancia Skyring, on the lake of that name, they headed west into a brewing storm. They victualled themselves with one big cheese for the one-week trip, but when it turned into two weeks they started conserving the cheese and caught fish.

They carried the deflated boat across a narrow isthmus into a system of freshwater lakes that occupy the centre of the peninsula from where they had a fine view of Mount Burney, a broken massif of heavily glaciated peaks and ridges. But they could approach no closer than ten miles. 'I'd been expecting a pretty little volcanic cone,' Shipton wrote, 'instead it looked more like Kangchenjunga, completely sheathed in glacier; one of the peaks, perhaps the highest, was a sharp white fang.' On their return voyage they encountered severe westerly gales and mountainous seas, white with spume. As usual they had engine trouble, so Marangunic made a mast out of a tree and used a tent as a sail, and considered they were 'close to death' surfing down the waves and in danger of broaching.

In the following years Shipton did a number of expeditions into more and more remote parts of Patagonia. In 1962–63, Jack Ewer and John Earle joined him on a second reconnaissance of Mount Burney, a mountain that had already titillated him. Again he took the Zodiac inflatable boat with which to navigate the freshwater lakes. As seemed to become a habit at the start of a trip, they had boat problems – forgetting spanners and spare parts, fouling the propeller, beaching the craft badly and soaking the packages it contained (including Earle's movie cameras and film).

But the clouds were so low throughout the trip that they could not even see their mountain. So Shipton decided they should try to walk right around it through unexplored country, rather than wait for the weather to clear in the hope they could try to climb it. If a clear day should happen, then they would dash for the top. In fact, during the next sixteen days the mountain remained shrouded in cloud. They were burdened, not only with the boat weighing 150 pounds, but with Earle's bulky and heavy camera equipment. Of the difficult ground they had to cover, Earle says, 'Eric moved very well on the treacherous, loose rock and shale. He always seemed in balance and used such little effort in comparison with our sliding and clawing progress.' Ewer was unhappy about the decision not to attempt the mountain, becoming disgruntled because the trip lacked the excitement and challenge of their ice cap crossing. But Shipton was quite content with their achievement of exploring so much new ground, finding uncharted glaciers, and getting a good picture of the layout of Mount Burney, of which they caught their first glimpse only as they were heading out of the forest.

On return to their dump on Skyring Sound they found that both foot pumps had perished so they had to inflate the boat by mouth which was exhausting and dizzying work, even taking only three or four minute relays each. On their way back to civilisation at Estancia Skyring, the home of Gerald Friedli and his family, they met Chris Bonington, fresh off a first ascent of the Central Tower of Paine. Recounting their adventure quite prosaically to Bonington, Shipton confessed that they had forgotten to take any salt to spice their simple diet of porridge for breakfast, a bit of chocolate and cheese for lunch, and a concentrated meat bar for supper. Bonington wrote in *The Next Horizon*, 'I shall never forget Shipton's look of quiet satisfaction when he remarked, "You know, we hardly noticed its absence at all. I think we might well leave it behind on our next trip."'

Next year Shipton had some free time (not an unusual state of affairs for him), so he decided to return to the Cordillera Darwin to try to climb Mount Bové, along with John Earle, Peter Bruchhausen (from his trip of three years before) and a young Chilean student. Bruchhausen again had a bad start. He collapsed near their camp from an allergy to mussels of which they had eaten plenteously; then high up on the glacier a strong gust blew him off his feet and into a crevasse; finally he slipped on some steep ice but luckily came to a halt unharmed. They had the faithful old Pyramid tent again and, despite its weight and awkwardness, found it a blessing in the ferocious winds. Using their familiar siege tactics they made first ascents of both Mount Bové and Mount Francis. Descending from the latter Shipton, who was carrying the tent on a pack frame, tried to leap a crevasse, just failed, and fell into it, landing on a ledge above a deep abyss. John Earle recounted in *Springs of Enchantment*, Shipton saying in a calm, faint voice, 'Er, I say, are you going to be able to get me out?' Extracting him, and the precious tent, took nearly an hour, and his toes were mildly frostbitten. Eventually they reached the Beagle Channel in time for their rendezvous with the

Chilean Navy. Back in Punta Arenas, Phyllis Wint was waiting for him on one of their trysts, and they all repaired to Tierra del Fuego to stay with the Bridges family at the Estancias Viamonte and Harberton.

When Shipton was traversing the Southern Patagonian Ice Cap with García and Marangunic in 1960, they frequently talked about the 'natural sequel' of doing a similar journey across the Northern Ice Cap. This would entail a shorter route, but severe terrain because of some high passes. So the three men teamed up again in 1963–64 together with Miguel Gomez, a Spanish mountaineer living in South America. It is anticlimactic to summarise this journey in a paragraph or two, because on its own it stands out as a remarkable piece of exploration. Yet so much of what happened is the same as has been described before on his other Patagonian journeys – endless relaying of outrageous loads, storms that only their Pyramid tent could withstand, being wet and cold for days on end – that this journey appears quite straightforward compared with the earlier ones. By now Shipton had refined his techniques of travel and learned from experience about moving through that inclement land.

They were dropped near the front of the San Rafael Glacier, flowing into the head of a long inlet, of which Charles Darwin wrote, 'It pushes its ice into the sea at a point on the coast where, within 500 miles, palms grow.' They ascended the glacier, which squeezed against forest that grew on its precipitous flanks, causing it to be deeply contorted with crevasses and chaotic, towering seracs. They used sledges and skis, and carried a rubber dinghy which they expected to need at the end of the journey for lake and river crossings. By Patagonian standards the weather was fair – fifteen fine days in six weeks. They managed to climb several peaks along the way in what Shipton describes as 'some of the loveliest mountain country I have seen in Patagonia or anywhere else'.

Eventually they came down off the ice cap to Lago Colonia through a maze of wide crevasses. The dinghy was too small to carry all of them, so they made a raft with their skis strapped to air mattresses, and towed it behind them; for oars they used snow shovels fixed to the end of poles, and anoraks hoisted as sails. The lake was very rough and at the far end they were hurled unceremoniously ashore by the breakers.

What, you may ask, was so extraordinary about Shipton's explorations in Patagonia, compared with his much more prestigious climbs in the Himalaya? First, the sheer physical stresses of travelling through the land itself, which had no pretty alpine paths, wide valleys, or trade routes to follow. He was either in dense *Nothofagus* forest, or negotiating glaciers as deeply crevassed as he had seen anywhere. Second, they carried by themselves huge loads of all their gear without the luxury of armies of porters and high altitude Sherpas. Third, the Patagonian weather was unremittingly foul, with blizzard followed by hurricane, by white-out, compared to the Himalaya where the monsoon is predictable almost to the day, and the weather at either end is often quite settled, except high on the mountains. Fourth, they were in remote country, on journeys to which they were totally committed, with no chance of rescue should anything serious happen to them because they had no radio, no messengers, no communication. Finally, Shipton was travelling with fit young men half his age, yet able to pull his weight as an equal. These were outstanding, rare journeys indeed.

Resulting from Shipton's good relations with Chile, built up during the years of his Patagonia travels, and his close association with the Chilean Navy, he was invited in 1964 to give geographical advice on a long-standing boundary dispute with Argentina. The Queen of England, or her counsels, was asked to arbitrate the matter, as had her great grandmother at the turn of the century. The immediate problem arose over a small and insignificant piece of mountainous country lying near Palena to the south of Esquel, and containing two obscure rivers, the Rio Engano and the Rio Encuentro, and a hill, the Cerro de la Virgen. But it was only a symptom of a more long-lasting dispute involving the entire frontiers of Patagonia. The original treaty of 1881 specified the frontier would follow the line of high peaks that formed the watershed between the Atlantic and the Pacific. Unfortunately in the southern Patagonian Andes, the drainage of the Continental Divide and the line of the high mountain peaks are not the same thing; Chile wanted the frontier as the former, Argentina the latter.

The Chilean Government flew Shipton, first class, to Santiago. Expecting some mountaineering, he wore his climbing boots and carried an ice axe which was stored away among the mink coats. Before his Chilean government business he was joined by Jack Ewer and his old friend George Lowe, then headmaster of a large boarding school in Santiago, for a couple of weeks on a glacier in Aisen province.

Thereafter he met his Chilean hosts, and spent time riding horseback through the lovely region of dispute, climbing gentle mountains and meeting the local people. Previously no one had bothered much with this Engano Valley where a small band of Chilean farmers had settled, until Argentina realised the settlers were in their territory, and made a fuss which turned into an international incident far out of proportion to its geographical or political importance.

Each side sent its mission to Palena, the main town of the region, for on-the-spot discussion of the case, which focused on which was the main river valley, and the volume of two contested streams. The commissions stayed in a luxurious bungalow specially built for the occasion, feasted on flown-in lobsters and shell fish, and swanned around the area by helicopter and small plane. They also recorded the names on the headstones in remote graveyards to see where the early settlers and explorers were buried. Predominantly immigrant Welsh names appeared in the Argentine cemeteries, Spanish names in the Chilean ones, evidence that weighed heavily when it came to decide where the divide should be made.

The tribunal met in London in the autumn of 1966 for the final debate, which took six weeks of legal wrangling between high powered (and paid) lawyers. Eventually the Queen's Award was made, with Chile retaining the land occupied by the settlers, and Argentina the larger uninhabited area. After two years of massive expense and labour (which was sheer delight to Shipton) both countries were pleased with their awards, and the matter was settled.

CHAPTER 17

The Celebrity Guide and Lecturer

1967–77

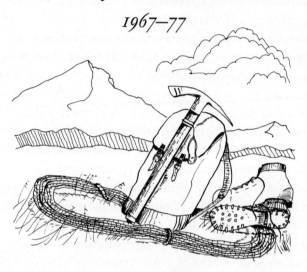

THE FINAL DECADE of Eric Shipton's life was a natural winding down of the intense activity he had sustained far longer than most people do in middle age. He had filled his fifties, which he claimed was the best decade of his life, with the Patagonia journeys, some of his toughest exploring of all. His sixties were a time to enjoy visiting interesting faraway places at other people's expense by leading trekking groups, or lecturing on cruise ships, accompanied by his constant and devoted partner, Phyllis Wint. He was now appreciated as a fount of Himalayan wisdom, sought by climbers planning journeys to distant ranges, a service he always provided generously.

Stimulated by a previous trip to Ecuador, when he had climbed to 16,000 feet on Cotopaxi, in 1965 Shipton made his first of three visits to the Galapagos Islands. There he met Roger Perry, director of the Charles Darwin Research Station, himself of an adventurous disposition, who was delighted to find a kindred companion for exploring the islands. Little was known of the rugged interiors of any of the larger islands, which lie on the Equator, 700 miles from the coast of Ecuador. Perry was keen to learn whether any giant tortoises inhabited the crater of the Volcàn Alcedo, the central of five volcanoes evenly spaced along the 100-mile length of Albemarle Island.

Shipton and Philip Hugh-Jones, an English doctor friend, flew to the Galapagos in an Ecuadorian military plane. The pilot, one of the junta, had difficulty in finding the islands so the two Englishmen helped navigate with a map and compass. On their arrival, Perry asked if they wanted to count tortoises on Albemarle Island. He provided the research station's vessel *Beagle* to put them ashore on a sandy beach (a rare commodity) where abounded sea lions, marine iguanas, scarlet crabs, flightless cormorants, blue-footed boobies, pelicans and penguins. He also sent along as a porter the research station handyman, Calapucho, an exiled Amazonian Indian.

Albemarle Island's coastal fringe consisted of cinder desert and huge fields of rough volcanic lava with small deposits of smooth pumice, but barren of vegetation except for the occasional cactus plant. The jagged rock was hard on their boots and made walking tedious. It was generally so porous that any rain was soaked up immediately. Without pools or streams, they had to carry all their drinking water, which necessarily limited the length of their stay on the island.

The slopes of the volcanoes were covered with dense thorn scrub and occasional open woodland. Shipton found lots of sleek and fat wild donkeys whose tracks made his passage easier through the undergrowth. The final climb to the rim of the Alcedo crater, fifteen miles in circumference and 1,000 feet deep, was up a gentle convex slope like all Galapagos volcanoes which have the shape of a turtle's shell due to the enormous size of the craters in proportion to their height. Along the crater rim they found seventy-nine tortoises, most longer than eighteen inches, suggesting a population of several thousand on the island. Shipton was impressed by their agility in clambering over steep ground, and also by their apparent deafness. Descending into the crater he struggled through undergrowth, following donkey tracks where possible, and found a geyser shooting jets of boiling water eighty feet high in the air every few seconds. This water fell and cooled in puddles where the donkeys could drink.

After five days the *Beagle* returned to their rendezvous with Roger Perry on board, wanting to join them in exploring neighbouring Narborough Island, again intent on looking for tortoises. Shipton hurt his back by slipping on some wet rocks while landing ashore, so his companions had to set off for the crater without him. But next day, in frustration at not feeling better from a day's rest, he decided to try the opposite treatment, and started climbing the crater with Calapucho, who quickly decided that mountaineering was not for him. Shipton's back improved steadily the higher he climbed. At the crater rim he was in dense mist, so, being only lightly dressed, he collected wood and settled down beside a blazing fire prepared to stoke it throughout the night.

'After dark the weather cleared and the moon, then in its first quarter, lit the scene about me,' Shipton wrote in *Animals Magazine*. 'The air was still and the silence complete. The walls of the crater, nearly 12 miles round, fell sheer into a cauldron of white mist which remained deep in the interior. With the dawn the mist dispersed and I saw the lake at the bottom of the crater, more than 2,000 feet below.' He refrained from climbing down into it because he had neither food nor water, and he started back after watching the sunrise. Perry and Hugh-Jones had reached the crater bottom where they spent the night at the edge of a sweet water lake, teeming with Galapagos pintail ducks.

Shipton returned to the Galapagos twice in subsequent years, and made further visits to the volcanic islands with Perry. Although insignificant by the scale and rigour of his other explorations, these trips were some of his most enjoyable and fruitful.

Being elected President of the Alpine Club in 1965 was an accolade from the mountaineering establishment, recognising Shipton's contribution to their sport and his return from a personal wilderness. He had mixed feelings about the honour. The prospect of having to talk in front of audiences filled him with dread (worse yet was to read aloud, an excruciating trial for most dyslexics). In fact, he managed to get through most Alpine Club meetings by asking the Honorary Secretary to read aloud anything important, claiming he had forgotten his glasses. He wormed out of giving a Valedictory Address to the club (Jack Longland said he was the only president on record ever to have done so) by arranging his next Patagonian trip during the occasion of the

Alpine Club dinner. Later he presided at a reception of a Polish delega-
tion of climbers and delivered a brief speech in Polish learnt on the
spur of the moment from his dinner neighbour, which was reminiscent
of his schoolboy struggles with Horace, and considerably easier than
having to read his own speech aloud.

His presidency covered an important milestone of the Alpine Club
(the world's oldest) when it merged with the Alpine Climbing Group, a
corps of Britain's best young climbers. The debates over whether to
allow such a cocky bunch of individualists through the respectable
doors of 74 South Audley Street raged long and vociferously. Despite
strong opposition from some older members, especially George Finch,
who (Shipton told Pamela) gave a violent tirade against modern youth
saying that they should all be flogged, the progressives won a convincing victory in favour of amalgamating the two clubs, by 208 votes for,
with sixteen against. Shipton held liberal and progressive views concerning mountaineering politics, and it was probably fortunate that he,
and not one of the old guard, was there to moderate the great debate.

Only once was he in serious danger of being drummed out of the
Alpine Club (if we discount his forgetting his subscripton when he was
in Kashgar, and sending Tom Longstaff a cheque for £4 to forward to
the Hon. Treas.). This was when John Earle invited him to appear on a
TV programme he was directing about the pre-war Everest expeditions.
For a prop they had borrowed from the Alpine Club the famous
Mallory ice axe found in 1933 during Shipton's first Everest expedition.
After the show Shipton offered to return the treasured item to the club.
In the flurry of unpacking his car at Tite Street he laid it on the pave-
ment and promptly forgot about it. He eventually remembered the ice
axe and went outside to fetch it, but it was gone. Next morning, after
Shipton had spent a sleepless night of worry, a policeman knocked on
the door bearing the ice axe, and said (as Earle records), 'Knowing you
to be a climbing gentleman, sir, I guessed that this was some form of
climbing implement. But I found it too late last night to return it to you
then.'

As President of the Alpine Club, Shipton attended the Matterhorn
Centenary celebrations in Zermatt and, though fearful of convivial
assemblies, he thoroughly enjoyed himself and made several new
friends. Among them was Bob Bates, the American mountaineer

known for his adventures on Mount McKinley and K2, who invited
Shipton to visit Alaska the next year. Bates and his climbing colleague,
Adams Carter, arranged for him to lecture in the eastern United States,
which paid for his Alaska expenses. At one talk the audience howled
with mirth when he confessed that he only came upon crampons late
in life, and had never once hit in a piton.

From Talkeetna, just outside Denali National Park, Don Sheldon,
the legendary bush pilot, landed them on Mount Russell from a ski
plane. From their drop-off they climbed fairly high on the mountain but
failed to reach the summit because they were stormbound for two
weeks under ten feet of snow, during which time Shipton cemented his
friendship with the Americans.

Simultaneously, his Chilean friend, Cedomir Marangunic, was geo-
logising with Ohio State University on the Sherman Glacier near
Cordova. So Shipton set off to visit him with two young Alaskan
companions, who took a long time bushwhacking through trackless
forest to the foot of the glacier. Marangunic tells how from his camp
he saw three unusual dark dots, which he thought were black bears,
climbing the glacier: then three hours later Shipton and his two friends
walked into the hut: 'They'd been walking for three days in the forest
absolutely lost, without food or tents. They were hungry and tired, and
slept in our sleeping bags for three hours. Then Eric said, "We've got
to go back now." So they left and we had no chance to chat.' But Shipton
had been impressed by the vastness of this mostly untrodden Alaskan
wilderness and its massive unclimbed mountain ranges.

Commercial mountain tourism, especially in the Himalaya, came into
vogue in the late 'sixties. Some of the leaders in the field were Mountain
Travel, a company founded by Colonel Jimmy Roberts in Nepal, and
Thomas Cook of London, who celebrated their centenary by running
a Cook's Tour to Everest base camp. Shipton was an obvious person to
lead such enterprises; he never pretended to be more than a figurehead,
and sensibly left all the organisation to the company. He felt his job was
to amble along the trail being pleasant and interesting to the clients, who
paid for their experience and bathed in the glow of rubbing shoulders
with the great explorer. His hands-off style made it difficult for less
prestigious leaders following in his footsteps, who were expected by
their employers to be much more active and organisational. Shipton led

several of these trips to Nepal, visiting the Everest and Annapurna regions.

After much pressing by his publisher, Hodder & Stoughton, he at last started to write the new volume of autobiography they had been requesting repeatedly (*Upon That Mountain* only took him up to the war). 'I haven't begun to think how I'll deal with my emotional tangles or the Everest do, but we'll just see how things shape,' he wrote to Pamela. Writing was always a chore, and he a great procrastinator. Although his later books do not have the flair of *Nanda Devi* or *Blank on the Map*, he always produced clear, well-researched, readable prose. Perhaps his biggest omission was an in-depth commentary on the politics of Central Asia that he might have written when he had plenty of time on his hands in Kashgar; there is only one brief chapter in *Mountains of Tartary* on that fascinating political crucible. *That Untravelled World* was very well received and reviewed. However, his emphasis is surprising; sometimes he spends pages describing an event of small importance, while disposing briefly of critical moments in his life, or even of large clumps of time.

That a dyslexic should acquire such mastery of words as Shipton did, is not as strange as it might seem now that the condition is more understood. Dyslexia has nothing to do with intelligence, everything to do with a neurological inability to connect words seen on a page with the words that should form in the brain and leave the mouth. Flaubert, Hans Christian Andersen and W. B. Yeats were all dyslexics. Pamela Freston again was his main sounding board, to whom he kept a steady flow of his book drafts. He corresponded with her to the end of his life; his letters were always affectionate, having lost the argumentative passions of their earlier years, always full of gossipy snippets (never mean) about their mutual friends, and occasionally reminiscing over the heady days when they were still lovers. She was certainly a crutch of support through his various self-inflicted personal crises, and she maintained an overwhelming influence on him – 'his policeman', Phyllis Wint called her.

However, *That Untravelled World* stirred up dormant controversy over the 1953 Everest leadership. Claude Elliott took deep exception to two words in one sentence of Charles Evans's review in the *Alpine Journal* of 1970, when he wrote, 'The Committee adopted the *unworthy device* of presenting him [Shipton] with a condition he could not accept and this deprived him of the leadership.' A review in the *Times Literary Supplement* also suggested some hanky-panky.

On 6 July 1971 Elliott delivered to Blakeney a long memo for the Alpine Club records, marked *Very Private,* and which 'should be shown to no one at all without the express consent of Goodfellow and myself, or of Goodfellow after I am dead'. Elliott expressed the feeling that 'it would be undesirable if a legend of bad, even dishonourable treatment of Shipton by the Committee would become established,' and he considered it 'highly important that this account should not get into the hands of any injudicious or publicity-seeking, or malicious person.' In fact, Elliott's account reveals nothing new that is not already available in the Blakeney papers in the British Library, leaves out certain pertinent nuances, and yet accepts some personal blame for the outcome of the unfortunate meeting of 28 July 1952 which reaffirmed Shipton as leader for Everest 1953.

Elliott concludes, 'It is however greatly to be hoped that no one will seek to revive this controversy and it can sink now into total oblivion.' One can sympathise with the sentiments of such a decent and gentle man as Elliott, yet the person most deeply affected by the whole shemozzle was Shipton. While wishing none of the epithets of the above paragraph, it is the responsibility of a biographer to present Shipton's view and the known facts of the circumstances of late 1952 which turned his life upside down and deprived him of the chance to be there when Everest, to which he had devoted so much of his life, was climbed.

Shipton became sought after frequently as a speaker (although only a mediocre performer, but still famous enough to attract an enthusiastic audience), and he made several lecture tours in the United States. The era of educational cruises had just begun, and he was approached by Lars Linblad of New York to be the guest lecturer on one of his small ships cruising the Chilean Channels, to the Galapagos, and later twice to Antarctica.

Phyllis Wint, his constant companion on all these cruises, was quite unconventional for her day. Diana, who called her 'the enigma of all time', together with many of his former lovers, could not understand why he should fall for Phyllis. Some attributed it to domestic convenience and the fact that she would let him go off on his travels on a whim and unimpeded. Certainly lack of fetters and demands was part of the bastion of their relationship, but that alone could not have held them together for twenty years. Phyllis was just not bothered by the other women in Shipton's life and felt no jealousy towards them, though she got a certain amusement from their machinations.

'Eric suggested marriage to me once, but we never mentioned it again,' Phyllis said. 'We were very close and happy, and it didn't really seem to matter. My children were much more concerned about us not being married than I was. Suddenly after we'd been together for about a year, Eric said to me, "I thought I'd never say these words again, but I love you. I don't know why, I can't help it, but I just do." He always wanted somebody to be close to; all his life he was looking for something that wasn't there.' Phyllis felt confident of his affection, despite his philandering track record, and her confidence was justified throughout their two decades of living together.

But things were not so comfortable between their children, and Phyllis's daughters admit to resenting the visits of the Shipton sons at The Haye. Both boys were living with Diana and David Drummond in Scotland during the holidays from boarding school. Nick, the image of his father, entered Sandhurst as an officer cadet in the Royal Engineers, going on to pass out of Shrivenham with first class honours. After six years in the army he became a science teacher specialising in physics. More recently he took up chiropractic medicine, and runs a thriving practice split between Bristol and Cardiff.

John, the rebel, admits he slid into a drug-taking hippie culture, with 'the ambition of becoming a beggar,' and was a constant source of anxiety to his father. Although academically bright, he was kicked out of every educational establishment he attended. He bummed round the world for a year, becoming a lighthouse keeper in New Zealand for a while, and then joined Bill Tilman's crew sailing to Greenland in *Baroque*, an experience he relished. Later he settled down to teacher training, married and went to Sudan and Iran to teach English. Latterly he has become a successful bluebell farmer in south-west Wales.

But during all the boys' growing up Shipton's parenting skills were marginal. He was kind yet distant, neglectful of the niceties of giving presents at Christmas and birthdays, and he could be quite thoughtless. The boys agree that they really never knew him intimately to the day he died. Nick was once deeply hurt when his father invited one of his friends' sons to accompany him on a trip, and not himself, who was longing to go. He did once take John (who for unknown reasons he always called Johann) to his old stamping grounds in the Alps, and taught him to eat raw eggs.

'Did anyone know him? What was he like as a person?' was Nick's heartfelt query in recent years. He summarised his feeling thus:

> Although spending only two or three weeks each year in his company, I recall these times with pleasure. They were usually spent in unusual places with interesting people, like the converted barn in the Pyrenees where, after the ritual of peeing into Franco's Spain, intelligent conversation flowed into the night. Even then we would frugally exist on processed dried food left over after a Patagonian expedition, instead of the fare offered in the French villages we passed.
>
> He did not find it easy to be close to us. It wasn't that he didn't want to, he just found it difficult. In some ways he was in awe of me and couldn't share my army experiences or university achievements. After I settled down as a school teacher and had a family, Eric's occasional contacts were brief and distantly benevolent. He was once found inside a playpen being a lion, while both his granddaughters played unconcernedly outside.
>
> I was always proud of Eric, but I carry the burden of association and comparison with such a larger than life character. It was a regret to us both, I think, that we didn't get to know each other better.

Shipton was not the Lothario he has been painted, though his powerful attraction to, and for, women is indisputable. Diana spoke very forthrightly about him. 'His sex life was very busy, yet I remained devoted to him. He totally was not a popper-into-bed. He had to get the person tied up. I'd say to him, "Why must you get so emotionally involved? You seem to want your women to be involved too, and that just isn't fair." He needed female adulation, and constant reaffirming for which I blame his mother.' Diana continued, 'I couldn't get right down to the depths of Eric. There was a gap somewhere; a big lump of what makes most people tick was missing. He was ruthless and had a need for greatness.' Diana was perhaps the only woman of his acquaintance who was not so mesmerised by his far-yonder, deep-set blue eyes that she could not be profoundly critical of him. And yet she loved him forever, and when she died two Polyphotos of him lay on her bedside table, even though they had been divorced for nearly three decades. She once told their mutual friends the Ransoms, 'Any woman who has ever been in love with Eric never falls out of love with him.'

In the early 'seventies Shipton continued to be invited on frequent trips abroad. Once he acted as Sherpa to a geologist visiting Lord Howe Island in the Tasman Sea off the east coast of Australia, visiting Ed Hillary in New Zealand on the way. He returned to Patagonia in 1972–73, and this time he did manage to climb Mount Burney with Roger Perry and a young New Zealander, Peter Radcliffe. His companions were, he told Pamela, 'a splendid combination, very considerate of an old man's frailties.' He was then sixty-five, still carrying packs of over 100 pounds weight.

The expedition got off to a bad start when Shipton left his ice axe in the back of a truck in which he was hitch-hiking. The precious tool was eventually located by a Mr Pickering, the incident of 'ice picks, pickups and Pickering' causing him much mirth, and the others considerable confusion. Radcliffe had brought an assortment of ice screws and other technical gadgets but none of the climbers had a rope; luckily they were able to rectify this at a ships' chandlers in Punta Arenas. Again they had the help of the Chilean Navy, to whom Shipton was now a legend, and frequently referred to as 'Sir Eric' (Odell would have approved).

On a rare windless, cloudless day they left their ice cave and climbed to Burney's summit ridge. This forms the crater rim of the quiescent volcano, crowned by a crescent of spectacular spires, which Radcliffe described as 'like being placed on a lower jaw full of seven major teeth, five canines and two molars'. After descending they went off to explore the Munoz Gamero peninsula, encountering 'sweeping curtains of rain turned to sleet', where Perry, who rarely goes anywhere without jacket and tie, considered the visibility 'a bit thick'. When Radcliffe looked outside the Pyramid tent he saw 'an exasperated Eric crouching and blowing at a futile pile of twigs and dead matches on the wet mossy beech forest floor'; however, he managed, with a Kiwi's rain forest tramping experience, to rekindle the fire from an ember. Then a fox raided their food dump and they were reduced to even shorter rations than usual.

On their return to England, Radcliffe was invited to stay with Shipton and Phyllis at The Haye, describing himself as 'a vagrant gardener-in-residence and hanger-on'. He continued, 'Eric would sometimes bung me in the Renault and hurtle along country lanes to look up some curious relics of his past, generally wealthy widows whose spouses, having run the Empire, had laid their bones to rest in a local church-yard. Showering gravel and pheasants to either side, we'd brake to a halt amongst a brace of black labradors and cloth-capped gardeners, to the tune of "Eric, darling, how wonderful." Scones and tea would follow, with minute discussions of which col they'd used to get out of the Nanda Devi Sanctuary.'

The next year Shipton was busy tripping round the world. He returned to Patagonia with Roger Perry to investigate a recent volcanic eruption of Mount Hudson; he went to Rhodesia to visit his sister, who had settled there, and to Kenya where he flew in a small plane over his mountain adventures of forty-three years before; and he lectured on some more *Linblad Explorer* cruises in the Chilean archipelago and the Galapagos.

In December 1976 Shipton at last fulfilled his already twice thwarted wish to visit Bhutan by leading a tour group there. He was now quite used to this way of having his trips subsidised. On the way there he met several of his old Sherpa friends from previous expeditions, Angtharkay in Kathmandu, and in Darjeeling Karma Paul and Tenzing Norgay – 'as sweet and courteous as ever'. He stayed in the Mount Everest Hotel in all its faded glory where he indulged in nostalgic memories of 'dancing cheek to cheek' with Pamela in the great ballroom. Then he moved on to Kalimpong to stay at the Himalayan Hotel where he had the pleasant surprise of finding Lhakpa Tenzing, who had been with him in the Karakoram and Kashgar. Together they walked up the hill to see 'Glenrilli', where he had first met Pamela at the Odlings' dinner party.

Although his visit to Bhutan was circumscribed by the very nature of such tours, he enjoyed the beautiful scenery of that remote and comparatively unvisited land whose people had so much in common with the Tibet he loved. There he met his friends John and Phoebe

Tyson, running a boys' school in Thimphu, the capital. But he developed a 'tummy upset', and went totally off his food; then he found a lump at the top of the scar of his gall bladder (which had been removed in Kunming). The lump grew quickly, yet for the rest of the trip he seemed as energetic as normal.

When he got back to England he began to feel very unwell, and wrote to Pamela, 'I've been rather under the weather with this bug of mine.' He went reluctantly to see a doctor, who found his liver to be enlarged, and told him he thought it might be due to hepatitis. A liver scan showed two more lumps, so he consulted a Harley Street surgeon, who admitted him to Guy's Hospital for further tests. At operation they found evidence of the spread of cancer, which turned out to have arisen in his prostate. So the doctors put him on treatment with female hormones, never a pleasant prospect.

The first two days after the operation he appeared to be doing well, but then he slumped, lost weight and slept a lot. He tried to persuade Phyllis to go to the country for a rest because she was very upset by his illness; not so Shipton, who said, 'If only these doctors would put a name to it I wouldn't mind. It's just bad when I don't know what's wrong.' He kept taking his daily walk, determined to get fit, despite the fact that he could only just make the half mile round the block from Tite Street, down to the Embankment, and home by way of Swan Walk and the Chelsea Physic Garden.

Many friends visited him and were appalled by his skeletal frame. Robert Cross said to him, 'Eric, how are you managing?'

'I know the minimum you need to keep alive,' he replied. 'I try to eat not less than that, but I'm not going to force down more. I'm trying to get the exercise I need.'

Meanwhile some of his lady friends hovered around and pressed him to leave his 'dreary, dingy basement flat' and go to the country. Phyllis certainly found his illness quite overwhelming, and was relieved and grateful when one of his friends offered to nurse him at her home in Wiltshire, near Pyt House and his old schoolboy haunts. In the same village lived Pamela Freston, who visited him regularly. He continued with his daily walks, but they became slower and shorter as he lost weight and strength. He faded visibly but he was in no pain, and Phyllis Wint spent unrestricted time with him.

On 28 March 1977, at 7.30 in the evening, Eric Shipton died peacefully. He was cremated in Salisbury and his ashes were scattered on the Fonthill Lakes, overlooking the part of England he loved above all else.

So passed the man whose name will always be associated with Mount Everest over the two decades from 1933–1953, arguably one of the greatest mountain explorers of all time. The final words must be Eric Shipton's, from his book, *Upon That Mountain*:

> He is lucky who, in the full tide of life, has experienced a measure of the active environment he most desires. In these days of upheaval and violent change, when the basic values of today are the vain and shattered dreams of tomorrow, there is much to be said for a philosophy which aims at living a full life while the opportunity offers. There are few treasures of more lasting worth than the experience of a way of life that is in itself wholly satisfying. Such, after all, are the only possessions of which no fate, no cosmic catastrophe can deprive us; nothing can alter the fact if for one moment in eternity we have really lived.

Appendix 1

Notes on Sources

THIS APPENDIX tells how I gathered my sources and wrote this book. I have also included some personal vignettes and incidents concerning Eric Shipton, either because they shed light on his and other characters involved in the book, or for simple amusement.

Author's Note (pp 1–4)
(p 2) On one occasion Sarah's mother, an intellectual and somewhat ascetic lady, was staying with us in Bristol when Eric arrived, as always unannounced, preferring to visit us in Clifton rather than stay across the Downs with Phyllis Wint and her lady friend, 'The Brigadier'. Within seconds his silent presence had reduced two normally calm women to a state of total dither as they scurried round making tea for him.

Nearby Bristol Zoo was much enjoyed by our children, and Eric would often accompany us there, his favourite spot being the gorilla house. One day he lingered staring down at the massive beast with huge eyebrows and deep set eyes like his own. Our children were becoming fractious, so I hurried along a reluctant Eric. On leaving he could not resist putting his eye to the keepers' peephole. Two inches away was the eye of the gorilla, catching a last glimpse of her new-found friend.

On another visit my then eight-year-old son, Adam, and I took Eric for a walk in Leigh Woods across the Brunel Suspension Bridge. At first Adam was impressed at being told he was going on an adventure with a famous explorer; later he became disillusioned when, to Eric's amusement, we became utterly disorientated, despite the help of our compass.

Chapter 1 Discovering Mountains (pp 5–10)
(p 7) In 1984 I was in Norway cross-country ski racing in the
Holmenkollen Marsj and stayed with Shipton's old schoolfellow,
Gustav Sommerfelt, who talked about their schooldays and their time
together in Kenya. He waved at me a bunch of letters from Shipton,
promising to let me see them 'some day'. He has since died, and, unfortunately, this precious correspondence is still cloistered in Oslo, unavailable.

Chapter 2 The Kenya Planter (pp 11–28)
Soon after meeting Gustav Sommerfelt, a serendipitous event occurred
which reignited my interest in writing the story of Eric Shipton. A
Yukon friend, while hiking the Chilkoot Pass, route of the Klondike
gold rush, met a family from Vancouver named Bridgman. On their
return to Whitehorse they all came to coffee at our house before flying
south. As Robin Bridgman was climbing our front steps he noticed my
ice axe which had lain there since the winter.

'I've got one of those at home,' he remarked casually, 'it belonged to
a chap called Shipton.'

Flabbergasted, I pursued the story and discovered that Robin's
mother was Madge Anderson, now Bridgman, whom I met later in her
apartment overlooking Stanley Park in Vancouver, British Columbia. I
discovered that she had been Eric's main girlfriend and correspondent
of his Kenya days, nicknamed Midget (after whom he named Midget
Peak on Mount Kenya). I could envisage this elegant, petite lady, now
in her mid-eighties, dancing her way through the hearts of many bach-
elor Kenya farmers. When we talked of Eric, she produced a wad of his
letters from 1928 to 1935 covering his adventures on Mount Kenya,
Ruwenzori, Kamet and Everest 1933, and we pored over several photograph albums with pictures of Eric and Bill Tilman at picnics and tennis
parties.

Much of this chapter draws from my interviews with Madge
Bridgman, and from her own autobiography, *The Winds of Change*.
Tilman's book *Snow on the Equator* gives a personal view by Shipton's
longtime companion of their shared adventures.

Sarah and I travelled round Mount Kenya in 1988 visiting many of
the places mentioned in the text.

Chapter 3 First Footing in the Himalaya (pp 29–39)
Frank Smythe's books *Kamet Conquered* and *Valley of Flowers* provided
much basic information for this chapter. Shipton's correspondence with
Madge Bridgman gives a personal glimpse of the Kamet expedition.

Raymond Greene (brother of Graham), formerly chairman of
Heinemann Medical, publisher of my book *Medical Care for Mountain
Climbers*, would occasionally take me out to lunch to discuss my MS,
and, incidentally, his Everest adventure. In a street close by his offices
were two restaurants. On the south side stood the White Tower, of
impeccable haute cuisine and cellar with a head waiter always referred
to as 'Mr'; to the north just off the Tottenham Court Road was a ham-
burger joint with formica-topped tables and tomato ketchup in nasty
individual plastic packages. By the side of the street we walked down
on our way to lunch, I knew instantly how my book was going.

Chapter 4 A Grim and Joyless Business (pp 40–51)
In 1981 I spent a weekend at the Dorset home of Tom Brocklebank, a
humorous, intellectual ex-Eton schoolmaster, who was an ardent
admirer and vociferous defender of Shipton. There I slept in a bed
recently vacated by Anthony Blunt, a schoolfriend of Tom's, to whom
he had offered a safe house in the wake of accusations of treason. Also
there I met Tom Longstaff's daughter, 'Dick' Worcester, who gave many
insights into TGL.

Once while on holiday in Ullapool in the remote Western Highlands
of Scotland I began negotiating with Tom Patey to join his general practice. He took me to visit Longstaff, then a nonagenarian, living with his
wife, Charmian, on a moor outside Achiltibuie. After remarking that the
only special equipment he took to Trisul (which he climbed in 1909) was
a spare pair of socks, a propos of nothing he confided in a raspy
whisper and with a glint in his eye, 'I've got seven married daughters,
and only one son-in-law I *hate*.'

Jack Longland, father of my university friend John, used to offer
open house in Bakewell to Cambridge University Mountaineering Club
climbers on outings to the Derbyshire gritstone outcrops. I interviewed
him much later at his home and, as usual, his opinions were forthright,
uncompromising and fun.

(p 41) Head-picking for lice, a normal and quite social event, was performed daily on our own children by our Sherpani ayah while we traversed Bhutan. So one is tempted to see Bailey's hand in this aspect of the complaint which reached London, and an attempt to ensure himself a quiet life.

Chapter 5 Into the Sanctuary (pp 52–62)
Much information for this chapter comes from Shipton's book *Nanda Devi*, and from his and Tilman's accounts in various geographical and alpine journals. Unfortunately, permission to enter the Nanda Devi Sanctuary nowadays is absolutely unobtainable, even for the vice-president of the Indian Mountaineering Federation, Suman Dubey, who was refused an entry permit for himself, another Indian climber and myself last spring.

Chapter 6 Old Leaders, Young Men (pp 63–75)
Everest: the Unfinished Adventure by Hugh Ruttledge was one source for this chapter. 1936 was the beginning of Shipton's lifelong correspondence with Pamela Freston; Celia Armitage, her daughter, made scores of his letters to her mother available to me. Barney Rosedale provided me with a copy of the diaries of Edwin Kempson, whom I had met previously in Marlborough. Charles Warren checked the text and maps for accuracy. Charlie Houston filled in details of the climb of Nanda Devi, much of which I had already heard from Noel Odell himself.
(p 66) In 1969, with one Sherpa companion, I walked up the Bhote Kosi to have a look at the South Faces of Cho Oyu and Gyachung Kang. We stopped to shelter from a snow storm at a low, stone-walled house with a sod roof set in the middle of some potato fields. An old man invited us in. He had a simian face and wore a battered Tibetan hat with two ear flaps tucked inside, and patched climbing breeches secured at the knees with red ties. He started to brew tea and boil potatoes on a fire of green juniper that made clouds of acrid smoke. We talked in Nepali, and our conversation quickly turned to the expeditions he had been on three decades before.

'Did you ever meet Eric Shipton?' I asked him.

'Shipton Sahib *mero ekdum ramro sati*,' he said. 'Shipton Sahib my very good friend.'

'What's your name?'

'Sen Tensing,' he replied.

I suggested he accompany us the following day to show us the peaks at the head of the valley. Being a friend of Shipton Sahib's had given me instant promotion in status. Sen Tensing drew out of a wooden chest an old pair of boots, and spent the rest of the evening repairing a wide split in the welts whilst regaling me with tall stories of his adventures with Eric Shipton, interspersed with intoning his religious mantras. He also pulled from the chest his treasured tiger book, a log of all his expeditions with handwritten recommendations from those leaders he had served, that read like pages from a history book of Himalayan mountaineering.

(p 73) Concerning shaking hands with Tilman on the summit, in the margin of my own copy of *The Ascent of Nanda Devi* Odell has written, 'It's true! N.E.O.'

Chapter 7 Peaks, Valleys and Glaciers (pp 76–86)
Shipton's *Blank on the Map*, his *Geographical Journal* article, and letters to Pamela Freston, gave light to this chapter.

(p 82) In September 1974 Shipton was slated to lead a Thomas Cook's tour to the Karakoram to retrace his former steps, but he was laid up in bed with a bad back. When I visited him in Tite Street he persuaded me to lead the trip in his place. At Heathrow Airport the disappointed faces of the clients on hearing that I was the substitute for their hero is something I prefer to forget. Escorting them along the steep, unstable, slippery slopes of the Braldu Gorge was extremely harrowing (Shipton himself described it thirty-five years before in *Blank on the Map* as 'very difficult country'), but when I later censured him for not warning me of this hazard he was singularly unsympathetic.

Chapter 8 A Vile Waste of Time (pp 87–95)
Tilman's book *Mount Everest 1938* and Shipton's serial letters to Pamela Freston provide most of the sources for this chapter.

Chapter 9 Karakoram Survey (pp 96–106)
Staying at the home of Scott and Anne Russell near Oxford, I learned much about this expedition, and of the general mountaineering scene in Britain over the next decade with which Scott was intimately involved. I read his book *Mountain Prospect* and he showed me many of his papers and those of George Finch, Anne's father.

Shipton wrote a detailed account of the expedition in the *Geographical Journal*, as well as letters to Diana, his wife-to-be. (There was now a lapse in his correspondence with Pamela Freston, while the wounds of their break-up healed.)

Beatrice Lumley (née Weir) spoke warmly about her friendship with Eric Shipton. Sitting on a garden seat at her home in Kent, a distant look came into her eyes – the same look shared by several of the women who adored Eric Shipton for a while but moved on with their lives, yet forever held a candle for him.

Chapter 10 The Consul-General (pp 107–124) and Chapter 11 The Great Game (pp 125–138)
Eric Shipton's *Mountains of Tartary* and Diana Shipton's *The Antique Land* were valuable sources for these chapters.

The Persia/Hungary period of Shipton's life was the least well documented of all until I visited John and Alison Shipton and their two charming teenage daughters at a farmhouse in a bluebell dell (the bulbs of which he farms) in West Wales. During supper, John pointed to a wooden chest lying under a pile of bric-à-brac, and said, 'That's all Diana's stuff. We haven't opened it since she died.' Thereupon we engaged in a frenzy of looking through photograph albums, newspaper cuttings, love letters, diaries, and particularly Eric's letters to Diana from Persia (few) and Hungary (many).

I have corresponded with several nameless senior diplomats concerning Shipton's activities during his Persia/Hungary service. All these Foreign Officers were very cautious about branding him as what we commoners call a 'spy'. However they left little doubt that perhaps he was doing more than just advising on cereal distribution and agriculture. Incidentally, he was later referred to in *Pravda* as 'Eric Shipton, the well-known spy'.

Shipton's report to the Government of India from Kashgar comes from the Public Records Office, and information about his appointment as Consul-General from the Oriental and India Office collections of the British Library.

I tried to locate Shipton's Danish assistant Hansen through e-mail, only to find that Hansen is the second most common name in Denmark.

Bob and Vera Ransom are a spry couple in their eighties living on Nob Hill in San Francisco with whom I had Chinese dimsum last autumn on my way to Patagonia. Evidently the impression of their two-week visit to Kashgar in 1946 stands out over all their subsequent worldwide travels. Bob's views of the British seem to have mellowed. They lent me many documents and some excellent photos of Eric and Diana.

I learned much about The Great Game from Peter Hopkirk over cappuccinos in a café on the Wandsworth Bridge Road which stood near the home of my tolerant and generous London hostess, Maybe Jehu, a niece of Beatrice Lumley. Joanna Lumley kindly checked all references to her mother.

Chapter 12 Everest from the South (pp 139–164)
First-hand accounts of this expedition come from interviews with Ed Hillary, George Lowe and Michael Ward.

Sarah and I met Ed and Louise Hillary in Darjeeling on our way to Bhutan in the spring of 1967. We had asked Sherpa Tenzing Norgay's daughter, Pem Pem, to find a Sherpani ayah to help with our children, Adam, aged three and a half, and Judith, eighteen months, during our forthcoming five-month journey across roadless Himalaya, which resulted in a book, *Two and Two Halves to Bhutan.*

Tenzing invited us to join a lunch party he was giving at the Gymkhana Club for the Hillary family and their helpers who had just come out of Solu Khumbu after spending the previous winter at Khumjung, building a new school. Tenzing seated himself at the bottom of the table, surrounded by children – his own, the Hillarys' and ours – whom he entertained for two hours without stopping. Together with the New Zealand party of school-builders, we then moved across to Kalimpong for a week at the Himalayan Hotel, being spoiled by the patrons, the MacDonald sisters, Auntie Vicky and Auntie Vera. I met Ed Hillary several times in the intervening years, the most recent being in Vancouver in November 1996 where he was fund-raising for his Himalayan Trust (work for which he became a Knight of the Garter) and especially for the hospital in Kunde, recently staffed by two doctors from Whitehorse, Yukon.

George Lowe's spirited accounts in this and the next chapter are reported unexpurgated. He has checked and added to my drafts of the accounts of these crucial years in the story of Everest.

Michael Ward has encouraged me, written me volumes of interesting letters, given his characteristically forthright opinions, and lent me maps and photos.

Charlie Houston supplied details about his trip with his father and Bill Tilman to Solu Khumbu, as did Jesuit Father Andy Bakewell, another participant. Charlie has been an authoritative source of information about high-altitude medicine, much of which I discussed with him personally when he was directing the High Altitude Physiology Study on Mount Logan, in the Yukon, in the late 'seventies and on many subsequent meetings. He, Tom Hornbein and Brownie Schoene, all distinguished American high-altitude climbers and medical men, along with Jim Milledge and Michael Ward, corrected Appendix 2 on the physiology of high altitude.

Information about Shipton's invitation of the New Zealanders in 1951 came from Scott Russell's archives. Jennifer Bourdillon allowed me to read her late husband Tom's account of his encounter with the yeti tracks and his personal views of Shipton. In 1951 Bourdillon and Shipton were walking together on the march in, when the normally silent Bourdillon described how he met his wife-to-be. One rainy day at Oxford, as a break from studying, he took a punt on the river. During the downpour he passed a girl punting in the opposite direction, and their eyes met for a second. Totally out of character, he turned around and caught up with her – and that was that.

Chapter 13 Crossroads on Cho Oyu (pp 165–184)
Reports on this expedition were written by Eric Shipton and Charles Evans in the *Geographical Journal*; Ed Hillary and George Lowe in the *New Zealand Alpine Journal*; and Ed Hillary in *Nothing Venture, Nothing Win*. Michael Ward has recently written in the *Alpine Journal* a thorough summary of the mapping and scientific events leading up to Everest 1953.

The anecdotes of this chapter come almost verbatim from George Lowe, who has commented on each draft.

In 1961 Tony Hagen and Peter Aufschnaiter were both employed by the Swiss Red Cross in Patan, Kathmandu, when Sarah and I were working just round the corner at Shanta Bhawan Hospital (where I looked after Woodrow Wilson Sayre after his near-fatal attempt on Everest). From Hagen I heard of this meeting with the British Ambassador, and from Aufschnaiter of his escape through Garhwal and subsequent seven years spent in Tibet together with Heinrich Harrer. Also at that time ex-Gurkha officers Jimmy Roberts and Charles Wylie were living and working in Kathmandu, both endless funds of Himalayan lore.

(p 174) I only met Pugh once, very briefly, but unforgettably. I was standing beside Noel Odell outside the Pen-y-Gwyrd Hotel one crisp, clear morning, recalling his recent happy visit to our home in the Yukon. Odell, then an octogenarian, had just recovered from major surgery, yet stood straight as a guardsman on parade. From the direction of the parking lot a red-haired figure approached us in a flurry of briefcases, rucksacks and boots – Griffith Pugh. Through bottle-bottom glasses he stared intently at Odell.

'Smythe, isn't it?' he said, thrusting forward his hand in greeting (Frank Smythe had been dead for nearly two decades). Then he disappeared into the hotel.

'Funny fellow that,' said Odell in his most urbane manner.

Chapter 14 Thruster John (pp 185–201)

The facts of this tumultuous episode in Eric Shipton's life are all open for scrutiny in the British Library, the Alpine Club Archives, and the Himalayan Committee minute books of the Royal Geographical Society Archives through the memos of Tom Blakeney, Peter Lloyd and Claude Elliott.

I interviewed the following for their opinion of this crucial time, some in 1981, others in 1996. Several of them reviewed the draft chapters: Tom Brocklebank, Roger Chorley, Raymond Greene, Alf Gregory, Ed Hillary, Emlyn Jones, Larry Kirwan, George Lowe, Peter Lloyd, Jack Longland, Jimmy Roberts, Scott Russell, Michael Ward, Charles Wylie.

John Hunt generously checked the draft of this chapter and suggested some factual changes.

Chapter 15 The Lakeland Warden (pp 202–213)

I was a boy on course 35 at the Outward Bound Mountain School in 1954, my first introduction to mountains. Rarely did we meet the

Warden, but one day he arrived quietly to watch our inept attempts to practise abseiling down a rocky outcrop near the school. He approached one of our patrol, a plumber-fitter from Grantham.

'And how do you usually spend your weekends at home, Terry?' Mr Shipton asked in his gentle, distant manner, his penetrating blue eyes staring out from under bristly overhanging eyebrows.

'The girlfriend, sir,' shot back the reply.

'Oh, it's a full time job, is it?' said Shipton without blinking.

To check on Shipton's Outward Bound time I visited the Mountain School in Eskdale and had help from Frank Dowlen, John Lagoe, Margaret Mossop, and John and Phoebe Tyson, and by letter from Roy Greenwood and David Ridgeway. At Robert Cross's house in Winchester I learned about Shipton's Shropshire sojourn in his own personal wilderness.

(p 212) On many occasions, Eric invited me to 'his' flat in Tite Street for lunch, which consisted of vegetable curry and popadoms. I was never introduced to the lady with straight black hair sitting silently and serenely on a pouffe in front of the gas fire doing the *Daily Telegraph* crossword. She did not look up, nor did we exchange a single word; I had no idea where she fitted into his domestic picture – nor did it interest me, I was so absorbed in our discussion of places more exotic than Chelsea. Later on I got to know Phyllis Wint well and became deeply fond of her, and she gave me many frank insights into her beloved companion of twenty years.

Chapter 16 Essays in Masochism (pp 214–241)
Shipton's two books, *Land of Tempest* and *Tierra del Fuego: the Fatal Lodestone* were sources of information, supplemented by interviews with Roger Perry, John Earle, and Philip Hugh-Jones. In October 1996 I travelled to Santiago to try to find Shipton's Chilean companions. I tracked down Cedomir Marangunic and talked with him of a friend for whom he evidently felt a deep affection. I then took a cargo boat through the Chilean Archipelago, from where both Tilman and Shipton had approached the Patagonian Ice Cap. From Puerto Natales I travelled by bus to Punta Arenas.

I had previously been in Tierra del Fuego, and visited Ushuaia and Estancia Harberton after returning from the Antarctic with Sarah when

I was lecturing on Wilderness Medicine aboard a cruise boat. Natalie and Thomas Goodall talked warmly of Shipton's visits to their estancias. While I was waiting for a bus in a hotel foyer in Commodoro Rivadavia a tall Chilean was standing at the reception speaking good English. I approached him and asked if he had ever met Eric Shipton; he had. His name was Gerald Friedli from Estancia Skyring.

Shipton became quite involved with the politics of Chile at a very sensitive time in her history, and wrote a controversial letter to *The Times* in defence of General Pinochet. At the same time he was consulted on the possibility of relocating Tibetan refugees to work in some high-altitude sulphur mines in the Andes, a project that never got beyond theory.

Chapter 17 The Celebrity Guide and Lecturer (pp 242–254)
(p 249) from John's Bryanston school report:

> The last boy who got over thirty punishment runs finished up head of house so none of us must give up hope. Most of the bitterness, surliness, and some of the ostentation has gone out of him. I'm not sure he does not *intend* to look like something out of the chorus of *Oliver*. But, ye gods, he does make it difficult for us. It's dirty shoes, untidy clothes, hair too long, black lists, lateness, just about the lot; and it's *so* disappointing after the improvements of the spring term. I believe he thinks he's showing more character by rebelling against the rules in such excessive fashion. It's a shame that one with so much academic intelligence should be so downright stupid as to think that.

Then after his expulsion:

> I'm sincerely sorry to have lost this harum-scarum fellow, but I've given up hope that he would turn a corner here. He confesses at present to a basically hedonistic outlook on life, but I feel this is not all bravado. His charm reflects a nature with a lot of real good and idealism and a capacity for loving. Best of luck, John.

Eric Shipton had several interviews with the BBC during his last decade, but two were of special interest to me. One was his review of

Slavomir Rawicz's book *The Long Walk*, a bestseller of the time. Based on his experience of both sides of the Himalaya, Shipton questioned Rawicz in detail about the violent contrast of geography, of which the latter seemed totally unaware. In summary Shipton said, 'Throughout the book there are so many improbable circumstances, so many geographical details which fail to match our knowledge of the areas travelled, that it is impossible to trace the boundary between fact and fantasy.' In essence he debunked the book, in his own gentle but firm manner.

He also appeared as a guest on BBC's perennially successful chat and music programme *Desert Island Discs*, and his castaway's selection throws light on the limited ranges of his musical tastes: 'Swanee' (Tommy Kinsman Orchestra), the ballet music from Gounod's *Faust*, Noel Coward's 'Room with a View', 'Dance, Little Lady', and 'London Pride', Chopin's Etude in E major, 'These Foolish Things' (Savoy Hotel Orpheans), 'The Glow Worm' (Boston Pops), and 'The Londonderry Air' – his special choice. The book he would have taken to the desert island was *The Human Situation* by W. McNeill Dixon, and the single permitted luxury item, a snorkel mask.

A memorial meeting was held for Eric Shipton at the Royal Geographical Society on 1 June 1977, organised by his son, Nick. The chairperson was Dorothy Middleton, and speakers were: Gustav Sommerfelt, John Auden, John Earle, Bob Ransom, Peter Boardman and Michael Ward.

On one of my infrequent visits to Jan Morris's Welsh hideaway she casually threw out the remark, 'Of course, I retype all my books three times from scratch.' Having an editor-ready MS of another book at hand, I decided that if such a paragon of the English language gets results that way perhaps I had better try the same. I returned home and was amazed at the difference the physical act of even one re-typing made. So I determined to do the same with this MS and, although I only re-typed completely twice, I am eternally grateful for Jan's wisdom and example.

I dictated the whole MS onto tape, twice, for my mother-in-law, Irene Fleming, a voluminous reader and an astute critic, who has recently lost her central vision. Likewise, through this laborious task I discovered a harvest of corrections which did not turn up on visual checking. The full script has also been read, to its profit, by Tony Armitage and Pat Paton.

After perusing the maps in dozens of travel books in my own library, I decided to draw my own sketch maps. In this task I have benefited from the expert advice of Ted Hatch, ex-cartographer of the RGS, and of Afan Jones and Gary Hewitt, both of Whitehorse. Only place names that appear in the text are on the maps. The spelling of such names, especially in Sherpa country, is perpetually confusing, but has been helped by Sherpas Norbu Tenzing and Mingma Temba, and by my Tibetan language teacher, Sonam Tobgyel Rimpoche.

Bruce Paton (voluntarily exiled from Scotland half a lifetime ago to Denver, Colorado), a retired cardio-thoracic surgeon and now president of the Wilderness Medicine Society, drew the chapter headings. We discovered in a chance conversation that both our missionary grandfathers met at the turn of the century in China.

Appendix 2

Science on Everest

So MUCH of this book has been concerned with Shipton's relationship with Mount Everest and his contribution to its successful climb after three decades of trying, that it seems shallow to gloss over the science that also contributed so much to that success, even if Shipton himself would not agree with its importance.

First some basic science of life in the thin, cold air on high. Our planet is surrounded by a diaphanous mantle of atmosphere, the gases of which exert a pressure on the surface of the earth. The air we breathe at sea level contains four parts of nitrogen, to one part of oxygen. As we climb, the 4:1 ratio of these gases does not change, but their density becomes less; fewer molecules are present, which means less weight of the air, and therefore lower barometric pressure. In other words fewer molecules exist in a given volume of air and the pressure exerted by them falls steadily. Thus an ordinary weather barometer can be used as an altimeter because it registers the pressure gases exert on the earth.

At the top of Mount Everest (29,028 feet, or 8,848 metres) the atmospheric pressure is about one third that at sea level. The atmosphere is thinner over the North and South Poles, where the pressure is the lower for any given altitude than over the Equator. Eventually, as we climb, the pressure will no longer be adequate to drive sufficient oxygen from the air into the blood and thereby into the tissues, especially the brain.

Acclimatisation is the physiological process that allows humans to adapt so they can live and work in the oxygen-thin atmosphere of high altitude. Life would be more difficult above about 10,000 feet, or 3,000 metres, without the physiological adjustments of acclimatisation, which compensate for the low pressure of oxygen in the air (hypoxia), and high-altitude mountaineering would be nearly impossible. Certainly no unacclimatised person could climb to the top of Mount Everest, or even survive there, without oxygen, a feat now achieved by well-trained, acclimatised mountaineers.

Low oxygen pressure in the atmosphere, and hence in the lungs and blood, increases the rate and depth of breathing. Initially the heart beats faster and more strongly, increasing the flow of blood to the lungs, and breathing deepens and quickens; but this soon settles back to normal. Bone marrow at high altitude produces more red cells and hemoglobin, which allows blood to carry more oxygen. The blood becomes more viscous, or sticky, and the circulation is sluggish because the volume of blood plasma falls. This is partly because more urine is passed, partly because of dehydration caused by sweating with heavy exercise and by overbreathing in the cold dry atmosphere, and partly because the expanding red cell mass takes space at the expense of plasma volume. Blood vessels in the calf muscles of stormbound climbers lying inactive in their tents, are susceptible to clotting, and some unlucky people even suffer strokes thereby.

Acclimatisation changes have one common purpose: to make optimum use of what little oxygen is available in the thin air on high. But ironically some of these adaptations defeat their own ends, for example, the blunted response of Sherpas to lowered oxygen pressure. Acclimatisation is quite idiosyncratic; it starts at different altitudes and proceeds at different rates in different people. Some are never troubled, provided they ascend slowly enough, while others for no obvious physical reason never acclimatise properly, however long they remain high, even at relatively low altitude. It is not progressive. After about three months at very high altitude, say above 20,000 feet or 6,000 metres, climbers steadily deteriorate; they sleep and work poorly, and lose appetite and weight. Retreat to the valleys for a long holiday is the solution.

Acute Mountain Sickness (AMS) strikes those who fail to adapt to high altitude and can kill the unwary, the bold and the previously healthy. It affects those who ascend too high too fast, and is usually cured by immediate descent. Oxygen and certain drugs may help, but should not be relied on for treatment. Mild AMS has vague, ill-defined symptoms but can drift subtly into Severe AMS, setting off a chain of events, the fundamental problem being that body water settles in the wrong places – the brain in High Altitude Cerebral Oedema, and/or the lungs in High Altitude Pulmonary Oedema, or the tissues of the face, hands and feet.

Appendix 3

Glossary

abseil — method of sliding down a steep place on a rope doubled through a sling (q.v.) fixed above. Also known as rappelling (French).

belay — a way of anchoring a climber to the mountain so s/he cannot be pulled off while safeguarding a moving companion.

bergschrund — a wide crevasse between the static mountain and a flowing glacier.

bhatti — a Nepali tea house or wayside 'hotel'.

chimney — a vertical fissure usually climbed by straddling, or wriggling upwards with the climber's back against one wall, feet against the other.

cirque — a mountain amphitheatre — also corrie (Scots), and cwm (Welsh).

col — the lowest part of a ridge or gap between two mountain peaks.

couloir — a steep, narrow gulley.

crampons — steel spikes fastened to the sole of a boot used for climbing hard snow and ice.

crevasse — a crack in a glacier, sometimes very deep, and often invisible because of snow covering.

cwm — Welsh word for cirque (q.v.).

dzong — a Tibetan or Bhutanese fortress lorded over by a dzongpen, or governor. It is the government and religious centre for a region and often also has a dungeon.

gendarme — a rock pinnacle on a mountain ridge.

icefall — a jumbled mass of tottering ice pinnacles formed where a glacier spills steeply over a lip, and constantly changing because of the downward flow of the glacier.

moraine – rocky debris pushed aside by an advancing glacier.

pitch – the distance between two belays.

piton – a metal spike hammered into rock, or screwed into ice, to which a belay can be attached.

serac – an ice pinnacle.

Sherpa – a race of originally Tibetan people living, particularly, on the south side of Mount Everest. By natural adaptation and innate skill they have become the preferred porters at high altitudes, and have more recently become mountain guides in their own right.

sirdar – the foreman of a group of porters.

sling – a loop of rope or webbing used in belaying techniques.

tricouni – a crenellated nail fixed to the welt of a climbing boot, commonly used in pre-WWII climbing but nowadays replaced by treaded rubber Vibram soles.

Tyrolean traverse – a way of stringing a rope over a crevasse, secured at both ends, by which the climber manoeuvres him/herself across.

wind-slab – snow compacted by strong winds and liable to avalanche by breaking away from the mountain in one huge slab.

yeti – the Abominable Snowman.

Bibliography

ABBREVIATIONS

AJ – Alpine Journal
GJ – Geographical Journal
HJ – Himalayan Journal
NZAJ – New Zealand Alpine Journal
AAJ – American Alpine Journal
GM – Geographical Magazine

All publications are from London unless indicated otherwise.

BOOKS BY ERIC SHIPTON

Nanda Devi (1936)
Blank on the Map (1938)
Upon That Mountain (1943)
Mountains of Tartary (1951)
The Mount Everest Reconnaissance Expedition 1951 (1952)
Land of Tempest (1963)
That Untravelled World (1969)
Tierra del Fuego – The Fatal Lodestone (1973)

CO-AUTHORED BOOKS

The True Book about Everest (1955)
The True Book about the North Pole (1957)
Mountain Conquest (1966)

ERIC SHIPTON'S CONTRIBUTIONS IN OTHER BOOKS

The Book of Modern Mountaineering (1968)
The World Atlas of Mountaineering (1969)

The only edition of Eric Shipton's work still in print is the collection under the title *The Six Mountain–Travel Books: Nanda Devi, Blank on the Map, Upon That Mountain, Mountains of Tartary, Everest Reconnaissance Expedition 1951, Land of Tempest*, published in 1985 by Diadem Books, London (ISBN 0-906371-56-2) and The Mountaineers, Seattle (ISBN 0-89886-075-X).

ARTICLES BY ERIC SHIPTON

AJ (1931)	'First Traverse of Twin Peaks of Mt Kenya'
AJ (1932)	'Mountains of the Moon'
AJ (1934)	'Lashar Plain'
AJ (1935)	'Nanda Devi Basin'
AJ (1937)	'Survey in Nanda Devi District'
GJ (1935)	'Nanda Devi and the Ganges Watershed'
AJ (1936)	'Mount Everest Recconnaisance 1935'
GJ (1936)	'Mount Everest Recconnaisance 1935'
HJ (1937)	'The Problem of Mount Everest'
GJ (1937)	'More Explorations Round Nanda Devi'
GJ (1938)	'The Shaksgam Expedition 1937'
GJ (1938)	'The Gyankar (Nyonno Ri) Range'
GJ (1938)	'Shaksgam 1937'
GJ (1940)	'Karakoram 1939'
GJ (1944)	'Note on Nanda Devi Photos'
AJ (1946)	'Letter from Kashgar'
HJ (1949)	'Ascent of Gordamah Peak in Northern Sikkim'
AJ (1948)	'The Arch'
AJ (1948)	'Muztagh Ata'
AJ (1950)	'Bogdo Ola'
GM (1952)	'The Everest Tigers'
GJ (1952)	'Everest: The 1951 Reconnaisance of the Southern Route'
GJ (1953)	'The Expedition to Cho Oyu'
GJ (1955)	'Norton of Everest – an Appreciation'
GJ (1956)	'Fact or Fantasy – Review of *The Long Walk*'
AJ (1958)	'Imperial College Karakoram Expedition 1957'
GJ (1959)	'Explorations in Patagonia'
AJ (1960)	'Two Visits to the Andes of Southern Patagonia'

GJ (1960)	'Volcanic Activity on the Patagonian Ice-cap'
AAJ (1962)	'Across the Patagonian Ice-cap'
AJ (1962)	'A Journey over the Patagonian Ice-cap'
AJ (1962)	'The Darwin Range of Tierra del Fuego'
GM (1962)	'Tierra del Fuego'
AJ (1963)	'Further Travels in Patagonia and Tierra del Fuego'
AAJ (1963)	'Tierra del Fuego'
AJ (1964)	'Crossing the Northern Patagonian Ice-cap'
AJ (1967)	'A Visit to Alaska'
AJ (1967)	'Some Reflections on Modern Climbing'
AJ (1975)	'Mount Burney'
AJ (1975)	Valedictory Address

OBITUARIES WRITTEN BY ERIC SHIPTON

GJ (1956)	Tom Bourdillon
GJ (1962)	Hugh Ruttledge
GJ (1964)	Tom Longstaff
GJ (1966)	Lawrence Wager
GJ (1966)	Noel Humphreys

BOOKS

Bryant, L.V., *New Zealanders and Everest* (1953)
Dittert, René, *Forerunners to Everest* (1954)
Earle, John, *Springs of Enchantment* (1981)
Greene, Raymond, *Moments of Being* (1974)
Hillary, Edmund, *High Adventure* (1955)
    Nothing Venture, Nothing Win (1975)
Hunt, John, *The Ascent of Everest* (1953)
    Life is Meeting ((1978)
Pares, Bip, *Himalayan Honeymoon* (1940)
Russell, Scott, *Mountain Prospect* (1946)
Ruttledge, Hugh, *Everest 1933* (1934)
    Everest: the Unfinished Adventure (1937)
Shipton, Diana, *The Antique Land* (1950)
Smythe, Frank, *Camp Six* (1937)
    Kamet Conquered (1932)
Tilman, H. W., *Snow on the Equator* (1937)
    The Ascent of Nanda Devi (1937)
    Mount Everest 1938 (1948)

Two Mountains and a River (1949)
China to Chitral (1951)
The Seven Mountain Travel Books (1983)
Unsworth, Walt, *Everest* (1981)
Ward, Michael, *In This Short Span* (1972)

ARTICLES

Bryant, L.V., 'The Mount Everest Reconnaissance Expedition 1935', *NZAJ* (1936)
Evans, Charles, 'Cho Oyu Expedition 1952', *AJ* (1953)
  Review of *That Untravelled World*, *AJ* (1970)
Hillary, Edmund, 'A New Approach to Everest', *NZAJ* (1952)
  'Attempt on Cho Oyu 1952', *NZAJ* (1953)
Lloyd, Peter, Review of Walt Unsworth's *Everest*, *AJ* (1982)
Lowe, George, 'The Barun Exploration', *NZAJ* (1953)
Murray, W. H., 'The Reconnaissance of Mount Everest 1951', *AJ* (1952)
Peaker, Gilbert, 'High Pasture', *AJ* (1944)
Pugh, Griffith, 'Report on the Cho Oyu Expedition 1952', Medical Research Council: London 1952
Radcliffe, Peter, 'Mount Burney', *NZAJ* (1973)
Russell, Scott, 'A Profile of Eric Shipton', *NZAJ* (1969)
Spender, Michael, 'The Shaksgam Expedition 1937', *HJ* (1938)
Tilman H.W., 'Explorations in the Nepal Himalayas', *GJ* (1951)
  'The Annapurna Himal and the South Side of Everest', *AJ* (1951)
  'Nanda Devi and the Sources of the Ganges', *HJ* (1935)
  'The Mountains of Sinkiang', *HJ* (1949)
  'Muztagh Ata', *HJ* (1949)
  'Crossing the Patagonian Ice-cap', *AJ* (1956)
Ward, Michael, 'Griffith Pugh – An 80th Birthday Tribute', *AJ* (1990)
  'The Exploration of the Nepalese Side of Everest', *AJ* (1992)
  'Contribution of Medical Science to the First Ascent of Everest', *AJ* (1993)
  'Exploration and Mapping of Everest', *AJ* (1994)
  'Everest 1951. Cartographic and photographic evidence of a new route from Nepal', *GJ* (1992)

OBITUARIES OF ERIC SHIPTON

The Times, 30 March 1977
AJ, 1978 by Charles Warren
GJ, 1977
NZAJ, 1977 by Edmund Hillary

AAJ, 1978 by Bob Bates
HJ, 1979
Mountain, 1977
Expedition, 1977 by Ingrid Cranfield
GM. 1977
Dictionary of National Biography by Peter Lloyd

Index